German Essays
on Science
in the 19th Century

The German Library: Volume 36

Volkmar Sander, General Editor

GERMAN ESSAYS
ON SCIENCE
IN THE 19TH CENTURY

Edited by
Wolfgang Schirmacher

CONTINUUM · NEW YORK

1996
The Continuum Publishing Company
370 Lexington Avenue, New York, NY 10017

The German Library is published in cooperation
with Deutsches Haus, New York University.
This volume has been supported by Inter Nationes, and a grant
from Robert Bosch Jubiläumsstiftung.

Printed in the United States of America

Library of Congress Cataloging-in-Publication Data

German essays on science in the 19th century /
edited by Wolfgang Schirmacher.
    p.   cm. — (German library ; v. 36)
    Includes bibliographical references.
    ISBN 0-8264-0744-7 (hardcover : alk. paper).
    —ISBN 0-8264-0745-5 (pbk. : alk. paper)
    1. Science—Germany—History—19th century. 2. Technology–
–Germany—History—19th century. 3. Humanities—Germany–
–History—19th century. 4. Social sciences—Germany—History—
19th century. I. Schirmacher, Wolfgang. II. Series.
Q127.G3G37   1996
500—dc20   95-47852
                                                                CIP

Acknowledgments will be found on page 311,
which constitutes an extension of the copyright page.

Contents

Introduction: Wolfgang Schirmacher ix
Translated by Virginia Cutrufelli

Natural History and Science

ALEXANDER VON HUMBOLDT
Reflections on the Enjoyment Presented
to Us by Nature 1
Translated by E. C. Otté

LORENZ OKEN
On the Utility of Natural History 22
Translated by Daniel Theisen

CARL RITTER
Attempt at a General Comparative Geography 31
Translated by Daniel Theisen

LEONHARD EULER
Of Mathematics in General 37
Translater unknown

KARL FRIEDRICH GAUSS
Foundations of Mathematics 42
Translated by G. Waldo Dunnington

JUSTUS VON LIEBIG
On the Study of the Natural Sciences   46
Translated by Daniel Theisen

ADELBERT VON CHAMISSO
A Survey of Botany and the Plant Kingdom   57
Translated by Daniel Theisen

CHRISTOPH VON HUFELAND
Duration of the Life of Plants   64
Translated by Erasmus Wilson

ALFRED E. BREHM
The Importance of Birds in the Economy of Nature   72
Translated by H. M. Labouchere and W. Jesse

RUDOLF VIRCHOW
The Task of the Natural Sciences   80
Translated by Daniel Theisen

PAUL EHRLICH
On Immunity with Special Reference to Cell Life   90
Translated by Charles Bolduan

HERMANN VON HELMHOLTZ
The Physiological Causes of Harmony in Music   108
Translated by Russell Kahl

ADAM MÜLLER
On the Art of Listening   130
Translated by Dennis R. Bormann and Elisabeth Leinfellner

GEORG CHRISTOPH LICHTENBERG
On Physiognomy   141
Translated by Daniel Theisen

Humanities, Social Sciences and Law

JOHANN HEINRICH PESTALOZZI
The Art of Human Education   167
Translated by Daniel Theisen

Contents · vii

JOHANN JAKOB BACHOFEN
My Life in Retrospect   171
Translated by Ralph Manheim

LEOPOLD VON RANKE
History and Philosophy   185
Translated by Roger Wines

JACOB BURCKHARDT
On Fortune and Misfortune in History   188
Translated by James Nichols

RUDOLF VON IHERING
The Struggle for Law   204
Translated by John J. Taylor

FRIEDRICH CARL VON SAVIGNY
Origin of Positive Law   212
Translated by Abraham Hayward

CARL VON CLAUSEWITZ
On Military Genius   217
Translated by Michael Howard and Peter Paret

Economy and Technology

FRIEDRICH LIST
Labor and the Division of Labor   235
Translated by Daniel Theisen

ERNST ABBE
Profit Sharing in Large Industry   250
Translated by Daniel Slager

JOSEPH VON FRAUNHOFER
Of the Refractive and the Dispersive Power of Glass   263
Translated by J. S. Ames

GOTTFRIED DAIMLER
On the Novelty of My Patent Number 28022: A Reply   272
Translated by Daniel Theisen

WERNER VON SIEMENS
Science, Technology, and Organization   281
Translator unknown

Biographies   301
Translated by Virginia Cutrufelli

Bibliography   310

Introduction

The nineteenth century saw the transition of German universities from pedagogical academies to research universities where laboratories were founded and directed by professional scientists. The eminent pathologist Rudolf Virchow reported that contemporary scholarship and textbook science had been almost exclusively French until 1830. In Germany, by contrast, natural history and science had followed the Romantic spirit of the age, favoring an intuitive communion with nature and celebrating the creative powers of imagination. It was a magical world vision destined to unveil the wonders of a living book called *nature*. But the spirit of scientific investigation embodied by Francis Bacon and Galileo, which for hundreds of years had been banished from the fields of medicine and science, returned in force. Both Immanuel Kant's philosophical rejection of a methodology based on beliefs, and the beginning of the industrial age, gave rise to a broad movement toward the study of science and promoted an active inquiry starting from the facts. The popularization of science through education introduced a new and universally practiced method of thinking, taking its cue from observations. A scientist poses the questions not to himself, to his intellect, but to the phenomenon, to the condition itself. The chemist Justus von Liebig stressed that "no art is as difficult as the art of observation." Such observation demands "a sober intellect and the practical knowledge" that comes only through experience. This fearless approach rooted in practice also stimulated the humanities, social sciences, and law, a field greatly changed by impressive reforms of founding figures. German science became dominant on the Continent and, as with German technology, a trademark known the world over.

It should be noted that writers, theorists, and physicians deeply influenced by Romanticism, such as Adelbert von Chamisso, Christoph von Hufeland, Adam Müller, Lorenz Oken, and Friedrich von Savigny, played a crucial role in this epochal turn to a scientific view of nature. Oken, whose genius was lauded by Goethe, studied natural history and introduced a genetic notion of consequence, having established that no phenomenon of nature is simply given. He discovered carbon to be the basis of living matter, and it is an ironic twist that a pantheistic mystic such as Oken became the founder of the exact science of evolution. Alexander von Humboldt and Carl Ritter co-founded earth science, and also comparative geography—not forgetting to include the cultural landscape. American painters as well as writers, Herman Melville for one, acknowledged Humboldt's impact on their work and followed him in his understanding of nature as an adventure. The Romantic poet Chamisso delved into the "plant kingdom" in a noble spirit, but recognized at the same time a need for utilization of his scientific knowledge. The pharmacist and "Royal Physician" Hufeland based his medicine on macrobiotics. The ecologically-minded Alfred Brehm, a zoologist who was respectfully named "father of the animals," gave credit to the "animal kingdom," which has no minor species in relation to the cycle of nature. For the great scientists of the nineteenth century, the study of science was like a journey to a distant land. Nature is a book written in unknown ciphers, Liebig pointed out, but he loved learning to read it. Many of his students founded large-scale chemical factories, or worked for them, and contributed to the international reputation of the German chemical industry. A modern science of life that turned to the concept of the cell, as initiated by Paul Ehrlich, was compelled to abandon all traits of a scientific romanticism still seeking the great unifying principle underlying nature, but in return it gained hard knowledge on immunity. The necessary mathematical cornerstone for such a successful research science was provided by the gifted mathematicians Leonhard Euler and Karl Friedrich Gauss.

That science in all its forms has to serve the betterment of the human condition, as Humboldt phrased it, was a shared belief among the scientists of the age. The physicist, astronomer, and witty observer of his time, Georg Christoph Lichtenberg, remarked that the intensity of the study of natural history had become "insane" in Germany, but he had great hopes for a future science of nature. "Be observant, perceive nothing in vain, measure and compare" was his advice. Hermann von Helmholtz re-founded physiology and investigated the role of sense organs such as the eye and the ear in the synthesis of knowledge. Adam Müller, a representative of political romanticism who proposed an aesthetization of politics, introduced rhetorics as the "art of listening." Modern pedagogy was developed by a Swiss "failure," a man whose name is now synonymous worldwide with pedagogical reform. "Life itself educates, and perception is the basis of all human knowledge," emphasized Heinrich Pestalozzi, who endorsed the "book of the mother." Johann Jakob Bachofen, who received his cross-disciplinary education in England, France, Italy, Switzerland, and Germany, advocated a return to simplicity and found in antiquity a functioning "Mother Right." Do not set yourself above history, was Bachofen's counsel, with which the great historians of the German language could only agree. True to the historical sources, Leopold von Ranke's search for objectivity had a lasting influence on Western historiography. The science of history is different from a philosophy of history and should display a fondness for the particular combined with an eye for the universal. Every historical time must be evaluated in its own terms, Ranke urged, and his Swiss colleague Jacob Burckhardt pointed to the element of chance, to fortune and misfortune in history. The scientists of the nineteenth century generally believed in the enlightened perception of progress, but Burckhardt criticized the underlying notion that the laws of culture are known or could be easily discovered.

The application of science in positive law, economy, and technology is part of the ambivalent success story of German science. Rudolf von Ihering followed the spirit of Savigny's historical school of law but gave it a dynamic interpretation. For Savigny, there is an organic connection between law and the being and character of the people of a certain period; but Ihering understood the living law as a struggle between war and peace. Every legal right has to be continually defended, and law is, therefore, "uninterrupted labor of the entire people." The philosopher of war, Carl von Clausewitz, would certainly agree with this political interpretation of law, since for him, war was the continuation of politics with other means. Without the economic resources and technological inventions developed principally in the nineteenth century, the two world wars would probably never have occurred. The life's work of the economist Friedrich List, exiled and a traveler between the New and the Old Worlds, was devoted to a political economy of capitalism, valuing labor and using protective tariffs. But the most important contribution to applied science came from German inventors such as Ernst Abbe, also a social reformer, and Joseph von Fraunhofer, both of whom revolutionized practical optics, Gottfried Daimler, who was one of the inventors of the automobile, and Werner von Siemens, who invested heavily in communication technology. In some cases, as with Daimler, the scientific principles of the functioning technology were unknown, but this proved no obstacle to an entrepreneurship that transformed Germany from a chiefly agricultural and handicrafts society to an industrial power. Experience counts in science as well as in technology and organization, and, as Clausewitz admonished, one must have the courage to follow the faint light. The self-critical admission of Rudolf Virchow, scientist turned statesman, that scientific thought has its limits and cannot explain the universe in its entirety, was ignored by his contemporaries but proved prophetic in the next century.

For his invaluable help in the selection of the essays in this volume and for its preparation for print, I wish to thank my research associate Sven Nebelung.

W. S.
Translated by Virginia Cutrufelli

NATURAL HISTORY AND SCIENCE

Alexander von Humboldt

Reflections on the Enjoyment Presented to Us by Nature

In reflecting upon the different degrees of enjoyment presented to us in the contemplation of nature, we find that the first place must be assigned to a sensation, which is wholly independent of an intimate acquaintance with the physical phenomena presented to our view, or of the peculiar character of the region surrounding us. In the uniform plain bounded only by a distant horizon, where the lowly heather, the cistus, or waving grasses, deck the soil; on the ocean shore, where the waves, softly rippling over the beach, leave a track, green with the weeds of the sea; everywhere, the mind is penetrated by the same sense of the grandeur and vast expanse of nature, revealing to the soul, by a mysterious inspiration, the existence of laws that regulate the forces of the universe. Mere communion with nature, mere contact with the free air, exercise a soothing yet strengthening influence on the wearied spirit, calm the storm of passion, and soften the heart when shaken by sorrow to its inmost depths. Everywhere, in every region of the globe, in every stage of intellectual culture, the same sources of enjoyment are alike vouchsafed to man. The earnest and solemn thoughts awakened by a communion with nature intuitively arise from a presentiment of the order and harmony pervading the whole uni-

2 · German Essays in Science in the 19th Century

verse, and from the contrast we draw between the narrow limits

verse, and from the contrast we draw between the narrow limits of our own existence and the image of infinity revealed on every side, whether we look upwards to the starry vault of heaven, scan the far-stretching plain before us, or seek to trace the dim horizon across the vast expanse of ocean.

The contemplation of the individual characteristics of the landscape, and of the conformation of the land in any definite region of the earth, gives rise to a different source of enjoyment, awakening impressions that are more vivid, better defined, and more congenial to certain phases of the mind, than those of which we have already spoken. At one time the heart is stirred by a sense of the grandeur of the face of nature, by the strife of the elements, or, as in Northern Asia, by the aspect of the dreary barrenness of the far-stretching steppes; at another time, softer emotions are excited by the contemplation of rich harvests wrested by the hand of man from the wild fertility of nature, or by the sight of human habitations raised beside some wild and foaming torrent. Here I regard less the degree of intensity, than the difference existing in the various sensations that derive their charm and permanence from the peculiar character of the scene.

If I might be allowed to abandon myself to the recollections of my own distant travels, I would instance, among the most striking scenes of nature, the calm sublimity of a tropical night, when the stars, not sparkling, as in our northern skies, shed their soft and planetary light over the gently-heaving ocean;—or I would recall the deep valleys of the Cordilleras, where the tall and slender palms pierce the leafy veil around them, and waving on high their feathery and arrowlike branches, form, as it were, "a forest above a forest"; or I would describe the summit of the Peak of Teneriffe, when a horizontal layer of clouds, dazzling in whiteness, has separated the cone of cinders from the plain below, and suddenly the ascending current pierces the cloudy veil, so that the eye of the traveller may range from the brink of the crater, along the vine-clad slopes of Orotava, to the orange-gardens and banana-groves that skirt the shore. In scenes like these, it is not the peaceful charm uniformly spread over the face of nature that moves the heart, but rather the peculiar physiognomy and conformation of the land, the features of the landscape, the ever-varying outline of the clouds, and their blending with the horizon of the sea, whether it lies spread before us like a smooth and shining mirror, or is dimly seen through the morning mist. All that the senses can but imperfectly comprehend, all that is most awful in such romantic scenes of nature, may become a source of enjoyment to man, by opening a wide field to the creative powers of his imagination. Impressions change with the varying movements of the mind, and we are led by a happy illusion to believe that we receive from the external world that with which we have ourselves invested it.

When far from our native country, after a long voyage, we tread for the first time the soil of a tropical land, we experience a certain feeling of surprise and gratification in recognizing, in the rocks that surround us, the same inclined schistose strata, and the same columnar basalt covered with cellular amygdaloids, that we had left in Europe, and whose identity of character, in latitudes so widely different, reminds us, that the solidification of the earth's crust is altogether independent of climatic influences. But these rocky masses of schist and of basalt are covered with vegetation of a character with which we are unacquainted, and of a physiognomy wholly unknown to us; and it is then, amid the colossal and majestic forms of an exotic flora, that we feel how wonderfully the flexibility of our nature fits us to receive new impressions, linked together by a certain secret analogy. We so readily perceive the affinity existing among all the forms of organic life, that although the sight of a vegetation similar to that of our native country might at first be most welcome to the eye, as the sweet familiar sounds of our mother tongue are to the ear, we nevertheless, by degrees, and almost imperceptibly, become familiarized with a new home and a new climate. As a true citizen of the world, man everywhere habituates himself to that which surrounds him; yet fearful, as it were, of breaking the links of association that bind him to the home of his childhood, the colonist applies to some few plants in a far distant clime the names he had been familiar with in his native land; and by the mysterious relations existing among all types of organization, the forms of exotic vegetation present themselves to his mind as nobler and more perfect developments of those he had loved in earlier days. Thus do the spontaneous impressions of the untutored mind lead, like the laborious deductions of cultivated intellect, to the same intimate persuasion, that one sole and indissoluble chain binds together all nature.

It may seem a rash attempt to endeavor to separate, into its different elements, the magic power exercised upon our minds by the physical world, since the character of the landscape, and of every imposing scene in nature, depends so materially upon the mutual relation of the ideas and sentiments simultaneously excited in the mind of the observer.

The powerful effect exercised by nature springs, as it were, from the connection and unity of the impressions and emotions produced; and we can only trace their different sources by analyzing the individuality of objects, and the diversity of forces. . . .

I will here limit myself to the consideration of a few of the general results whose combination constitutes the *physical delineation of the torrid zone.* That which, in the vagueness of our impressions, loses all distinctness of form, like some distant mountain shrouded from view by a veil of mist, is clearly revealed by the light of mind, which by its scrutiny into the causes of phenomena learns to resolve and analyze their different elements, assigning to each its individual character. Thus in the sphere of natural investigation, as in poetry and painting, the delineation of that which appeals most strongly to the imagination, derives its collective interest from the vivid truthfulness with which the individual features are portrayed.

The regions of the torrid zone not only give rise to the most powerful impressions by their organic richness and their abundant fertility, but they likewise afford the inestimable advantage of revealing to man, by the uniformity of the variations of the atmosphere and the development of vital forces, and by the contrasts of climate and vegetation exhibited at different elevations, the invariability of the laws that regulate the course of the heavenly bodies, reflected, as it were, in terrestrial phenomena. Let us dwell then for a few moments on the proofs of this regularity, which is such, that it may be submitted to numerical calculation and computation.

In the burning plains that rise but little above the level of the sea, reign the families of the banana, the cycas, and the palm, of which the number of species comprised in the flora of tropical regions has been so wonderfully increased in the present day, by the zeal of botanical travelers. To these groups succeed, in the Alpine valleys and the humid and shaded clefts on the slopes of the Cordilleras, the tree-ferns, whose thick cylindrical trunks and delicate lacelike foliage stand out in bold relief against the azure of the sky, and the cinchona, from which we derive the febrifuge bark. The medicinal strength of this bark is said to increase in proportion to the degree of moisture imparted to the foliage of the tree by the light mists which form the upper surface of the clouds resting over the plains. Everywhere around, the confines of the forest are encircled by broad bands of social plants, as the delicate aralia, the thibaudia and the myrtle-leaved andromeda, while the Alpine rose, the magnificent befaria, weaves a purple girdle round the spiry peaks. In the cold regions of the Paramos, which is continually exposed to the fury of storms and winds, we find that flowering shrubs and herbaceous plants, bearing large and variegated blossoms, have given place to monocotyledons, whose slender spikes constitute the sole covering of the soil. This is the zone of the grasses, one vast savannah extending over the immense mountain plateaux, and reflecting a yellow, almost golden tinge, to the slopes of the Cordilleras, on which graze the lama and the cattle domesticated by the European colonist. Where the naked trachyte rock pierces the grassy turf and penetrates into those higher strata of air which are supposed to be less charged with carbonic acid, we meet only with plants of an inferior organization, as lichens, lecideas, and the brightly-colored dustlike lepraria, scattered around in circular patches. Islets of fresh-fallen snow, varying in form and extent, arrest the last feeble traces of vegetable development, and to these succeeds the region of perpetual snow, whose elevation undergoes but little change, and may be easily determined. It is but rarely that the elastic forces at work within the interior of our globe, have succeeded in breaking through the spiral domes, which, resplendent in the brightness of eternal snow, crown the summits of the Cordilleras—and even where these subterranean forces have opened a permanent communication with the atmosphere, through circular craters or long fissures, they rarely send forth currents of lava, but merely eject ignited scoriae, steam, sulphuretted hydrogen gas, and jets of carbonic acid.

In the earliest stages of civilization the grand and imposing spectacle presented to the minds of the inhabitants of the tropics could only awaken feelings of astonishment and awe. It might perhaps be supposed, as we have already said, that the periodical return of the same phenomena, and the uniform manner in which they arrange themselves in successive groups, would have enabled man more readily to attain to a knowledge of the laws of nature; but as far as tradition and history guide us, we do not find that any application was made of the advantages presented by these favored regions. Recent researches have rendered it very doubtful whether the primitive seat of Hindu civilization—one of the most remarkable phases in the progress of mankind—was actually within the tropics. Airyana Vaedjo, the ancient cradle of the Zend, was situated to the northwest of the upper Indus, and after the great religious schism, that is to say, after the separation of the Iranians from the Brahminical institution, the language that had previously been common to them and to the Hindus, assumed among the latter people (together with the literature, habits, and condition of society) an individual form in the Magodha or Madhya Desa, a district that is bounded by the great chain of Himalaya and the smaller range of the Vindhya. In less ancient times the Sanscrit language and civilization advanced towards the southeast, penetrating further within the torid zone, as my brother Wilhelm von Humboldt has shown in his great work on the Kavi and other languages of analogous structure.

Notwithstanding the obstacles opposed in northern latitudes to the discovery of the laws of nature, owing to the excessive complication of phenomena, and the perpetual local variations that, in these climates, affect the movements of the atmosphere and the distribution of organic forms; it is to the inhabitants of a small section of the temperate zone, that the rest of mankind owe the earliest revelation of an intimate and rational acquaintance with the forces governing the physical world. Moreover, it is from the same zone (which is apparently more favorable to the progress of reason, the softening of manners, and the security of public liberty), that the germs of civilization have been carried to the regions of the tropics, as much by the migratory movement of races as by the establishment of colonies, differing widely in their institution from those of the Phoenicians or Greeks.

In speaking of the influence exercised by the succession of phenomena on the greater or lesser facility of recognizing the causes producing them, I have touched upon that important stage of our communion with the external world, when the enjoyment arising from a knowledge of the laws, and the mutual connection of phenomena, associates itself with the charm of a simple contemplation of nature. That which for a long time remains merely an object of vague intuition, by degrees acquires the certainty of positive truth; and man, as has said, amid ceaseless change, seeks the unchanging pole.

In order to trace to its primitive source the enjoyment derived from the exercise of thought, it is sufficient to cast a rapid glance on the earliest dawnings of the philosophy of nature, or of the ancient doctrine of the cosmos. We find even among the most savage nations (as my own travels enable me to attest), a certain vague, terror-stricken sense of the all-powerful unity of natural forces, and of the existence of an invisible, spiritual essence manifested in these forces, whether in unfolding the flower and maturing the fruit of the nutrient tree, in upheaving the soil of the forest, or in rending the clouds with the might of the storm. We may here trace the revelation of a bond of union, linking together the visible world and that higher spiritual world which escapes the grasp of the senses. The two become unconsciously blended together, developing in the mind of man, as a simple product of ideal conception, and independently of the aid of observation, the first germ of a *Philosophy of Nature*.

Among nations least advanced in civilization, the imagination revels in strange and fantastic creations; and by its predilection for symbols, alike influences ideas and language. Instead of examining, men are led to conjecture, dogmatize, and interpret supposed facts that have never been observed. The inner world of thought and of feeling does not reflect the image of the external world in its primitive purity. That which in some regions of the earth manifested itself as the rudiments of natural philosophy, only to a small number of persons endowed with superior intelligence, appears in other regions, and among entire races of men, to be the result of mystic tendencies and instinctive intuitions. An intimate communion with nature, and the vivid and deep emotions thus awakened, are likewise the source from which have sprung the first impulses towards the worship and deification of the destroying and preserving forces of the universe. But by degrees as man, after having passed through the different gradations of intellectual development, arrives at the free enjoyment of the regulating power of reflection, and learns by gradual progress, as it were, to separate the world of ideas from that of sensations, he no longer rests satisfied merely with a vague presentiment of the harmonious unity of natural forces; thought begins to fulfill its noble mission; and observation, aided by reason, endeavors to trace phenomena to the causes from which they spring.

The history of science teaches us the difficulties that have opposed the progress of this active spirit of inquiry. Inaccurate and imperfect observations have led by false inductions to the great number of physical views that have been perpetuated as popular prejudices among all classes of society. Thus by the side of a solid and scientific knowledge of natural phenomena there has been preserved a system of the pretended results of observation, which is so much the more difficult to shake, as it denies the validity of the facts by which it may be refuted. This empiricism, the melancholy heritage transmitted to us from former times, invariably contends for the truth of its axioms with the arrogance of a narrow-minded spirit. Physical philosophy, on the other hand, when based upon science, doubts because it seeks to investigate, distinguishes between that which is certain and that which is merely probable, and strives incessantly to perfect theory by extending the circle of observation.

This assemblage of imperfect dogmas bequeathed by one age to another—this physical philosophy, which is composed of popular prejudices,—is not only injurious because it perpetuates error with the obstinacy engendered by the evidence of ill observed facts, but also because it hinders the mind from attaining to higher views of nature. Instead of seeking to discover the *mean* or *medium* point, around which oscillate, in apparent independence of forces, all the phenomena of the external world, this system delights in multiplying exceptions to the law, and seeks, amid phenomena and in organic forms, for something beyond the marvel of a regular succession, and an internal and progressive development. Ever inclined to believe that the order of nature is disturbed, it refuses to recognize in the present any analogy with the past, and guided by its own varying hypotheses, seeks at hazard, either in the interior of the globe or in the regions of space, for the cause of these pretended perturbations.

It is the special object of the present work to combat those errors which derive their source from a vicious empiricism and from imperfect inductions. The higher enjoyments yielded by the study of nature depend upon the correctness and the depth of our views, and upon the extent of the subjects that may be comprehended in a single glance. Increased mental cultivation has given rise, in all classes of society, to an increased desire of embellishing life by augmenting the mass of ideas, and by multiplying means for their generalization; and this sentiment fully refutes the vague accusations advanced against the age in which we live, showing that other interests, besides the material wants of life, occupy the minds of men. It is almost with reluctance that I am about to speak of a sentiment, which appears to arise from narrow-minded views, or from a certain weak and morbid sentimentality—I allude to the *fear* entertained by some persons, that nature may by degrees lose a portion of the charm and magic of her power, as we learn more and more how to unveil her secrets, comprehend the mechanism of the movements of the heavenly bodies, and estimate numerically the intensity of natural forces. It is true that, properly speaking, the forces of nature can only exercise a magical power over us, as long as their action is shrouded in mystery and darkness, and does not admit of being classed among the conditions with which experience has made us acquainted. The effect of such a power is, therefore, to excite the imagination, but that, assuredly, is not the faculty of mind we would evoke to preside over the laborious and elaborate observations by which we strive to attain to a knowledge of the greatness and excellence of the laws of the universe.

The astronomer who, by the aid of the heliometer or a double-refracting prism, determines the diameter of planetary bodies, who measures patiently, year after year, the meridian altitude and the relative distances of stars, or who seeks a telescopic comet in a group of nebulae, does not feel his imagination more excited—and this is the very guarantee of the precision of his labors—than the botanist who counts the divisions of the calyx, or the number of stamens in a flower, or examines the connected or the separate teeth of the peristoma surrounding the capsule of a moss. Yet the multiplied angular measurements, on the one hand, and the detail or organic relations on the other, alike aid in preparing the way for the attainment of higher views of the laws of the universe.

We must not confound the disposition of mind in the observer at the time he is pursuing his labors, with the ulterior greatness of the views resulting from investigation and the exercise of thought. The physical philosopher measures with admirable sagacity the waves of light of unequal length which by interference mutually strengthen or destroy each other, even with respect to their chemical actions: the astronomer, armed with powerful telescopes, penetrates the regions of space, contemplates, on the extremest confines of our solar system, the satellites of Uranus, or decomposes faintly sparkling points into double stars differing in color. The botanist discovers the constancy of the gyratory motion of the chara in the greater number of vegetable cells, and recognizes in the genera and natural families of plants the intimate relations of organic forms. The vault of heaven, studded with nebulae and stars, and the rich vegetable mantle that covers the soil in the climate of palms, cannot surely fail to produce on the minds of these laborious observers of nature, an impression more imposing and more worthy of the majesty of creation, than on those who are unaccustomed to investigate the great mutual relations of phenomena. I cannot, therefore, agree with Burke when he says, "it is our ignorance of natural things that causes all our admiration, and chiefly excites our passions."

While the illusion of the senses would make the stars stationary in the vault of heaven, astronomy by her aspiring labors has assigned indefinite bounds to space; and if she has set limits to the great nebula to which our solar system belongs, it has only been to show us in those remote regions of space, which appear to expand in proportion to the increase of our optic powers, islet on islet of scattered nebulae. The feeling of the sublime, so far as it arises from a contemplation of the distance of the stars, of their greatness and physical extent, reflects itself in the feeling of the infinite, which belongs to another sphere of ideas included in the domain of mind. The solemn and imposing impressions excited by this sentiment, are owing to the combination of which we have spoken, and to the analogous character of the enjoyment and emotions awakened in us, whether we float on the surface of the great deep, stand on some lonely mountain summit enveloped in the half-transparent vapory veil of the atmosphere, or by the aid of powerful optical instruments scan the regions of space, and see the remote nebulous mass resolve itself into worlds of stars.

The mere accumulation of unconnected observations of details, devoid of generalization of ideas, may doubtlessly have tended to create and foster the deeply-rooted prejudice, that the study of the exact sciences must necessarily chill the feelings, and diminish the nobler enjoyments, attendant upon a contemplation of nature. Those who still cherish such erroneous views in the present age, and amid the progress of public opinion, and the advancement of all branches of knowledge, fail in duly appreciating the value of every enlargement of the sphere of intellect, and the importance of the detail of isolated facts in leading us on to general results.

The fear of sacrificing the free enjoyment of nature, under the influence of scientific reasoning, is often associated with an apprehension, that every mind may not be capable of grasping the truths of the philosophy of nature. It is certainly true that in the midst of the universal fluctuation of phenomena and vital forces—in that inextricable network of organisms by turns developed and destroyed—each step that we make in the more intimate knowledge of nature, leads us to the entrance of new labyrinths; but the excitement produced by a presentiment of discovery, the vague intuition of the mysteries to be unfolded, and the multiplicity of the paths before us, all tend to stimulate the exercise of thought in every stage of knowledge. The discovery of each separate law of nature leads to the establishment of some other more general law, or at least indicates to the intelligent observer its existence. Nature, as a celebrated physiologist has defined it, and as the word was interpreted by the Greeks and Romans, is "that which is ever growing and ever unfolding itself in new forms."

The series of organic types becomes extended or perfected, in proportion as hitherto unknown regions are laid open to our view by the labors and researches of travelers and observers; as living organisms are compared with those which have disappeared in the great revolutions of our planet; and as microscopes are made more perfect and are more extensively and efficiently employed. In the midst of this immense variety, and this periodic transformation of animal and vegetable productions, we see incessantly revealed the primordial mystery of all organic development, that same great problem of metamorphosis which Goethe has treated with more than common sagacity, and to the solution of which man is urged by his desire by reducing vital forms to the smallest number of fundamental types. As men contemplate the riches of nature, and see the mass of observations incessantly increasing before them, they become impressed with the intimate conviction that the surface and the interior of the earth, the depths of the ocean, and the regions of air will still, when thousands and thousands of years have passed away, open to the scientific observer untrodden paths of discovery. The regret of Alexander cannot be applied to the progress of observation and intelligence. General considerations, whether they treat of the agglomeration of matter in the heavenly bodies, or of the geographical distribution of terrestrial organisms, are not only in themselves more attractive than special studies, but they also afford superior advantages to those who are unable to devote much time to occupations of this nature. The different branches of the study of natural history are only accessible in certain positions of social life, and do not at every season and in every climate present like enjoyments. Thus, in the dreary regions of the north, man is deprived for a long period of the year of the spectacle presented by the activity of the productive forces of organic nature; and if the mind be directed to one sole class of objects, the most animated narratives of voyages in distant lands will fail to interest and attract us, if they do not touch upon the subjects to which we are most partial.

As the history of nations—if it were always able to trace events to their true causes—might solve the ever-recurring enigma of the oscillations experienced by the alternately progressive and retrograde movement of human society, so might also the physical description of the world, the science of the cosmos, if it were grasped by a powerful intellect, and based upon a knowledge of all the results of discovery up to a given period, succeed in dispelling a portion of the contradictions, which, at first sight, appear to arise from the complication of phenomena and the multitude of the perturbations simultaneously manifested.

The knowledge of the laws of nature, whether we can trace them in the alternate ebb and flow of the ocean, in the measured path of comets, or in the mutual attractions of multiple stars, alike increases our sense of the calm of nature, while the chimera so long cherished by the human mind in its early and intuitive contemplations, the belief in a "discord of the elements," seems gradually to vanish in proportion as science extends her empire. General views lead us habitually to consider each organism as a part of the entire creation, and to recognize in the plant or the animal, not merely an isolated species, but a form linked in the chain of being to other forms either living or extinct. They aid us in comprehending the relations that exist between the most recent discoveries and those which have prepared the way for them. Although fixed to one point of space, we eagerly grasp at a knowledge of that which has been observed in different and far distant regions. We delight in tracking the course of the bold mariner through seas of polar ice, or in following him to the summit of that volcano of the antarctic pole, whose fires may be seen from afar, even at midday. It is by an acquaintance with the results of distant voyages, that we may learn to comprehend some of the marvels of terrestrial magnetism, and be thus led to appreciate the importance of the establishments of the numerous observatories, which in the present day, cover both hemispheres, and are designed to note the simultaneous occurrence of perturbations, and the frequency and duration of magnetic storms. . . .

The views of comparative geography have been specially enlarged by that admirable work, *Erdkunde im Verhältniss zur Natur und zur Geschichte,* in which Carl Ritter so ably delineates the physiognomy of our globe, and shows the influence of its external configuration on the physical phenomena on its surface, on the migrations, laws, and manners, of nations, and on all the principal historical events enacted upon the face of the earth.

France possesses an immortal work, *L'Exposition du Système du Monde,* in which the author has combined the results of the highest astronomical and mathematical labors, and presented them to his readers free from all processes of demonstration. The structure of the heavens is here reduced to the simple solution of a great problem in mechanics; yet Laplace's work has never yet been accused of incompleteness and want of profundity.

The distinction between dissimilar subjects, and the separation of the general from the special are not only conducive to the attainment of perspicuity in the composition of a physical history of the universe, but are also the means by which a character of greater elevation may be imparted to the study of nature. By the suppression of all unnecessary detail, the great masses are better seen, and the reasoning faculty is enabled to grasp all that might otherwise escape the limited range of the senses.

The exposition of general results has, it must be owned, been singularly facilitated by the happy revolution experienced since the close of the last century, in the condition of all the special sciences, more particularly of geology, chemistry, and descriptive natural history. In proportion as laws admit of more general application, and as sciences mutually enrich each other, and by their extension become connected together in more numerous and more intimate relations, the development of general truths may be given with conciseness devoid of superficiality. On being first examined, all phenomena appear to be isolated, and it is only by the result of a multiplicity of observations, combined by reason, that we are able to trace the mutual relations existing between them. If, however, in the present age, which is so strongly characterized by a brilliant course of scientific discoveries, we perceive a want of connection in the phenomena of certain sciences, we may anticipate the revelation of new facts, whose importance will probably be commensurate with the attention directed to these branches of study. Expectations of this nature may be entertained with regard to meteorology, several parts of optics, and to radiating heat, and electromagnetism, since the admirable discoveries of Melloni and Faraday. A fertile field is here opened to discovery, although the voltaic pile has already taught us the intimate connection existing between electric, magnetic, and chemical phenomena. Who will venture to affirm that we have any precise knowledge, in the present day, of that part of the atmosphere which is not oxygen, or that thousands of gaseous substances affecting our organs may not be mixed with the nitrogen, or finally, that we have even discovered the whole number of the forces which pervade the universe?

It is not the purpose of this essay on the physical history of the world to reduce all sensible phenomena to a small number of abstract principles, based on reason only. The physical history of the universe, whose exposition I attempt to develop, does not pretend to rise to the perilous abstractions of a purely rational science of nature, and is simply a *physical geography, combined with a description of the regions of space and the bodies occupying them.* Devoid of the profoundness of a purely speculative philosophy, my essay on the cosmos treats of the contemplation of the universe, and is based upon a rational empiricism, that is to say, upon the results of the facts registered by science, and tested by the operations of the intellect. It is within these limits alone that the work, which I now venture to undertake, appertains to the sphere of labor, to which I have devoted myself throughout the course of my long scientific career. This path of enquiry is not unknown to me, although it may be pursued by others with greater success. The unity which I seek to attain in the development of the great phenomena of the universe, is analogous to that which historical composition is capable of acquiring. All points relating to the accidental individualities, and the essential variations of the actual, whether in the form and arrangement of natural objects in the struggle of man against the elements, or of nations against nations, do not admit of being based only on a *rational foundation*—that is to say, of being deduced from ideas alone.

It seems to me that a like degree of empiricism attaches to the Description of the Universe and to Civil History; but in reflecting upon physical phenomena and events, and tracing their causes by the process of reason, we become more and more convinced of the truth of the ancient doctrine, that the forces inherent in matter, and those which govern the moral world, exercise their action under the control of primordial necessity, and in accordance with movements occurring periodically after longer or shorter intervals.

It is this necessity, this occult but permanent connection, this periodical recurrence in the progressive development of forms, phenomena, and events, which constitute *nature,* obedient to the first impulse imparted to it. Physics, as the term signifies, is limited to the explanation of the phenomena of the material world by the properties of matter. The ultimate object of the experimental science is, therefore, to discover laws, and to trace their progressive generalization. All that exceeds this goes beyond the province of the physical description of the universe, and appertains to a range of higher speculative views. . . .

The study of a science that promises to lead us through the vast range of creation may be compared to a journey in a far distant land. Before we set forth we consider, and often with distrust, our own strength and that of the guide we have chosen. But the apprehensions which have originated in the abundance and the difficulties attached to the subjects we would embrace, recede from view as we remember that with the increase of observations in the present day, there has also arisen a more intimate knowledge of the connection existing among all phenomena. It has not unfrequently happened, that the researches made at remote distances have often and unexpectedly thrown light upon subjects which had long resisted the attempts made to explain them, within the narrow limits of our own sphere of observation. Organic forms that had long remained isolated, both in the animal and vegetable kingdom, have been connected by the discovery of intermediate links or stages of transition. The geography of beings endowed with life attains completeness, as we see the species, genera, and entire families belonging to one hemisphere, reflected, as it were, in analogous animal and vegetable forms in the opposite hemisphere. These are, so to speak, the *equivalents* which mutually personate and replace one another in the great series of organisms. These connecting links and stages of transition may be traced, alternately, in a deficiency or an excess of development of certain parts, in the mode of junction of distinct organs, in the differences in the balance of forces, or in a resemblance to intermediate forms which are not permanent, but merely characteristic of certain phases of normal development.

Passing from the consideration of beings endowed with life to that of inorganic bodies, we find many striking illustrations of the high state of advancement to which modern geology has attained. We thus see, according to the grand views of Eli de Beaumont, how chains of mountains dividing different climates and floras and different races of man, reveal to us their *relative age,* both by the character of the sedimentary strata they have uplifted, and by the directions which they follow over the long fissures with which the earth's crust is furrowed. Relations of superposition of trachyte and of syenitic porphyry, of diorite and of serpentine, which remain doubtful when considered in the auriferous soil of Hungary, in the rich platinum districts of the Oural, and on the south-western declivity of the Siberian Altaï, are elucidated by the observations that have been made on the plateaux of Mexico and Antioquia, and in the unhealthy ravines of Choco. The most important facts on which the physical history of the world has been based in modern times, have not been accumulated by chance. It has at length been fully acknowledged, and the conviction is characteristic of the age, that the narratives of distant travels, too long occupied in the mere recital of hazardous adventures, can only be made a source of instruction, where the traveler is acquainted with the condition of the science he would enlarge, and is guided by reason in his researches.

It is by this tendency to generalization, which is only dangerous in its abuse, that a great portion of the physical knowledge already acquired may be made the common property of all classes of society; but in order to render the instruction imparted by these means commensurate with the importance of the subject, it is desirable to deviate as widely as possible from the imperfect compilations designated, till the close of the eighteenth century, by the inappropriate term of *popular knowledge.* I take pleasure in persuading myself that scientific subjects may be treated of in language at once dignified, grave and animated, and that those who are restricted within the circumscribed limits of ordinary life, and have long remained strangers to an intimate communion with nature, may thus have opened to them one of the richest sources of enjoyment by which the mind is invigorated by the acquisition of new ideas. Communion with nature awakens within us perceptive faculties that had long lain dormant; and we thus comprehend at a single glance the influence exercised by physical discoveries on the enlargement of the sphere of intellect, and perceive how a judicious application of mechanics, chemistry, and other sciences may be made conducive to national prosperity.

A more accurate knowledge of the connection of physical phenomena will also tend to remove the prevalent error that all branches of natural science are not equally important in relation to general cultivation and industrial progress. An arbitrary distinction is frequently made between the various degrees of importance appertaining to mathematical sciences, to the study of organized beings, the knowledge of electromagnetism, and investigations of the general properties of matter in its different conditions of molecular aggregation; and it is not uncommon presumptuously to affix a supposed stigma upon researches of this nature, by terming them "purely theoretical," forgetting, although the fact has been long attested, that in the observation of a phenomenon, which at first sight appears to be wholly isolated, may be concealed the germ of a great discovery. When Aloysio Galvani first stimulated the nervous fibre by the accidental contact of two heterogeneous metals, his contemporaries could never have anticipated, that the action of the voltaic pile would discover to us, in the alkalies, metals of a silvery luster, so light as to swim on water, and eminently inflammable; or that it would become a powerful instrument of chemical analysis, and at the same time a thermoscope, and a magnet. When Huyghens first observed, in 1678, the phenomenon of the polarization of light, exhibited in the difference between the two rays into which a pencil of light divides itself in passing through a double refracting crystal, it could not have been foreseen, that a century and a half later the great philosopher, Arago, would by his discovery of *chromatic polarization,* be led to discern, by means of a small fragment of Iceland spar, whether solar light emanates from a solid body, or a gaseous covering; or whether comets transmit light directly, or merely by reflection.

An equal appreciation of all branches of the mathematical, physical and natural sciences, is a special requirement of the present age, in which the material wealth and the growing prosperity of nations are principally based upon a more enlightened employment of the products and forces of nature. The most superficial glance at the present condition of Europe shows that a diminution, or even a total annihilation of national prosperity, must be the award of those states who shrink with slothful indifference from the great struggle of rival nations in the career of the industrial arts. It is with nations as with nature, which, according to a happy expression of Goethe, "knows no pause in progress and development, and attaches her curse on all inaction." The propagation of an earnest and sound knowledge of science can therefore alone avert the dangers of which I have spoken. Man cannot act upon nature, or appropriate forces to his own use, without comprehending their full extent, and having an intimate acquaintance with the laws of the physical world. Bacon has said that, in human societies, knowledge is power. Both must rise and sink together. But the knowledge that results from the free action of thought, is at once the delight and the indestructible prerogative of man; and in forming part of the wealth of mankind, it not unfrequently serves as a substitute for the natural riches, which are but sparingly scattered over the earth. Those states which take no active part in the general industrial movement, in the choice and preparation of natural substances, or in the application of mechanics and chemistry, and among whom this activity is not appreciated by all classes of society, will infallibly see their prosperity diminish in proportion as neighboring countries become strengthened and invigorated under the genial influence of arts and sciences.

As in nobler spheres of thought and sentiment, in philosophy, poetry, and the fine arts, the object at which we aim ought to be an inward one—an ennoblement of the intellect—so ought we likewise, in our pursuit of science, to strive after a knowledge of the laws and the principles of unity that pervade the vital forces of the universe; and it is by such a course that physical studies may be made subservient to the progress of industry, which is a conquest of mind over matter. By a happy connection of causes and effects, we often see the useful linked to the beautiful and the exalted. The improvement of agriculture in the hands of free men, and on properties of a moderate extent—the flourishing state of the mechanical arts freed from the trammels of municipal restrictions—the increased impetus imparted to commerce by the multiplied means of contact of nations with each other—are all brilliant results of the intellectual progress of mankind, and of the amelioration of political institutions, in which this progress is reflected. The picture presented by modern history ought to convince those who are tardy in awakening to the truth of the lesson it teaches.

Nor let it be feared, that the marked predilection for the study of nature, and for industrial progress, which is so characteristic of the present age, should necessarily have a tendency to retard the noble exertions of the intellect in the domains of philosophy, classical history, and antiquity; or to deprive the arts by which life is embellished of the vivifying breath of imagination. Where all the germs of civilization are developed beneath the aegis of free institutions and wise legislation, there is no cause for apprehending that any one branch of knowledge should be cultivated to the prejudice of others. All afford the state precious fruits, whether they yield nourishment to man and constitute his physical wealth, or whether, more permanent in their nature, they transmit in the works of mind the glory of nations to remotest posterity. The Spartans, notwithstanding their Doric austerity, prayed the gods to grant them "the beautiful with the good."

I will no longer dwell upon the considerations of the influence exercised by the mathematical and physical sciences on all that appertains to the material wants of social life; for the vast extent of the course on which I am entering forbids me to insist further upon the utility of these applications. Accustomed to distant excursions, I may, perhaps, have erred in describing the path before us as more smooth and pleasant than it really is, for such is wont to be the practice of those who delight in guiding others to the summits of lofty mountains: they praise the view even when great parts of the distant plains lie hidden by clouds, knowing that this half-transparent vapory veil imparts to the scene a certain charm from the power exercised by the imagination over the domain of the senses. In like manner, from the height occupied by the physical history of the world, all parts of the horizon will not appear equally clear and well-defined. This indistinctness will not, however, be wholly owing to the present imperfect state of some of the sciences, but in part, likewise, to the unskilfulness of the guide who has imprudently ventured to ascend these lofty summits.

The object of this essay is not, however, solely to draw attention to the importance and greatness of the physical history of the universe, for in the present day these are too well understood to be contested, but likewise to prove how, without detriment to the stability of special studies, we may be enabled to generalize our ideas by concentrating them in one common focus, and thus arrive at a point of view from which all the organisms and forces of nature may be seen as one living active whole, animated by one sole impulse. "Nature," as Schelling remarks in his poetic discourse on art, "is not an inert mass; and to him, who can comprehend her vast sublimity, she reveals herself as the creative force of the universe—before all time, eternal, ever active, she calls to life all things, whether perishable or imperishable."

By uniting, under one point of view, both the phenomena of our own globe and those presented in the regions of space, we embrace the limits of the science of the cosmos, and convert the physical history of the globe into the physical history of the universe; the one term being modeled upon that of the other. This science of the cosmos is not, however, to be regarded as a mere encyclopedic aggregation of the most important and general results that have been collected together from special branches of knowledge. These results are nothing more than the materials for a vast edifice, and their combination cannot constitute the physical history of the world, whose exalted part it is to show the simultaneous action and the connecting links of the forces which pervade the universe. The distribution of organic types in different climates and at different elevations—that is to say, the geography of plants and animals—differs as widely from botany and descriptive zoology as geology does from mineralogy, properly so called. The physical history of the universe must not, therefore, be confounded with the *Encyclopedias of the Natural Sciences,* as they have hitherto been compiled, and whose title is as vague as their limits are ill-defined. In the work before us, partial facts will be considered only in relation to the whole. The higher the point of view the greater is the necessity for a systematic mode of treating the subject in language at once animated and picturesque.

But thought and language have ever been most intimately allied. If language, by its originality of structure, and its native richness, can, in its delineations, interpret thought with grace and clearness, and if, by its happy flexibility, it can paint with vivid truthfulness the objects of the external world, it reacts at the same time upon thought, and animates it, as it were, with the breath of life. It is this mutual reaction which makes words more than mere signs and forms of thought; and the beneficent influence of a language is most strikingly manifested on its native soil, where it has sprung spontaneously from the minds of the people, whose character it embodies. Proud of a country that seeks to concentrate her strength in intellectual unity, the writer recalls with delight the advantages he has enjoyed in being permitted to express his thoughts in his native language; and truly happy is he, who, in attempting to give a lucid exposition of the great phenomena of the universe, is able to draw from the depths of a language, which through the free exercise of thought, and by the effusions of creative fancy, has for centuries past exercised so powerful an influence over the destinies of man.

Translated by E. C. Otté

Lorenz Oken

On the Utility of Natural History

Wherever I may browse in the encomia to natural history, I see nothing but a base praising of the profit this discipline affords when the craftsman and the artisan bring with them some knowledge of it into their workshops. If the occasional incidental glance is cast to its influence upon the sciences, it remains nevertheless in the background. The temporal profitability to tradesmen is emphasized, as though one wanted to use this profitability to attract the common people, who are not yet able to comprehend more noble ends. This would be a feasible course of action to take if one were dealing with a people who, having just emerged from the state of savagery, stood tottering on the threshold to the state of communal existence.

We may, however, believe to our encouragement that the education of the German people has progressed further than those extollers and proponents of natural history have the cheek to allow; that the German seeks in the sciences not base utility, which oppresses the spirit and even the body, but that he recognizes the noble, consummate, gratifying, enriching value of the sciences, the value which avails itself to all spiritual and bodily aspirations, and that he honors, acquires, and cultivates these sciences for their own sake. If indeed a base conception of natural history does yet exist among our people, then it has been placed there by the teachers of this science, who fail to recognize its true value. Can anything attest more to the utter lack of all truly scholarly disposition, of all truly scientific spirit than the questionable attempt to tear out isolated fragments of natural history and to treat them as an independent discipline? What will become of our science, what will become of our education, if in the end they consist of nothing more than natural history for dyers, or foresters, or factory owners; if in place of mineralogy, which teaches us solely about the existence of our planet, about its formation, about the nature of its components, and thereby about all possible uses, if in place of this consummate science we are given a mineralogy for masons, for dyers, for apothecaries?! What will become of botany, if nothing more is taught or learned than economic, medical, forestrial, or kitchen botany?! Of all the sciences, zoology has been the most successful in preserving its scientific essence, but doubtlessly for the sole reason that it is itself so scientifically constructed that any subdisciplines that may be wrenched from its general framework, be they in and of themselves useful or harmful, could never be treated as whole, independent sciences.

This fragmentation of natural history leads to a loss of all scientific cohesiveness and of a sense thereof, and only the motives of profiteering and greed misuse such lax and isolated knowledge. Love of science is lost, and anyone who does not want to learn a corresponding trade knows nothing but that he does not need that knowledge. This miseducation must needs become general, and lead to a situation where one would regard this knowledge not as universally necessary to a truly human education, but as merely of limited significance, affording advantage to this or that interest, and would in the end be dismissed by someone who considers himself to belong to a different field.

Such a distorted view of this science would of necessity lead even educated, learned men to believe that only the future doctor would need to learn natural history, and botany in particular, because it serves only him; that no one else would have any use for it. This distorted view would of necessity lead the doctor to believe that for him, only those areas of natural history pertaining to medicine were necessary, that general natural history belonged solely to the realm of the scholar. If in the end this science is deemed to be of use only to doctors, and if only those aspects that are useful to doctors are deemed useful at all, then it is easy to see that such a profiteering scholarship will result in no one at all cultivating science as a whole.

The fragmentation of natural history and its debasement to a venture of mere profit, however, not only bring about the destruction of the scientific spirit, but lead to the downfall of the isolated, detached, trade-oriented branches as well. How can the system of botany be taught with any comprehensibility within the framework of medicinal botany? How can an economic or a hunter's zoology ever be taught, since the majority of the animals that are absolutely essential to the construction of the system occur neither in the economy nor in the game preserve? Thus do these pseudoscientific branches fall apart, and degenerate into a senseless listing, describing, and naming of animals.

Far be it from me, however, to dismiss as useless, let alone as pernicious, these isolated elaborations of natural science and their application to the trades, to agriculture, etc. On the contrary, I hold them to be useful and necessary, but not in the form in which they are now being pursued. They must never want to develop into sciences in their own right, they must always keep in mind their essential relationship to science in general, of which they are but branches. One must never teach them without stressing the primacy of science in general; otherwise, one runs the risk of misguiding young minds and eradicating the people's true appreciation for the sciences.

But I do unconditionally hold these isolated branches to be pernicious when it comes to the education of scholars. The scholar is not to be made into a mere tradesman, nor the physician into a mere writer of prescriptions, the theologian into a mere reciter of sermons, the jurist into a mere copier of laws, the philologist into a mere word maker, the metaphysician into a mere tinkerer of formulas. Each should be a creator in his field, each should carry the treasure of human knowledge within himself, out of which he independently brings forth what the tradesman reproduces. But what can the physician bring forth independently in his science when he knows nothing but the names of a few hundred medicinal herbs? How can the theologian open the eyes of his congregation to the power and the goodness of the creator when he knows nothing of the wonders of nature, revealed in all fullness in each stone, in each plant, and in the eyes of each animal? How can the jurist ever be able to come to decisions in litigation regarding objects of nature and damages thereto when he has no knowledge of these? How can the philologist or the historian ever explain anything about the teachings of the ancients, imbued as they were with the wisdom of nature, if he does not know what they knew? How, finally, can the metaphysician ever hope to produce anything better than fables about nature if the level of his knowledge is no higher than that of those previously mentioned?

The knowledge of nature is for each and every person a necessity. For the tradesman, further and specialized development of this knowledge is necessary for him to carry out his work, but for the scholar from any field, mere specialization is a detriment. He, the scholar, has been appointed to stand watch over the sanctity of the sciences; this sanctity lies, however, only in the integrity, in the wholeness of the sciences, not in the specialized, isolated refinement, which serves only the profit motive and those of clever ignorance.

I shall leave it to others to speak at length on the practical utility of natural history and to list and name those plants and animals that yield to us monetary benefits, and shall direct myself towards the higher utility.

Philosophy's return to that object with which it occupied itself in the grayest days of antiquity, namely nature, is a conquest of the most recent modernity, which holds for us the promise of a return of that same auspicious era for the sciences that had blossomed for them before ignorant sophistry and hairsplitting scholasticism succeeded in thrusting aside the natural sciences. But hardly had a sense for the philosophical study of nature been awakened when, as happens with all new, promising prospects, a vacuous swarm took the floor, spouting formulas and empty, baroque notions about nature; almost to the point where this science, hardly having awakened, threatened to sink back into its old slumber on account of the mischief to which it was subjected at the hands of its ignorant adherents. So discouraged were the more well-informed of the scholars, and so poorly had the vacuous ones portrayed natural history, that the object of their portrayal was anything but natural history!

These times are over! One can no longer rely on empty formulas, grandiloquent phrases, baroque words, and inadequate content to make one's fortune in Germany. Perhaps one can try one's luck with these ruses in another country. Natural philosophy has taken a turn that is thoroughly real, onto a course that can only be pursued with the help of a rich treasure of extensive knowledge of nature. The times are over in which ignorant speculators from the ranks of the aesthetes can try their luck; that which has yielded only chaff and bubbles has been scattered by the winds, and what remains is strong and unified enough to exterminate everything that should ever again endeavor to bring about such a phantasmic period in natural philosophy.

The stranger to the natural sciences, physics, and natural history can no longer hope to understand the doctrine of natural philosophy. Even less should such a person be allowed to speak on these topics. Thus, the number of those who cultivate natural philosophy will initially decrease, until the science education in our German schools has had the chance to establish a firmer footing and prevail; but then the number, be it small or large, will consist not of gapers and fortune hunters, but of solid scientists, with whom natural philosophy will be forever secure, and through whom natural philosophy will be able to reap respect from any person of reason.

But all philosophy must begin with natural philosophy, and end with it as well, or else all philosophy is but natural philosophy. Without it, all metaphysics is a monstrosity. Morals, however, natural law, religion and art, in the most comprehensive sense ethics, all of these are but the blossoms of natural philosophy. None of those sciences can be grasped without the latter, much less delineated, by one who is not imbued with both. Our religious, our moral, our legal circumstances are, as are those of art, predelineated in the divine laws of nature, and can be clearly developed only through the philosophy of nature; without these they are nothing but chimeras and phantasms.

Whoever has not attained a deep, ardent devotion in religion and art, a clear insight into morality, law, and heroism, a divine reassurance in the face of the problem of the world, is no natural philosopher. But it is in that direction that every man of learning strives; it is indeed the very essence of the learned to fathom the world and the intellect, without which all education is in vain. This state, however, cannot be attained through the versions of sciences specialized for the trades, through the breadwinning sciences, but only through the pure, complete science that teaches everything that falls within its scope, without base intentions.

But anyone in possession of the whole science is likewise in possession of the specialized ones, the breadwinning sciences as well; but he, however, knows not the latter without the former. Whoever knows botany knows medicinal botany as well, and forestial botany, and economic botany. He knows these solely because he has produced them from within himself, while the other, who knows only these, has done nothing but memorize them like a child. The same holds for mineralogy, the same for zoology. The education of the learned one, who is without a doubt identical with the scholar, is a whole education, not a piecemeal education; it is a masterpiece, not the work of a day laborer.

The supreme, indeed, the only value of natural history is ultimately to elevate a people to a universal education, and only natural history can make such an education complete. Until now, the value of natural history had always been solely a particular one: its role in the establishment of a true professional scholarship. It is about time, though, that it accomplished for the people as a whole what it has accomplished in this role: harmony with oneself and with the world, clear knowledge of one's own and others' humanity, of the essential natures of animals, plants, and minerals, their relationships to each other, to humanity, and to the entire world of the intellect; a general education towards earnest humaneness, towards masculine resignation, towards the power of insight over the power of force, towards love of the whole, since only the whole is the true object of natural science, and not towards love of the wretched individual, which just like any selfishly profiteering science is destined to perish.

There is a confession that, shameful as it may be, I must make, if natural science is to be accorded its due honor. As much as we can assure ourselves that individual education in our midst has risen to a level superior to that of all other nations, we cannot deny that the majority of foreign peoples known to us enjoy a great advantage over us when it comes to universal education and heroic resignation to insight. But what is the individual in the turmoil of the whole? A weak, yes, a ridiculed voice in the desert!

It is just this excessive preponderance of education among the learned that robs the competent people of its organ of understanding, which erects an impenetrable barrier between the two classes, a barrier that among the foreigners, owing to the even distribution of education within their societies, does not exist. For the unity of a people to be brought about, all that is required is that those of high position be understood, regardless of whether they are to be counted more among the masses or among the learned. With the foreigners, the former seems to be the case; as far as we are concerned, neither is the case. Those of higher position have outstripped those of lower position, two camps have formed and have become alien to one another, cooperation is lacking, failure and ineptitude are everywhere, obtuseness here, arrogance there. That is the reason why the German does not respect or appreciate anything a German has accomplished, why he marvels and emulates only the foreigners. He attributes their accomplishments to their harmony and their educational style, which renders even the masses receptive to the educational level of the higher minds.

It is from this alienation between the two classes that all our misfortune emanates. The striving for higher education on the part of the lower classes is commendable, but for them, no intermediate step is available. They can aspire to a higher education only through a *salto mortale,* but when they do, they find themselves drifting about in an unfamiliar world in which they no more attain understanding than those from the upper classes condescend to try and understand them. Everyone isolates himself and loses his sense of purpose. Education is not able to transcend the individual, intelligence serves only profit, self-interest displaces public spirit, bitter rage displaces honesty, assertion, even assertion of the lowest existence, displaces honor. We need only see how completely the main pillars of the state have lost their orientation! The scholar carries on science in the manner of a day laborer, the clergy is becoming bourgeois, the nobility is sinking to the level of peasants! All of this has resulted from the previously described tension of our education.

But in what way does the foreigners' education, which leads them to mutual understanding and fortune in their endeavors, differ from our own? The answer lies obviously and uncontestably in their science education. Among those peoples, the study of all positive sciences, particularly the physical sciences and natural history, has attained dominance, especially in education; it has become fashionable among those from all walks of life, whereas in our society, the study of these sciences has been taken up on the one hand by a limited circle of scholars, and has become on the other hand a mere plaything for children or an instrument of profiteering for the proprietors of factories.

We, however, to speak only of the education that is currently in fashion, and with which both classes are equally afflicted, have entered the period of affectation and unclever cleverness; we lack a sound foundation and the proper steadfastness. Clever prattle about everything, even about the natural sciences, passes for universal education, something that everyone is grasping for and that anyone can acquire cheaply. But real education demands earnest endeavor. Nature does not play; even less so does the march of humanity, which tramples those peoples who do not understand it, who are not aware that humanity only reenacts that which a relentlessly geometrizing nature has already enacted. How can one who has not integrated nature into himself, who is not himself nature, ever hope to be human, how can he fit into nature's plan, how can he endure in the face of her elements?

If we have indeed lacked the insight into the value of the positive sciences, if we have not on the basis of these sciences recognized that they alone can render humanity consummate, then we now have the experience before us that has delivered us a rude awakening. A people that does not know how to coexist with nature, a people that desires only to manipulate or to master nature, such a people cannot hold its own against other peoples! He who does not know nature cannot conquer her, and neither can he know the character and the power of those peoples who do understand each other.

Oh, that the Germans might one day begin to plant at the root, instead of merely pruning and trimming the branches of a gnarled trunk! Might they produce objects instead of verbiage, deeds instead of cunning cleverness, promote an education in nature before a humanistic education! The blossom cannot grow without the stem!

A good, noble, solid foundation has been laid to this purpose: the education of antiquity, in which the Germans excel. Only a barbarian would want to suppress this method, but how easily does it degenerate into a mere virtuosity in the coining of words, how easily does the study of antiquity, through which the mind is made receptive to all real education, degenerate into a mere pedantic, slavish learning of dead languages, to the letters of which one clings without penetrating to the deeper message!

Whatever may have been said to the contrary, languages are nothing but the means to the education that emanates solely from reality, of which the languages are merely designations. We at the universities can be anything but grateful to those forms of education that allow the pupil to choose the fields of his rudimentary knowledge with unguided arbitrariness, for treating the natural sciences without rigor and as matters of secondary importance, thus inducing the young mind to fail to appreciate the exceeding value of these sciences. We can be anything but grateful to those who provide us with nothing but mouthpieces; the German people can be anything but grateful, for what it requires is men. What we require is a spirit cognizant of the necessity of the real, a love for rigor in the natural sciences, and enthusiasm for the good cause—good since it is forced upon us by nature and by preponderant nations.

But even a memory weighted down with thousands of names can be of no service to us. True education in natural history consists not in a register of names, not in the knowledge of all products of nature, even less in the profiteering that can be carried out therewith; it consists in the comprehension of nature as a whole, in the global view of the interrelationships of her primary organs, in the recognition of her relationships to man and to the state, to which end the knowledge of all characteristic organs and the enumeration and the natural ordering of all families of animals, plants, and minerals is of course required. But the petty lumping together and dividing up of all species of creatures, together with the thereby necessitated neglect of their inner structure, the significance of their own organization and their sequential relationship to other families or species; this lumping together and dividing up is not only not necessary, but actually detrimental to the spirit of natural history and to the general ennoblement of a people. With natural history, what is of primary importance is not what one may add to it in the course of time. The knowledge of minerals does not exist for its own sake, but for the sake of geology; botany must needs reach its consummation in plant physiology; zoology has only to prepare the way for comparative and philosophical zoology. These sciences, as they are now being taught and as they must always be taught, must not be allowed to remain in isolation. The head and the soul that they all lack must be added, if an education of thinking and judgment, not merely the training of memory, is to be established, if a point of mediation in education is to be created, through which mutual understanding between the classes can be fostered.

Translated by Daniel Theisen

Carl Ritter

Attempt at a General Comparative Geography

If it is acknowledged that each and every person of morals, for the carrying out of his occupation, must maintain an awareness of the measure of his powers, and of what is external to him or of his environment, as well as his relationship to it, and if this is acknowledged likewise to hold true for all of those who through earnest endeavor would succeed in anything, then it is clear that every association of persons as well, that every people, must become conscious of their own internal and external powers, as well as those of their neighbors, and of their relationship to all conditions acting upon them from without, if they are not to wander astray of their true goal.

Blind striving and unconscious wanting do not, for all the exertion and activity they may give rise to, impart that power that leads to just existence and earnest endeavor. A more developed striving is called for, a more conscious wanting, one that would correspond to the aforementioned power, that would manifest itself, where clarity meets truth, in noble, great, and memorable deeds, deeds that belong to the realm of eternity. It is not the confused multiplicity of unrestrained forces, but the intuitive perception of measure and law in the infinite profusion and power that imbues even the physical aspects of our being with a thrilling presentiment of the divine.

But the earnest will of man, and the knowledge of what corresponds to his inherent power in what is external to him, as well as the mutual permeation and enhancement of both, these can only emerge from the serious struggle for deeper knowledge of the self, and from the contemplation of the human and of everything that has revealed itself in the history of humanity.

Just as every individual, owing to his or her nature, is not able to rise to every task nor called upon to do so, neither is any one people able to achieve every goal and be crowned with the laurels of fame and fortune. It is characteristic of human nature that in each individual dwells a set of traits shared by no other individual. By developing these traits, the individual becomes more perfect; this hold true for peoples just as much as it does for individuals. The greatness of man, moral and otherwise, lies in the consummate development of these characteristic traits, as does the national character, the national greatness of a people. This consummate development warms and illuminates the present and the future, not pursuant to temporal and spatial, but to moral greatness, and casts its shining rays deep into the entire realm of the present-day lives of the peoples and of unfolding history.

Character, however, is not something a people can give to itself, just as it is not something an individual can give to himself; all either can do is to maintain the independence of such a character. Character itself, however, emanates from a power higher than that of man in all his insignificance. But it lies only in his power, and what is more, in his vocation, to become aware of this character in life, for without this awareness, his endeavors can never succeed.

The character of a people can only be discerned on the basis of its nature, on the basis of its relationship with itself, with its constituent members, with its environments, and, because no people can be conceived of without a state and a fatherland, on the basis of its relationship to both of these, and on the basis of the relationship of both of these to neighboring lands and states.

Here reveals itself the influence that nature must needs exert upon peoples, to a much higher degree, it must be noted, than it does upon individuals, because here masses are working upon masses, so to speak, and the personality of the people as a body stands out above that of the individual.

This influence has been recognized, and has always been an important object of investigation for the history of peoples, states, and mankind in general; it has, in our day as well, become a topic of ardent discussion.

But nature everywhere exerts her power in a gradual fashion, and does so more in secret than by the bright light of day. The seed sprouts underground, and within the protective husk of the bud lies the preformed impulse for the creation of a yet another new generation. Thus are her conditions and actions, wherever one looks, deeper than they appear, more simple than they look in their initial diversity, and with astonishingly far-reaching consequences. The quiet force she exerts requires an equally quiet soul into which she can instill the impressions of her phenomena; only such a soul can penetrate undisturbed to the center of her lawful regularity.

Often, nothing is needed to contemplate such a similarly formed soul but an outward sign, the right vision, the sincere word, because like understands like. But now, at least, nature is no longer quite so close to man; she has become to him a mysterious entity, and only in the large-scale coordination of her forces, only in the coherence of her phenomena does she allow herself to be contemplated. Only then does she cast light and radiate life onto all the paths upon which human zeal dares to tread; her radiance becomes then a blinding star, the fullness of which human zeal is not, in the end, able to fathom. Then she illuminates all the prevailing conditions of creation, which we are wont to designate animate and inanimate nature, and begins to answer our questions, above all our questions pertaining to humanity.

Should it not be worth the effort, for the sake of human history and the history of the various nations, to proceed for a change from a hitherto disregarded aspect, from that of the earth in its essential relationship to people, from the arena of its general activity, i.e., its surface, and to strive to comprehend the image and the life of nature in all her interconnections as sharply and as exactly as individual powers allow, and to follow the course of her simplest and most general geographical laws in her static, dynamic, and animated formations?

The earth, existing independently of man, is the arena for all occurrences of nature; it was so before his arrival, and it would be so even without him. The law governing its formations can therefore not emanate from man. In a science of the earth, the earth itself must be inquired of its laws. The monuments raised upon it by nature, as well as their hieroglyphs, must be observed and described, and their construction decoded. Its surfaces, its depths, its heights must be measured, its forms must be classified according to their essential characteristics, and the observers of all times and of all peoples must be heard and understood, as indeed must the peoples themselves in what they reveal to these observers, and in what through these peoples has been made known about the earth. The facts, those that proceed from the aforementioned, as well as those that have long since been passed down to us, must, in their often repressed and forgotten multitude, diversity, and unity, be arranged into a lucid whole.

Then the result would emerge by itself from each individual member, from each progression; the result, whose truth would prove itself in localized occurrences of nature and as a reflection in the life of those peoples whose existence and particular character coincide with this or that progression of characteristic geological formation. For determined as they are by a higher order, peoples as well as individuals emerge, through the influence of an activity of nature and of reason, from the spiritual and from the physical element alike into the all-consuming circle of the life of the world. After all, each organism forms itself in accordance with its inner coherence and its external environment, and makes itself known in the law and in the form that condition and enhance one another, since nowhere in it does chance prevail.

Not only in the limited circle of the valley or the mountain range, or of a people and a state do these reciprocal conditions exert their influence upon their histories, but in all plains and elevations, among all peoples and states, from the time of their conception right up to the present day. All of them are subject to the same influence of nature, and if this seems to express itself, or is expressed, in only one or the other point, so then is it every bit as certain that this influence has operated everywhere and at all times under a deeper cover of concealment, just as the once unknown God, who had of course been omnipresent all along, operates in a higher world.

Just as God was initially only known and revered on the basis of His individual works, without having yet been seen by mortal eye, so shall one day the disunity of the thousands of competing forces of nature be resolved, the unity of such forces being at present obscured to our eyes, and this unity shall enter the realm of human wisdom.

Armed with this belief, all striving for a comprehensive overview of the workings of nature in all their interconnections, as weak as this striving may be, can be fruitful, as long as it is guided by the spirit of truth, and only in this regard can an endeavor such as the present one be taken up with love by the contemporaries, only in this way can its content be given life.

It is not up to the individual to fulfill such a task. To the end of fathoming this task, more or less every person of any depth makes, through his life's work, his contribution to the well-being of the succeeding generation. All the individual can do is join in this task with the powers that have been given him, and in the course of faithful historical development inquire into the unity of law in the diversity of phenomena.

The palm of renown belongs, in recognition of their status as the heroes of history, to those intellectual explorers, who, furnished with deep power of soul and great strength of character, and proceeding from the complexity of isolated occurrences, from the thought process and the history of the isolated individual, or of one people, or of the community of peoples, were through their deeds able to illuminate and illustrate human nature from its unconscious depths to its dizzying heights, and who through their demonstration of the characteristic course of development leading to the attainment of the highest pinnacles of morality and nationhood, were able to become immortal teachers to all the peoples of the earth.

Perhaps the time will come when equally strong characters, by encompassing the world of nature as well as the world of morals with their penetrating gaze, looking forward and backward from out of the totality of globally historical occurrences, will be able to show to each people, in light of this general given situation, the necessary course of development they themselves must take in their respective places on this earth, if they too are to attain the prosperity granted to each and every faithful people by the eternally just power of fate.

To the end of bringing ourselves closer to such a truly great goal, a goal aspired to by so many, the highest task of the wisdom of state, a goal that in all its greatness shines over to us from a dark prehistoric world only in the songs of the prophets with their enthusiastic gaze towards nature and towards history; to the end of once again bringing ourselves closer to a lost goal such as this one, this path, which along with its results is being presented here, can serve within the realm of the sciences as one of the preparatory means.

It is a path that admittedly appears at first sight meandering, yet it proceeds, speaking in a human sense, from its starting point quite solidly in the direction of the point to which it leads; and even if it does not lead to its final goal, the prospects and the knowledge that can be attained by proceeding along it appear to be not at all insignificant. Without straying off into the endlessness of individual experience, it proceeds only step by step from specialized experience, and thus becomes the curve expressive of the general law, through which the multiplicity of experience or of the material world can be mastered and wielded in service of the higher purpose.

But not the general law of only one, but rather of all essential forms in which nature appears—on the largest scale on the surface of the earth, as well as on the smallest scale in each particular locality thereon—should become the object of investigation along this path. For only by drawing upon the totality of the general laws governing all the basic and main types of the inanimate as well as the animate surface of the earth can the harmony of the entire, full world of phenomena be expressed.

And if the idea of the entire human race is utterly unthinkable without the earth, then the individual, the nation, being as it is much more dependant upon the earth, as well as the state, fettered as it is to the nature of its country, none of these will ever be able to aspire to full harmony with themselves without an awareness of their true relationship to the earth.

Or in other words, only this accord between people and fatherland, between the relationship of the state to nature and to human existence, or to physics and politics, only this accord has, proceeding from the one side throughout the history of the world, given rise to and promoted the flourishing of peoples and states.

And where this accord no longer springs forth unconsciously, bound up with the organic development of the various peoples, as it perhaps did in an earlier period of prehistory, the law of this accord, this eternal tetrakis, must, as the necessity of the present day commands, be discovered through serious scientific study, as the inexhaustible source of all harmony and must be inscribed into human consciousness.

Translated by Daniel Theisen

Leonhard Euler

Of Mathematics in General

Whatever is capable of increase or diminution, is called *magnitude* or *quantity*.

A sum of money, for instance, is a quantity, since we may increase it or diminish it. The same may be said with respect to any given weight, and other things of this nature.

From this definition, it is evident, that there must be so many different kinds of magnitude as to render it difficult even to enumerate them: and this is the origin of the different branches of mathematics, each being employed on a particular kind of magnitude. Mathematics, in general, is the *science of quantity;* or, the science that investigates the means of measuring quantity.

Now we cannot measure or determine any quantity, except by considering some other quantity of the same kind as known, and pointing out their mutual relation. If it were proposed, for example, to determine the quantity of a sum of money, we should take some known piece of money (as a dollar, a crown, a ducat, or some other coin,) and show how many of these pieces are contained in the given sum. In the same manner, if it were proposed to determine the quantity of a weight, we should take a certain known weight; for example, a pound, an ounce, etc. and then show how many times one of these weights is contained in that which we are endeavoring to ascertain. If we wished to measure any length or extension, we should make use of some known length, as a foot for example.

So that the determination, or the measure of magnitude of all kinds, is reduced to this: fix at pleasure upon any one known magnitude of the same species with that which is to be determined, and consider it as the *measure or unit;* then, determine the proportion of the proposed magnitude to this known measure. This proportion is always expressed by numbers; so that a number is nothing but the proportion of one magnitude to another arbitrarily assumed as the unit.

From this it appears, that all magnitudes may be expressed by numbers; and that the foundation of all the mathematical sciences must be laid in a complete treatise on the science of numbers; and in an accurate examination of the different possible methods of calculation.

This fundamental part of mathematics is called analysis, or algebra.

In algebra then we consider only numbers that represent quantities, without regarding the different kinds of quantity. These are the subjects of other branches of the mathematics.

Arithmetic treats of numbers in particular, and is the *science of numbers properly so called;* but this science extends only to certain methods of calculation which occur in common practice: algebra, on the contrary, comprehends in general all the cases which can exist in the doctrine and calculation of numbers.

* * *

The principal object of algebra, as well as of all the parts of mathematics, is to determine the value of quantities that were before unknown. This is obtained by considering attentively the conditions given, which are always expressed in known numbers. For this reason algebra has been defined, *the science which teaches how to determine unknown quantities by means of known quantities.*

The definition, which we have now given, agrees with all that has been hitherto laid down. We have always seen the knowledge of certain quantities lead to that of other quantities, which before might have been considered as unknown.

Of this, addition will readily furnish an example. To find the sum of two or more given numbers, we had to seek for an unknown number which should be equal to those known numbers taken together.

In subtraction we sought for a number which should be equal to the difference of two known numbers.

A multitude of other examples are presented by multiplication, division, the involution of powers, and the extraction of roots. The question is always reduced to finding, by means of known quantities, another quantity till then unknown.

In the last section also, different questions were resolved, in which it was required to determine a number, that could not be deduced from the knowledge of other given numbers, except under certain conditions.

All those questions were reduced to finding, by the aid of some given numbers, a new number which should have a certain connection with them; and this connection was determined by certain conditions, or properties, which were to agree with the quantity sought.

When we have a question to resolve, we represent the number sought by one of the last letters of the alphabet, and then consider in what manner the given conditions can form an equality between two quantities. This equality, which is represented by a kind of formula, called an *equation*, enables us at last to determine the value of the number sought, and consequently to resolve the question. Sometimes several numbers are sought; but they are found in the same manner by equations.

Let us endeavor to explain this further by an example. Suppose the following question or *problem* was proposed.

Twenty persons, men and women, dine at a tavern; the share of the reckoning for one man is 8 sous, that for one woman is 7 sous, and the whole reckoning amounts to 7 livres 5 sous; required, the number of men, and also of women?

In order to resolve this question, let us suppose that the number of men is $=x$; and now considering this number as known, we shall proceed in the same manner as if we wished to try whether it corresponded with the conditions of the question. Now, the number of men being $=x$, and the men and women making together twenty persons, it is easy to determine the number of the women, having only to subtract that of the men from 20, that is to say, the number of women $=20-x$.

But each man spends 8 sous; wherefore x men spend $8x$ sous.

And, since each woman spends 7 sous, $20-x$ women must spend $140-7x$ sous.

So that adding together $8x$ and $140-7x$, we see that the whole 20 persons must spend $140+x$ sous. Now, we know already how much they have spent; namely, 7 livres 5 sous, or 145 sous; there must be an equality therefore between $140 + x$ and 145; that is to say, we have the equation $140 + x = 145$, and thence we easily deduce $x = 5$.

So that the company consisted of 5 men and 15 women.

Another question of the same kind.

Twenty persons, men and women, go to a tavern; the men spend 24 florins, and the women as much; but it is found that each man has spent 1 florin more than each woman. Required, the number of men and the number of women?

Let the number of men $= x$.

That of the women will be $= 20 - x$.

Now these x men having spent 24 florins, the share of each man is $\frac{24}{x}$ florins.

Further, the $20 - x$ women having also spent 24 florins, the share of each woman is $\frac{24}{20-x}$ florins.

But we know that the share of each woman is one florin less than that of each man; if, therefore, we subtract 1 from the share of a man, we must obtain that of a woman; and consequently $\frac{24}{x} - 1 = \frac{24}{20-x}$. This, therefore, is the equation from which we are to deduce the value of x. This value is not found with the same ease as in the preceding question; but we shall soon see that $x = 8$, which value corresponds to the equation; for $\frac{24}{8} - 1 = \frac{24}{12}$ includes the equality $2 = 2$.

It is evident how essential it is, in all problems, to consider the circumstances of the question attentively, in order to deduce from it an equation, that shall express by letters the numbers sought or unknown. After that, the whole art consists in resolving those equations, or deriving from them the values of the unknown numbers; and this shall be the subject of the present section.

We must remark, in the first place, the diversity which subsists among the questions themselves. In some, we seek only for one unknown quantiy; in others, we have to find two, or more; and it is to be observed, with regard to this last case, that in order to determine them all, we must deduce from the circumstances, or the conditions of the problem, as many equations as there are unknown quantities.

It must have already been perceived, that an equation consists of two parts separated by the sign of equality, =, to show that those two quantities are equal to one another. We are often obliged to perform a great number of transformations on those two parts, in order to deduce from them the value of the unknown quantity; but these transformations must be all founded on the following principles; that *two quantities remain equal, whether we add to them, or subtract from them equal quantities; whether we multiply them, or divide them by the same number; whether we raise them both to the same power, or extract their roots of the same degree.*

The equations, which are resolved most easily, are those in which the unknown quantity does not exceed the first power, after the terms of the equation have been properly arranged; and we call them *simple equations,* or *equations of the first degree.* But if, after having reduced and ordered an equation, we find in it the square, or the second power of the unknown quantity, it may be called an *equation of the second degree,* which is more difficult to resolve.

Translator unknown

Karl Friedrich Gauss

Foundations of Mathematics

1. The subject of mathematics includes all extensive magnitudes (those in which parts can be conceived); intensive magnitudes (all nonextensive magnitudes) insofar as they are dependent on the extensives. To the former class of magnitudes belong: space or geometrical magnitudes which include lines, surfaces, solids, and angles; to the latter: velocity, density, rigidity, pitch and timbre of tones, intensity of tones and of light, probability, etc.

2. A magnitude in itself cannot become the subject of a scientific investigation; mathematics considers magnitudes only in reference to each other. The relationship of magnitudes to each other which they have only insofar as they are magnitudes, is called an arithmetical relationship. In geometrical magnitudes there occurs a relation in respect to position and this is called a geometric relationship. It is clear that geometric magnitudes can also have arithmetical relationships to each other.

3. Mathematics really teaches general truths which concern the relations of magnitudes and the purpose of it is to present magnitudes which have known relationships to known magnitudes or to magnitudes known to these, i.e., to make a presentation of them possible. But now we can have a presentation of a magnitude in a twofold manner, either by direct perception (a direct presentation), or by comparison with others, by direct perception of given magnitudes (indirect presentation). Accordingly the duty of the mathematician is either really to present the magnitude sought or to indicate the way one proceeds from the presentation of a magnitude directly

given to the presentation of the magnitude sought (arithmetical presentation). This latter occurs by means of numbers, which show how many times one must repeatedly present the directly given magnitude* to get a presentation of the magnitude sought. That magnitude one calls unity and the process measuring.

4. These various relations of magnitudes and the various modes of presenting magnitudes are the foundations of both major disciplines of mathematics. Arithmetic regards magnitudes in arithmetical relations and presents them arithmetically; geometry regards magnitudes in geometric relations and presents them geometrically. To present geometrically magnitudes which have arithmetical relations, which was so customary among the ancients, is no longer the custom at present, otherwise one would have to regard this as a part of geometry. On the contrary, one applies the arithmetical mode of presentation most frequently to magnitudes in geometrical relationships, e.g., in trigonometry, also in the theory of curves, which are regarded as geometric disciplines. That moderns have thus preferred the arithmetical presentation rather than the geometrical, does not occur without reason, especially since our method of counting (the base ten) is so much easier than that of the ancients.

5. Since a great difference can occur among the arithmetical relations of magnitudes to each other, the parts of the arithmetical sciences are of a very different nature. Most important is the circumstance of whether in this relationship the concept of the infinite must be presupposed or not; the first case belongs to the calculation of the infinite, or higher mathematics, the latter to common or lower mathematics. I omit the further subdivisions which may be deduced from the foregoing concepts.

6. In arithmetic one accordingly determines all magnitudes by indicating how many times one must repeat or combine a known magnitude (unit) or an aliquot part of it, in order to get a magnitude equal to it, i.e., one expresses it by a number and in this way the real subject of arithmetic is number. So that it may become possible to abstract from the meaning of the unit magnitudes which are determined by various units, there must be means of reducing to one. This problem will be solved in due course.

---

*Occasionally, also, how many times one must conceive a part of the same as repeated, which then gives the idea of the broken number (fraction).

7. Since the relations of magnitudes are the real subject of mathematics, we have to acquaint ourselves with the most important of these relations and especially with those which due to their simplicity are regarded as the elements of the others, although even here the first (addition and subtraction) really are fundamental to the others (multiplication and division).

8. The simplest relation among magnitudes is unquestionably that of the whole and its parts, which is a direct consequence of the idea of the extensive magnitude. The fundamental theorem in this relation, which one can regard as an axiom, is that "the parts united in any order if none be omitted, are equal to the whole." The first species of calculation, addition, teaches how to find the whole from the parts; in the second species, subtraction, it is shown how to find from the whole and one part, the other. In respect to addition the parts are called the "summing" magnitudes, the whole the sum or the aggregate; in respect to subtraction the whole is called the major or minuend, the known part the minor (subtrahend), the part sought the difference, residue, or remainder. It is clear that minor and difference may be interchanged.

9. Next to the relation between the whole and its parts, one has to note the relation between the simple and the complex, which likewise gives two species of reckoning. In this relation we have to look at three magnitudes, the simple, the complex and the number, which indicates what kind of a complex it is. Multiplication teaches how to find the second from the first and last; division teaches how to find the last from the first two. In respect to multiplication the simple is called the multiplicand; the number which determines the species of the complex, the multiplier; both are called factors; the complex, the product. In respect to division the simple is called the divisor; the number which determines the species of the complex, the quotient, and the complex, the dividend.

10. The most attractive truths which concern multiplication are the following:

(1) The multiplier times the multiplicand gives the product, which gives the multiplication of the latter by the first, or the factors can be interchanged:

$$a.b = b.a$$

(2) If the multiplier is a product, then instead of multiplying the multiplicand by the multiplier, one can multiply the multipli-

cand by one factor of the multiplier and the product thus obtained by the second factor:

$$(a.b).c = a.(b.c)$$

(3) A product of several factors remains unchanged in whatever order one takes these factors:

$$a.b.c.d = a.d.c.b = c.b.a.d, \text{ etc.}$$

(4) It is equivalent whether one multiplies the multiplicand (immediately), or its parts singly by the multiplier, and adds the products thus obtained:

$$(a + b).c = ac + bc$$

(5) It is equivalent whether one multiplies the multiplicand by the multiplier (immediately) or singly by its parts; and adds the products:

$$a(b + c) = ab + ac$$

11. Division teaches how to find the magnitude (from the complex and the simple) which determines the species of the complex. Here, therefore, three magnitudes are completely in the same relation to each other, as in multiplication, and what is proved of them there must also be valid here, only that one uses here the names current in this species of reckoning, instead of those customary in multiplication. If it is proved there that multiplier and multiplicand may be interchanged (i.e., the simple may be regarded as a determining magnitude of the complex and the determining magnitude of the complex as the simple) this means as much as allowing the quotient and divisor to be interchanged; and consequently if the quotient and divisor are given, one finds the divisor completely by the same operation as though the divisor and dividend were given. Therefore one sees that, although three combinations are possible, nevertheless only two species of reckoning arise.

Translated by G. Waldo Dunnington

Justus von Liebig

On the Study of the Natural Sciences

Nature is for most of you at this moment, as I must presuppose, a book written in unknown ciphers, a book that you want to understand, that you would like to learn to read. The words and symbols with which it speaks to us, however, are ciphers of a special kind; the phenomena with which you will have to become acquainted are peculiar ones indeed. A series of these phenomena, which occur when a small number of bodies are brought together with others, can be thought of as the alphabet with which we decipher the book. All the names of things or substances that you will hear will be of no value to you in your endeavor to understand, if you neglect to acquaint yourself with their meaning. The name "air," for example, atmospheric air, is for the chemist an aggregate of properties; no mortal eye has ever seen a molecule of air, for the act of seeing requires certain effects upon the eye to manifest themselves, certain properties that air molecules lack. But air molecules possess other properties, ones that are brought to light by chemistry, and through these other properties the chemist perceives not only the presence of air molecules where no one else would perceive them, but also shows that this invisible and intangible matter is composed of several similar, equally invisible kinds of matter. He succeeds, through thorough familiarity with their properties, in separating them, weighing them, and making their presence perceptible to every other eye. He shows you that the kind of air that burns in our street lamps consists of five or six completely different kinds of air. He shows you that one component of air, which is used in the breathing process, represents one of the most important conditions for animal life, and that a product of the respiration process is the most immediate condition for plant life. He shows you the intimate interconnection of the visible and the invisible material world, of the existence of which our forefathers had no idea. He is able to do all this because he has come to know the language and the characteristics of these substances through visible or through perceptible phenomena, which appear, in the presence of or through combination with other substances, more distinctly than the sound of a string you might pluck, and every bit as comprehensible as the black lines and symbols with which you reveal your invisible thoughts to a friend separated from you by a distance of thousands of miles. It is through this quite peculiar language of phenomena that you shall become acquainted with chemistry.

Each of the new names you shall hear has its significance for the understanding of natural phenomena. The names *oxygen, chlorine, iodine, mercury, lead,* must gradually become for you embodiments of properties that these bodies possess in and of themselves, or which appear under certain circumstances, in a similar manner to which the word "church" evokes, in one who entertains the proper conception thereof, not only a notion of the external and internal qualities of a building, but a multitude of interrelationships as well, which have nothing whatsoever to do with the stone, wood, and iron the building consists of.

The questions inquiring into the causes of natural phenomena, into the sources of life of plants and animals, into the origins of their sustenance, the conditions of their existence, and the changes in nature to which we belong by virtue of our physical bodies and with which we coexist in perpetual interaction—these questions are so befitting of the active human intellect that the sciences that provide satisfactory answers to them exert more influence on the culture of the intellect than any of the others. From this aspect as well, chemistry represents for the educated person a rich source of fresh, perpetually self-rejuvenating knowledge, thorough acquaintance with it manifests itself like a sixth bodily sense that allows you to perceive innumerable phenomena that remain invisible and concealed to those not yet so endowed. Chemistry leads you into the realm of quiet forces, through whose power all coming into being and passing away on the earth is determined, and upon whose action the production of the most essential necessities of life and of the body politic rests. A simple acquaintance with the composition of bodies enables you to solve problems that a few years ago were considered unsolvable.

A field, upon which we cultivate the same plant a number of years in succession, will become infertile for this plant in three years, another field perhaps in four, in seven, in ten, in a hundred years. One field yields wheat, but not beans; it yields barley, but not tobacco; a third field yields rich harvests of beets, but no clover!

The acquaintance with the composition of the soil and that of the ash of the plant enables you to see why the field, when the soil is not fertilized, gradually loses its fertility for a given plant, why one plant thrives in this field while another does not.

Chemistry imparts knowledge of the means by which the fertility of the soil can be restored.

Chemistry's task in physiology is to answer the question of the measure in which the organic form is dependant upon its component parts, to show what changes foodstuffs undergo when they are transformed into blood, what changes the blood's components are subject to when they are transformed into components of organs.

The nutritive value of a food, the operation of a medicament, that of the poisons, all of these properties are bound to something material, to certain elements that are responsible for these activities. The vital properties of an organ, of each and every animal fluid, are contingent upon their mixtures, i.e., their composition. Each and every cause of illness brings about a decomposition, a change in the composition. The application of medicaments aims at the restoration of the original composition; their operation is contingent upon their composition. Quinine contains the very same elements as strychnine, but in different proportions. The former is a most valuable medicament, the latter a deadly poison.

One of the most important problems for chemistry is to determine how and in what way the medicinal and the toxic properties of a substance are contingent upon its chemical composition, to determine the relationship between the effect and the components. A noteworthy step in this respect has already been made: we know with the greatest certainty that the seeds, herbs, roots, and tubers that serve as nourishment for animals and humans contain certain components in which the same elements in the same weight ratio as in the main components of the blood are to be found, that the nutritive value of a foodstuff is contingent upon the amount of these components, that everything we call food must contain one of these substances if it is to sustain life. But if the nutritive properties of human food or animal feed are contingent upon substances of a certain invariable composition, the obvious conclusion is that the medicinal properties of cinchona bark, opium, etc., and their effect on the nerve material, on the brain and the spinal cord are contingent upon causes similar to the effects that the components of food exert upon the apparatus through which the production of blood is facilitated.

Modern chemistry has made the most remarkable discoveries in this respect: it has proven that substances are present in the muscular system and in the spleen that are not found in plants, but that in their components and their composition are exceedingly similar to certain components of tea and coffee, cinchina bark and opium; so similar, in fact, that the science of chemistry places the organic bases produced in the bodies of animals in one and the same class with those derived from plants. Chemistry has at last succeeded in synthesizing urea, one of the main products of the animal vital process, from its component elements and with all of its properties, outside of the body. Since these discoveries, the organism can offer to the scientist a host of things yet unfathomed, but nothing unfathomable.

We now know that chemical forces play an essentially formative role in all life forms, that through chemistry it is possible to arrive at effective methods of treatment. Indeed, together with the fields of anatomy and physiology, we shall succeed in unveiling the wonders of the living body and in attaining a true insight into the vital processes.

Believe me, believe me on the basis of my experience of nearly thirty years, on the basis of my detailed knowledge of the history of the natural sciences: if a scientist ever succeeded in enriching his life through his research, this success was based solely on a method of investigation that can be said to be responsible for bringing about the extraordinary advances made in the last fifty years by the trades, by industry, by the fields of mechanics and natural science. These are the paths of knowledge and research for which we have Francis Bacon and Galileo to thank, which for hundreds of years had been banished from the fields of medicine and science by a false philosophy, but which now through their victories in the interest of humanity are gaining more and more ground. German natural philosophy: we look back upon it as we would upon a dead tree, which had borne the most beautiful foliage, the finest blossoms, but no fruit. With an unending expenditure of intellect and acuity, nothing but images was created; but even the most radiant colors, as Goethe claims in his theory of color, are nothing but blurred light. We, however, want and seek the pure light, the light that is truth.

For millennia, people have occupied themselves with explaining the phenomena of nature, but the explanations of the philosophical schools, from Aristotle right on into our day, have nothing in common with ours.

That which causes a body to fall, says Aristotle, is heaviness. But heaviness is the striving, immanent to the body, toward downward movement (the striving to fall). A stone falls because it is heavy; i.e., because it has a striving to move downwards; i.e., because it falls. Opium brings about sleep, because it is a body that possesses a sedative property; i.e., because it makes one sleep. The caustic properties of calcined lime stem from a thing known as "causticum." The sour taste of acids stems from the fact that acidic substances contain "acidum universale." What one saw in the effect was given a word, and this word was called the cause and it explained the effect. A thing gave gold its color, a thing gave it immutability; one sought to extract from mercury, so as to transform it into silver, the thing that made it liquid; one thing made a body hard, one thing (the spiritus rector) gave bodies their smell, another thing, phlogiston, was the cause of combustibility.

Insofar as the innumerable effects one perceived were ascribed to an equal number of hidden qualities or things, the investigation of the actual causes was provided with a ready-made goal; one knew from the start what one was looking for.

The role of explanation was played by a word, the role of truth was taken by blind faith, by a thoughtless parroting of totally unproven notions. Reason and experience admittedly compel us to believe the truth of a host of events we have not experienced ourselves, to believe facts that have been uncovered by others and that we have never observed ourselves. We believe indeed in all events, occurrences, and facts reported by reliable persons, as long as they do not contradict known laws of nature, or when their effects have been observed in some way or at some time by us or by some other reliable person. We believe in the existence of Julius Caesar, whom we have never seen, not only because his contemporaries saw him, but because his existence has been established by events, the effects of which upon the history of humanity are still being felt centuries after his time. But we do not believe in ghosts, even though thousands of people have seen ghosts, because we know on the basis of the theory of light that even corporeal matter with a certain degree of fineness, such as atmospheric air, can no longer be seen and because an incorporeal entity no longer possesses the property of being able to reflect light, the primary prerequisite to being seen. The belief that sees ghosts—this belief, gentlemen, does not belong to the realm of science; it is knowledge's worst enemy, for knowledge is the death of this belief.

The explanations of the modern scientist are infinitely different from those of earlier times. Modern science sets no store by even the most trenchant constructions of the intellect; it views as its task a kind of knowledge that can only be attained through untiring work and effort.

When the scientist of today wants to explain a phenomenon of nature, the burning of a light, the growth of a plant, the freezing of water, the fading of a color, the rusting of iron, he poses the question not to himself, to his intellect, but to the phenomenon, to the condition itself.

The scientist of today, when he wants to explain a phenomenon, inquires into what precedes this phenomenon, and into what follows it. He calls what precedes it "cause" or "condition," and what follows it "effect."

The growth of a plant is preceded by an embryo, a seed; prerequisite to this growth is soil. Without the atmosphere, without moisture, the plant will not grow. Soil and atmosphere are not conditions in and of themselves; there are calcareous soils, clay soils, sandy soils, each different from the rest in their properties and their composition. The word *soil*, as you can see, is a collective term for a whole list of conditions; a fertile soil contains them in the proportions necessary for the nourishment of the plant, and an infertile soil lacks several or all of these conditions. In order to produce the effect of fertility, all of these conditions must be present.

In the same way, the word *atmosphere* comprises a majority of conditions. The scientist asks, "What are these conditions?" and by showing and proving which specific roles certain components of soil, atmosphere, and water play in the growth of the plant, he explains the growth, how the plant increases in mass, insofar as this is explainable to the intellect.

When the smith places an iron bar in his forge until it glows white, and then takes it out again, it throws off sparks and covers itself with a black, porous crust, which flies off as hammer scales when the bar is struck with a hammer; the iron burns. Under similar conditions, the oil in our lamps burns with a bright flame. The scientist asks, "What precedes the burning of iron, of oil, and what follows it?" What are the conditions, what are the results of their combustion? The iron, the oil, the air, and a higher temperature precede the combustion of the iron, the oil. What is iron, what is oil? There are many types of oils. The word *oil* is a collective term for certain vegetable or animal substances that contain three components distinct in nature. Only one component of the atmosphere takes part in the combustion.

In combustion, iron increases in weight; the air in which it is burned decreases in weight by the same amount. The air in which oil is burned increases in weight by the weight of the oil burned.

The result of the combustion of iron and of oil is consequently clear; the burned iron is iron that has incorporated into itself a component of the air; the burned oil is air that has incorporated into itself the components of the oil. The generation of light and heat (the phenomenon of fire) accompanied the transfer of the component of air to the iron, and the transfer of the components of the oil to the air. A major portion of the phenomenon of combustion is herewith explained, and by asking further questions as to where the heat and light come from during combustion, why the iron does not burn up while the oil in a lamp does, why the iron burns with flying sparks while the oil burns with a flame; and by solving these questions in a very similar way, the scientist explains these phenomena in their respective parts.

The scientist of today explains by searching for the causes that have preceded the phenomena: the sensibly perceptible causes he calls conditions; the causes that cannot be so apprehended he calls forces.

According to this method, the cause of the common cold is not the inflammation of the nasal mucous membranes, for this is merely a definition of the word "cold." The explanation of the fever comprises in its meaning not an image, nor a description of the febrile state, or of the fever symptoms. It is a matter of finding out what has preceded the febrile state and what makes it persist; it is a matter of finding out, in the description of the respiratory process, which role is played by air and blood in the production of animal heat.

When the causes of a phenomenon are unknown or have not been thoroughly investigated, the scientist leaves the question open. When he finds iron in the blood, calcium in the bones of animals, without knowing where these elements come from, he does not say that they are products of the life process. When he is not able to determine the origin of microscopic animals, he does not say that they are the products of spontaneous generation. When he finds burned human remains in a locked room and cannot determine what has happened, he does not say that they have spontaneously combusted. He considers such forms of inference or explanation to be self-deception or masking of ignorance, because to explain something means to make it clear, and this entails light or insight, and because the explanation of a process cannot rest upon complete unfamiliarity with this process.

The determination of the causes of a phenomenon is the first requisite to its explanation. These causes must be sought out and established through observation. This seeking out and observation comprise the art of the scientist; the skilled formulation of questions attests to his intellect. Just consider how difficult it is to search for an object you lost yesterday, or a week ago. The surest way to find it is not to tear up the floor of your house, nor to tear your house down and sift through the rubble. You are most likely to find the object when you think back to where it was you last saw it and had it in your hand. By searching without thinking you will perhaps find it; by thinking and then searching you will guarantee your success. Similarly, in the search for the cause of a phenomenon, thinking is the only reliable guide: through observation you come to discern the perceptible landmarks along the way.

No art is as difficult as the art of observation: it demands an educated, sober intellect and the practical knowledge that comes only through practice and experience. For the observer is not one who sees with his eyes the thing before him, but rather one who sees what parts constitute the thing, and the relationship of these parts to the whole. Some overlook out of carelessness half of what is there; others report more than they see, because they confuse what they see with what they imagine; still others see the parts of the whole, but put things together that should in fact be kept separate. In the Görlitz trial in Darmstadt, the women who had undressed and washed the body of the victim saw neither arms nor head on the corpse; another witness saw one arm and a head the size of a fist, and a third witness (a doctor) saw both arms and a head every bit as large as a normal female skull. These differing testimonies clearly demonstrate the educational level of the witnesses, their ability to observe. Observation can be compared to a piece of glass, which, when it is to be made into a mirror, must be ground very flat and with the utmost care if the image it reflects is to be pure and undistorted.

One who observes a clock sees not only the pendulum swinging back and forth, the dial, and the moving hands; even a child can see these. He sees also the parts of the clock, the relationship between the counterweight and the wheelwork, and between the pendulum and the moving hands.

Since the sensory and nervous apparatus are the tools of the observer's mental processes, through which tools the impressions on which he bases his deductions and inferences are received and propagated, so does it lie in the nature of the matter that persons whose nervous systems are not completely healthy can in no way be qualified for the activity of observation. It is thus understandable that the new Od theory has not been able to find acceptance in the field of natural science. None of the phenomena which the Od is said to bring about have ever been seen or perceived by the discoverer of the Od, nor have they ever been perceived by any persons with sound minds and the honest will to perceive them. His "sensitives" are not able to describe for themselves what they see or experience; they must first be led, their attention must be drawn to the individual components and peculiarities of the phenomena by the questions of the interrogator, who himself, however, does not see, nor has ever seen, the phenomena. No person of sense can believe that the existence of a new force of nature can be grounded upon such a false method, upon clairvoyant and emotional phenomena evoked in weak-nerved and ill persons.

When the observer has determined the cause of a phenomenon and is able to unite its conditions, his next step is to prove, in an attempt to recreate the phenomenon at will, the correctness of his observations by means of the experiment. To make a series of experiments often entails dissecting a thought into its component parts and testing this thought by means of a perceptible phenomenon. The scientist makes experiments to prove the truth of his interpretation; he makes experiments to show a phenomenon in all its different components. If he is able to demonstrate for a series of phenomena that they are all effects of the same cause, he arrives at a simple expression of these phenomena, which in this case is known as a law of nature. We refer to a simple property as a law of nature when this property serves to explain one or more phenomena of nature.

We attribute, for example, the rising of mercury in a Torcelli's tube and the rising of a balloon to the law that the air has weight. In keeping with our experience, however, a single phenomenon of nature is never produced by a single cause, but is always brought about by the interplay of several laws of nature. The representation of the interconnection of these laws of nature is known as the theory of phenomenon. The theory of the barometer comprises three laws of nature: the law that air is heavy, the law that pressure upon liquids exerts itself uniformly in all directions, the law that pressure operating in one direction, when it is not canceled out by a counter-pressure of equal intensity, brings about a movement that persists until equilibrium is established. The theory of the balloon rests upon the last-mentioned law, upon the law that air is heavy, and upon a fourth law as well, that a body floating in a fluid loses an amount of weight equal to that of the fluid it displaces. A theory is the representation of the interconnection of all those laws of nature through whose interplay a phenomenon or a process is determined.

Thorough familiarity with a fact or a process enables you to explain to yourself other facts and processes; every property of a body can potentially furnish a key to open a locked door, but the theory is the master key, which opens all doors. You can see how greatly the concept of theory in a scientific sense differs from the word "theory" in its colloquial usage. In the latter sense, it is frequently used to mean the exact opposite of experience or practice; it often denotes the lack of familiarity with facts and laws of nature. For our purposes, theory is the sum of all practice; it rests upon the most thorough knowledge of facts and laws of nature, and it proceeds from this knowledge. When I use the word "practice" here in opposition to the word "theory," which means insight, I am not referring to the practical skill of an individual in some art or craft. A practical physicist can give the mechanic exact and detailed instructions on how to construct an accurate thermometer or barometer, can tell him how to calibrate the tube and which properties the mercury must have, without being able to make a thermometer himself, for he has never learned glassblowing. The practical chemist tells the manufacturer of sulfuric acid, with the utmost certainty and assurance, how much sulfur may be burned in a given stream of air going through a sulfur furnace in order to obtain the maximum amount of sulfuric acid, yet this does not mean that such a chemist can himself undertake its profitable commercial manufacture. He tells the farmer what components his soil must contain to be able to produce the greatest possible harvest of potatoes, without knowing when the potatoes must be planted in the spring. He produces quinine from cinchona bark without having the faintest idea of the proper dosages for various illnesses. He acquaints the physiologist with the nature and the properties of the blood components or the secretions in the healthy and the sick body, without knowing anything of the symptoms of illness and their bearing on the life processes. This type of practice, which is founded upon the technical application of the laws of nature, sets the standard for the skill of the glassblower, the manufacturer of sulfuric acid, for the experience of the farmer and the doctor, and for the knowledge of the physiologist, but it cannot be used to measure the practical aptitude of the chemist. He should, in a practical sense, know the laws of nature, the ways to explore them, and the fundamentals of their application, and for this reason the study of the other branches of natural science and the familiarity with mathematics and the chemical trades are indispensable.

Translated by Daniel Theisen

Adelbert von Chamisso

A Survey of Botany
and the Plant Kingdom

We have resolved to become acquainted with the most useful and the most destructive plants brought forth by the soil of our fatherland, precisely for the sake of the usefulness or destructiveness, for our purposes, which may grow out of them. We shall, to our advantage, borrow upon this knowledge from the natural history of plant and herbal lore.

The end of herbal lore itself, insofar as it is a science, is solely knowledge, not the practical benefits that may grow out of this knowledge. Curiosity is one of the more noble aspects of the intellect, and it is through this curiosity that man, as a creature of reason, distinguishes himself from the other animals. These other animals, in keeping with their nature, blindly give themselves over to the demands dictated by the imperatives of their survival and the procreation of their species. Man strives for knowledge; he longs for truth for its own sake; he wants to know about the things that surround him and present themselves to his senses, solely for the sake of knowledge. Science is the gratification of this pure urge of his higher nature.

There is, however, not but o n e science, but many sciences, for the totality of things cannot be simultaneously conceived in its entirety and comprehended in all its details.

It is evident that by disinterestedly striving through science to expand his particular intellectual discipline, man will also increase the very means of his power, and each science proves to be a source of unexpected usefulness. The astronomical expert wants only to measure and weigh the heavenly bodies that move through space; he inquires only into the laws of their orbits and the forces they obey, and yet he teaches the seaman to guide himself with such certainty over the vast surface of the ocean that after a journey of several months, he can confidently name the point on the coast that will shortly appear over the horizon. The botanical expert sets out for distant, unexplored shores to discover new plant species, and thereby increase the number of known species. Once on shore, he finds himself in an unknown botanical environment, yet he can immediately show the seaman which plants can be used for nourishment or for medicinal purposes, and which ones should be avoided.

It would behoove us, briefly digressing from our primary aim, to seize the opportunity to take a general look at the science from which we intend to derive benefit, and its object, the plant kingdom or the totality of plants. We do not presume to want to delve into the science per se; we wish only to become acquainted with its limits and its scope, as well as the tasks that it sets itself and the methods by which these tasks are to be accomplished.

Man can be looked upon as an agent in the household of nature. Together with those animal and plant species that he has appropriated for his use and that he raises and breeds for his own purposes, many other species, in the manner of parasites, enjoy his meticulous care and follow him on his wanderings as far as they can, until they reach the limits set to each and every one of them by the climate they are able to endure. For man himself, this weak, naked animal, who is master by virtue of his intellect, is confined by no other limit in his dominion, the earth, than the polar ice, which represents an absolute boundary to all life forms.

Wherever man, the moral creature, may wander, the countenance of nature transforms itself before him. His domesticated animals and his useful plants follow him; the forests are cleared, the wildlife is scared off, his plantings and crops spread out about his dwelling; rats, mice, and various types of insects settle in with him under his roof, several species of swallows, finches, larks, and partridges place themselves under his protection and enjoy as guests the fruits of his labor. Among the plants that he cultivates in his gardens and fields, a host of other plants proliferate as weeds, which voluntarily join and share the same fate with them. Finally, his subjects leave him and spread beyond the pale of the area he has cultivated, and even the wilderness untrodden by his foot is transformed. Countless herds of once domesticated, now wild horses and cattle populate the interior plains of America, and the plains of Chile are graced with forests of apple trees, whose seeds have been spread by the cattle.

We cannot fathom, under an unblazing sky, upon an unfertile earth, the region of this transformation under the influence of a more powerful sun. For half of the yearly cycle, winter suppresses all life for us. The tree bared of leaves slumbers in its buds, the perennial in its root, the herb only in its seed. The insect slumbers in its egg or its cocoon; a few insect larvae hide themselves in the depths of the earth or the waters. Aquatic life slumbers under the ice. Most birds have migrated, most mammals are hibernating, as are the amphibians. A few of the more robust species of warm-blooded animals pitifully mourn the hard times. Spring is the awakening from a long, drawn-out illness. That man has been able to settle, and even endure in the wintry lands, is incomprehensible to those who have experienced the milder warmth which the greater part of the inhabitable earth uninterruptedly enjoys. In the tropics, where the only missing prerequisite to life is moisture, nature works and creates irresistibly. Life progresses irresistibly; profusion is only limitation. Newly introduced species are either suppressed, or else they spread quickly, and soon one can no longer distinguish between what was originally native and what was foreign but has become wild.

The history of our domesticated animals and plants is inextricably bound up with that of our race and our wanderings. If natural history can teach us anything about the fatherland of the former, then it would at the same time be able to give us an account of ourselves and of the infancy of our civilization. But its silence, too, is instructive.

The summits of our mountains, of the Pyrenees, the Alps, the Caucasus, etc., upon which most species of arctic flora again appear, are separated from the polar lands by vast plains covered with vegetation of a much different kind. No continuous mountain ridge, no bridge affords passage to these plants from their arctic to their alpine habitats, and we can give no account of the way their migration has taken place. Now if we compare the flora of the Alps with that of the far North, we find that the majority of the species that predominate in and are characteristic of the latter are the same ones that constitute the main component of the vegetation in the former; several species, however, are lacking, and their place is taken by others. We find the majority of the nordic genera again, of which several have grown in significance, insofar as they have diversified into a greater number of species; a few genera have failed to appear, and a few new ones have joined the ranks. A few of the rarer species of the North, which occur there only in certain confined regions, can be found in our mountains, likewise bound to specific, isolated locations, and the odd plant has been found only on the northeast cape of Asia, on Unalaska, or on the shore of Baffin Bay, and on a single mountaintop in the Pyrenees, the Alps, the Carpathians, or the Caucasus.

The high mountain ranges of America run from north to south and form in the western part of this continent a projecting ridge that extends almost uninterrupted from the arctic regions to the southernmost point of land. The dominant plant forms in the northern frigid and temperate zones follow along this ridge and cross the tropics; coniferous and oak forests can still be found in the highlands of Mexico, oaks in Peru, and many arctic genera are still to be found among the tropical-alpine flora, but the species are peculiar to their respective regions. We mention here by way of example: the nordic forms from the families of the heathers and carnations, the ranunculi, gentians, alchemillas, and veronicas.

In the upper regions of the forests in these high mountain ranges, gregariously living plants maintain dominance in places, as they do under our nordic skies; as soon as one descends into the valley, however, the species mingle more and more, and the forest soon consists of innumerable opposing plant forms, some of which may well be called characteristic, but none of which could be called predominant. The palmlike, treelike ferns climb to a considerable height; the palms and the gigantic herbaceous bananas with broad unlobed leaves (the pisang, musa, and others) inhabit flat ground. Many of the larger families, which in our regions are represented only by worts, herbs, and shrubs, produce tall trees; even the grasses take on a treelike form, and the bamboo (bambusa), related to the reeds and rushes, one of the few gregarious plants of this nature, forms with densely clustered, tall, slender, windblown stalks impenetrable groves. The mangrove (rhizophora), another gregarious plant, sends down from its branches aerial roots, which it transforms into new stalks; it covers low shores and salt marshes with dense, strangely intertwined thickets. Mimosas with compound pinnate leaves, fig trees with entire leaves, palms and other tree forms in infinite diversity and abundance crowd together in profuse growth into forests; ferns, grasses, juncacae, and countless other plants, reaching the height of a man, fill the spaces between the trunks; twisting, climbing, winding species from all families and genera, enlisting the help of outside supports, lift themselves up throughout these spaces, sway back down from the branches, and weave between the earth, the trunks, and the treetops a fabulous, impenetrable net; ferns, arums, orchids, opuntiae, and other plants take up residence in the trees of the forest and form in their crowns fabulous hanging gardens; other plants, finally, duplicate the form of our maidenhair ferns (cuscuta) on a large scale and drape with golden or silvery tresses the heads of aged trees. The opuntiae (cactus) inhabit exclusively the New World. Plants from other natural families, species of spurge (euphorbia) and others imitate in the Old World their bizarre forms.

Wherever moisture is lacking in the tropics, the earth remains naked and barren. Thus in the Old World, in Africa and Arabia, vast, oceanlike deserts are to be found, in which but here and there sparse vegetation persists. The savannas, which in some areas of the torrid zone take the place of our meadows or heaths, are unirrigated, deforested tracts of land covered with high grass, but burned fallow by the sun and without flowers. Their scant flora consists of a few types of grasses and various low plants that subsist in their midst and in the protection of their shade.

The vegetation in the southern hemisphere is very different from that in the northern. The gregarious plants are much rarer; our spruces and pines are absent; they are represented only by different genera of conifers, which reach a far lower level of significance. A tree of this tribe, nevertheless, covers the mountain ranges of South America with tall forests, and forms the exclusive constituent of these forests; another species of this genus is found in Australia and on its neighboring islands. The amentaceous trees are likewise absent; they reappear on the southernmost point of the New World, being represented by a beech and a dwarf birch native to Tierra del Fuego.

Only insignificant points of land, isolated by vast seas, extend in the southern hemisphere beyond the tropics. The vegetation on each is peculiar to its respective region and extremely varied; in America, the mountain range seems to separate two distinct florae. The small area of these foothills gives rise to a comparatively very large number of plant species, and the regions of dispersion of many of these are exceptionally limited. The florae with which we are acquainted from the Cape of Good Hope and from southern Australia are extraordinarily abundant. A few combined plant families as well as others, which, while peculiar to their respective lands, are nevertheless interrelated, give these florae, as diverse as they otherwise are, a certain similarity. Faint traces of this similarity are yet to be found on the west coast of America; they disappear completely to the east of the mountains. It would not be appropriate to carry out this comparison any further.

Life forms appear to have spread from the continents to the islands of the adjacent seas. The further from the mainland the islands are, and the smaller their size and the lesser their elevation above sea level, the poorer is the nature to be found upon them. Mammals, with the exception of the ubiquitous rat and the bats, have migrated only to those islands closest to the coasts; land birds are rarely to be found on the most distant ones. Their flora is always sparser than their latitude would normally dictate; indeed, as previously mentioned, in proportion to their distance from the mainland and to their smaller area.

The East Indian islands and Australia are to be considered as mainland and as being linked to the adjacent Asiatic continent. A continuous chain of larger and smaller islands in the northern and western areas of the South Pacific stretches along the coast of the mainland and is to be regarded as a prefatory shore of this mainland. The islands of this vast oceanic basin, which lie scattered over a third of the torrid zone between Asia and America, which form in the west more tightly clustered groups and chains, and which in the east are separated by a vast, barren ocean from the American coast, appear to belong to the Old World, and it is from there that they have received their flora. All characteristic plant forms, nearly all genera, and most species can be traced back to the east Asian or the Australian continents, and the easternmost of these islands are the most meagerly endowed. It is to be noted that the migration of plants to these islands must consequently have occurred against the prevailing winds, which in the tropics blow from east to west, and against the ocean current, which obeys the prevailing winds. The islands of this ocean are either volcanic highlands or low banks of a type of limestone that the sea continuously creates from coral fragments cemented together. The latter are the most numerous; the poverty of nature on these islands is so great that on one chain of such islands, stretching, incidentally, for thirty German miles, no more than fifty-eight species of wildgrowing plants were found.

Translated by Daniel Theisen

Christoph von Hufeland

Duration of the Life of Plants

In order to prove and confirm what has been before said, let me now be permitted to take a view of all the classes of the organized world, and endeavor to establish on solid principles what I have asserted. This will give us an opportunity of becoming acquainted with the most important collateral circumstances which have an influence in prolonging or shortening life. How infinitely various is the duration of the different organized beings! Between the mold, which lives only a couple of hours, and the cedar, which can attain to the age of a thousand years, what a difference; how numberless the intermediate degrees; what a variety of life! The grounds, however, of this longer or shorter duration must lie in the structure of each being. This is an important and interesting circumstance, but at the same time of the utmost extent. I must, therefore, content myself with deducing from it the principal data, and exhibiting them in our present point of view.

In this respect, plants, that immense world of creation, that first degree of organized beings which nourish themselves by internal appropriation, form an individual and propagate their race, first present themselves to our view. What infinite variety of shape, organization, size, and duration! According to the latest discoveries and calculations, they amount to forty thousand genera and species at least!

They may all, however, be reduced, according to their duration of life, into three principal classes: annual, or properly only semiannual, which grow up in spring, and die in autumn; biennial, which die at the end of the second year; and, lastly, perennial, the duration of which extends from four to a thousand years.

All plants of a soft watery constitution, and which have fine tender organs, have a short life, and last only one or at most two years: those alone which have stronger organs and tougher juices exist longer; but wood is absolutely necessary in order to attain to the highest degree of vegetable existence.

Even among those which live only one or two years a remarkable difference may be observed. Those which are of a cold insipid nature, and destitute of smell, live, under like circumstances, not so long as the strong-scented balsamic plants, which contain more essential oil and spirits. Lettuce, wheat, oats, barley, and all kinds of corn, live no more than a year; but, on the other hand, thyme, mint, hyssop, balm, wormwood, marjoram, sage, etc., can live two years, and even longer.

Shrubs and small trees can live sixty years, and some even twice that number. The vine attains to sixty or a hundred years, and continues fruitful at the greatest age. This is the case also with rosemary. The acanthus and ivy, however, can exceed the age of a hundred. Among many such, for example, as the different kinds of *rubus*,* it is difficult to determine the age, as the branches creep along the ground, and always form new plants, so that it is almost impossible to distinguish the new from the old: and by these means they make their existence as it were perennial.

Those which attain to the highest age are the greatest, strongest, and hardest trees; such as the oak, the lime-tree, the beech, the chestnut, the elm, the plane tree, the cedar, the olive, the palm, the mulberry tree, and the baobab.† We may with certainty affirm, that some of the cedars of Lebanon, the celebrated chestnut tree *di centi cavalli* in Sicily, and several of the sacred oaks under which the ancient Germans performed their religious ceremonies, may have attained to the age of a thousand years and more. These are the most venerable, the only now existing testimonies of the ancient

---

*Common bramble, blackberry, raspberry.

†This newly discovered tree *(Adansonia digitata)* seems to be one of those which live to the greatest age. Its trunk acquires the thickness of twenty-five feet in diameter; and Adanson, in the middle of the present century, found trees only six feet in diameter, which had cut on them the names of sea-faring people who had visited them in the fifteenth and sixteenth centuries, yet these incisions had become very little extended.

world, and inspire us with reverence and awe when the rustling wind plays through their silvery locks, which once served to overshade the Druids and our wild ancestors clothed in their bearskins.

All trees of a rapid growth, such as the fir, the birch, the horse chestnut, and the like, yield always less solid and durable wood, and the period of their existence is shorter. The oak, which is the slowest in growing of all, has the hardest wood, and its life is of the longest duration.

Smaller vegetables have, in general, a shorter life than those which are large, tall, and spreading.

Those trees which have the hardest and most durable wood are, however, not always those which live longest. The beech, for example, the cypress, the juniper, the walnut, and the pear-tree, do not live so lóng as the lime-tree, though its wood be softer.

Those which produce juicy, tender, and delicate fruit, are, in general, shorter-lived than those which are barren, or which bear fruit entirely useless. And among the former, those which bear nuts or acorns become older than those which produce berries and fruit with stones.

Even these short-lived trees, the apple, the pear, the apricot, the peach, the cherry, etc., can, under very favorable circumstances, prolong their life to sixty years; especially when they are freed from the moss which grows upon them.

We may establish it as a general rule, that those trees which are long in producing leaves and fruit, and which also do not soon lose them, become older than those in which both these changes take place speedily. Those, likewise, which are cultivated, have, in general, a shorter existence than those which grow wild; and those which produce sour, harsh fruit, live longer than those which produce sweet.

It is highly worthy of remark, that when the earth is dug up every year around the roots of a tree, it becomes more vigorous and fruitful; but the duration of its life is shortened. On the other hand, if this be done every five or ten years, it will live the longer. In the like manner, frequent watering and manuring promotes fruitfulness, but it injures the duration of life.

One, also, by frequently lopping off the branches and buds, may contribute very much to the duration of the life of a shrub; so that small, short-lived plants, such as lavender, hyssop, and the like, if annually pruned, may prolong their life to the age of forty years.

It is also to be remarked, that when one turns up the earth, which has remained long untouched and unchanged, around the roots of old trees, and makes it softer and looser, they will produce fresher and more vigorous leaves, and become, as it were, again young.

When we consider with attention these observations, derived from experience, it is perfectly evident how much they confirm the above established principles of life and vital duration, and that they coincide perfectly with these ideas.

Our first grand principle was, the greater the quantity of vital power, and the solidity of the organs, the longer will be the duration of life; and we now find in Nature that the greatest, the most perfect, and the best-formed productions, in which also we must allow the greatest abundance of the vital power, and those which have the strongest and most durable organs, are precisely those which enjoy the longest life; as, for example, the oak and the cedar.

The bulk of the corporeal mass evidently appears here to contribute to the duration of life, and on the three following grounds:

(1) Bulk shows a greater provision of the vital or plastic power.

(2) Bulk gives more vital capacity, more surface, more external access.

(3) The greater mass a body has, the more time is required before it can be wasted by its external and internal consumptive and destructive powers.

We, however, find that a plant may have very strong and durable organs, and yet not live so long as one the organs of which are of less solidity. Of this we have an instance in the lime-tree, which lives much longer than the beech or the cypress.

This now leads to a law of the utmost importance for organized life and our future research; which is, that, in the organized world, a certain degree only of solidity promotes the duration of life, and that too high a degree of tenacity shortens it. In general, however, and among unorganized beings, it is undoubtedly certain the more solid a body is the greater will be its duration; but in organized beings, where the duration of existence consists in continual activity of the organs and circulation of the juices, this observation is limited, and too great a degree of solidity in the organs, and toughness in the juices, makes them sooner immovable and unfit for discharging their functions, produces obstructions and brings on premature old age, and even death.

It is not, however, merely on the quantity of the power and the organs that the vital power depends. We have already seen that a great deal, in particular, depends on the speedier or slower consumption, and on perfect or more imperfect restoration. Is this, therefore, confirmed in the vegetable kingdom?

It is, in the fullest manner; and we here find this general law: the more intensive life a plant has, the stronger and speedier is its internal consumption, the sooner it decays, and the shorter is its duration: on the other hand, the more capacity a plant has, either internally or externally, to regenerate itself, the longer it will preserve its existence.

I shall now proceed to treat, in the first place, on the law of *consumption*. Plants in general have a very weak intensive life, which consists only in the functions of growth, propagation, and receiving nourishment. They are subject to no arbitrary changing of place, no regular circulation, no muscular or nervous motion. The function of generation is, beyond dispute, the highest degree of their internal consumption, the utmost stretch of their intensive life. But how speedily is it followed by decomposition and annihilation! Nature appears here to make, as it were, the greatest exertion of her plastic power, and to show the ne plus ultra of the highest finishing and of bringing to perfection.

What tenderness and delicacy in the structure of the flower; what elegance and splendor of colors astonish us often in the most inconsiderable plant, to which we never could have ascribed such expansion. These are, as it were, the dress of ceremony, with which the plant celebrates its greatest festival, but with which it also often exhausts its whole stock of vital power, either for ever, or at least for a long time.

All plants, without exception, lose, immediately after this catastrophe, the vigor of vegetation; and begin to be stationary, which is the commencement of their dissolution. In all annual plants complete death follows; among the larger plants and trees, a temporal death at least, or a torpor of half a year, until, by the great strength of their regenerating power, they are again put in a condition to shoot forth new leaves and flowers.

On the same principles it may be explained, how all plants which acquire early the power of generation die also soonest: and it is an invariable law for the duration of life in the vegetable kingdom, that the earlier and speedier a plant comes to flower, the shorter time will its life continue; but the later it flowers, its existence will be of the longer duration. All those that flower immediately, the first year, die also the same year: and those that flower for the first time the second year, die also the second. Those trees only, and woody shrubs, which first begin to generate in the sixth, ninth, or twelfth year, become old; and among these, those genera that arrive latest at the period of propagation become likewise the oldest. A highly important observation, which, in part, fully confirms my ideas of consumption, and gives an instructive hint in regard to our future research.

An answer may now be given to that important question, What influence has *cultivation* on the longer or shorter duration of the life of plants?

Culture and art, upon the whole, shorten life; and it may be admitted as a fundamental principle, that in general all wild plants, left to themselves, live longer than those which are cultivated. Every kind of culture, however, does not shorten life; for, by careful attention, a plant which lives only one or two years in the open air, may be preserved much longer: and this is a very remarkable proof, that, even in the vegetable kingdom, it is possible to prolong life by a certain kind of treatment. But the question now is, In what consists the difference of that culture which prolongs life, and that which shortens it? This may be of importance to us in the following research, and may be referred to our first fundamental principle. The more cultivation strengthens intensive life and internal consumption, and at the same time makes the organization more delicate, the more is it prejudicial to the duration of life. This we observe to be the case in all hothouse plants, which, by warmth, manure, and other arts, are forced to a continual internal activity; so that they produce earlier, oftener, and more exquisite fruit than is natural for them. The case is the same, when, without forcing, by external causes, a higher degree of perfection and delicacy than belonged to its nature is communicated to the internal organization of a plant, merely by certain operations and arts, such, for example, as ingrafting, propping, and the art used in regard to full flowers. This kind of culture shortens the duration also.

Cultivation, on the other hand, may be the greatest means of prolonging life, if it do not strengthen the intensive life of a plant, or if it retard and moderate in any manner its internal consumption; if it lessen the too great natural toughness or hardness of the organs or matter to such a degree that they continue longer pliable and proper for their functions; and if it keep off destructive influences, and supply it with better means of regeneration. Thus, by the help of culture, a being may attain to a greater extent of life than it could have acquired according to its natural state and destination.

The duration of the life of plants may be prolonged, therefore, in the three following ways:

(1) If, by often pruning the branches, we guard against too rapid consumption. By these means we deprive the plant of a part of those organs by which it would exhaust too speedily its vital power, and we concentrate the power as it were within it.

(2) If we thereby check, or at least retard its flowering, and prevent a waste of the power of generation. This, we know, is the highest degree of vital consumption among plants; and we thus doubly contribute to the prolongation of life—first, by preventing this power from being exhausted; and, secondly, by obliging it to return back and to act as a means of support or nourishment.

(3) If we keep off the destructive influence of frost, the want of nourishment, and an irregular atmosphere, and preserve it by art, in an uniform, moderate, mean condition. Though we hereby somewhat increase the intensive life, we nevertheless create a richer source of regeneration.

Lastly, the fourth grand point on which the duration of every being, and also of a plant, depends, is its greater or less capacity to *restore* itself and to renew its parts.

In this respect, the vegetable world may be divided into two grand classes. The first do not possess this capacity; and these are the annual plants, or those which live only a year, and which die immediately after they have performed the function of generation.

The second class, on the other hand, which possess this great faculty of regenerating themselves annually; of producing new leaves, branches, and flowers, can attain to the astonishing age of a thousand years and upward. Such plants may be considered as organized masses of earth, from which an immense number of plants, but perfectly analogous to each mass, spring out every year. And in this regulation the wisdom of Nature appears great and divine.

When we reflect that, as experience teaches us, a period of eight or ten years is required in order to produce that degree of perfection in the organs and in the purification of the juices necessary in a tree before it can bring forth flowers and fruit, if it were subjected to the same laws of decay as other vegetable productions, and if a tree died immediately after it had generated, how ill-rewarded would the culture of it be; and how little proportion would the expense of preparation and time bear to the result! In such a case, fruit indeed would be uncommon.

To guard against this, Nature has wisely established, that the first plant acquires gradually such a consistence and solidity that at last the place of the earth is supplied by the trunk, from which an abundance of new plants spring out every year under the form of buds and buttons.

By this a double advantage is obtained. First, because these plants spring from a mass of earth already organized, they immediately receive juices assimilated and prepared, and can therefore employ them in the production of flowers and fruit, which with sap derived immediately from the earth would be impossible.

Secondly, these delicate plants, which in reality we may consider as so many annuals, die again after the process of fructification is completed, and yet the vegetable itself, or the stem, continues perennial. Nature, therefore, remains here true to her fundamental law, that the function of generation exhausts the vital power of single individuals, and yet the whole is perennial.

In a word, the result of all these observations is, that the great age of a plant depends on the following points:

(1) It must grow slowly.
(2) It must propagate itself slowly, and late.
(3) It must have a certain degree of solidity and duration in its organs, a sufficiency of wood, and the sap must not be too watery.
(4) It must be large, and have considerable extension.
(5) It must rise into the atmosphere.

By the contrary of all these the duration of life is shortened.

Translated by Eramus Wilson

Alfred E. Brehm

You call them thieves and pillagers; but know
They are the wingèd wardens of your farms,
Who from the corn-fields drive the insidious foe,
And from your harvests keep a hundred harms;
Even the blackest of them all, the crow,
Renders good service as your man-at-arms,
Crushing the beetle in his coat of mail;
And crying havoc on the slug and snail.
                              —*Henry Wadsworth Longfellow*

The Importance of Birds
in the Economy of Nature

One of the German governments has lately done what the Egyptians did thousands of years ago, and the Indians and Americans have done for centuries. They passed a law for the preservation of birds. By this act they acknowledged the importance of these useful creatures, and recognized the benefits which we directly and indirectly derive from them.

Michelet, in his extravaganza on the bird, sketches, with a superficiality truly French, the most gloomy pictures by way of demonstrating the utility of this creature; for my part I do not consider it necessary, especially towards my German—and, therefore, educated—readers, to express what M. Michelet, by a number of horrible tales, has sought to do. The importance of the bird-world to the whole of animated nature is immeasurable. "They are," says Tschudi, in his inimitable work on the "Zoology of the Alps," "the representatives of life, brightness, and joyous movement, throughout the universal globe. Without them the mountains would be desolate and utterly devoid of charm. The first thing man seeks is life; inanimate masses crush his spirit, the lifeless desert saddens him. Imagine our woods and meadows, rocks and streams, robbed of their merry tribe of feathered inhabitants, and we at once lose one of those links which connect us with the lower organic and inorganic world." What birds are to man beyond this I will seek to depict further on. It suffices at present to prove, by sheer statistics, the benefits he receives from them when he treats them really as the "lord of the creation" ought to do.

Tschudi looks upon birds as a connecting link existing between the highest and lowest conditions of life. This view must be taken in the widest sense. They stand between the two, working on either side; in the one case beneficially, in the other the reverse. The true guardians of equilibrium in the animal kingdom, they avert and prevent the dangerous attacks of the lower orders of animated nature, especially the superabundant increase of insect life. This mighty army, which preys even upon itself, is really only in some degree kept at bay by the feathered tribe. To permit the insect world to make undue headway would amount to destroying Nature, for in that case, the plant world, on which her existence depends, would cease to exist. The whole of remaining creation combined would not be able to arrest the destruction caused by insect-life so effectually as birds. Up to the present time we are acquainted with about 1,400 species of mammals and 800 of reptiles, whereas the birds amount to 8000. It is now a recognized fact that insectivorous birds form the most numerous class, and are the most widely distributed. It is, therefore, easy to conceive the usefulness of the bird, when I state that three-fourths of the most numerous classes are either partially or wholly insectivorous; besides which, as I have before said, many birds daily devour from three to four times their own weight of insect-food. Take, for instance, the quantity devoured by a single pair of Titmice in a day, and we find it amounts on an average to 2,000 insects per diem; this, by simple calculation, gives us a yearly total of 730,000 insects which are destroyed by this pair. Add to this the fact that one pair of Titmice will produce in one season no fewer than ten young birds, whose yearly nourishment will, together with that of the parent birds, give a grand total of about four millions of insects. This statement proves to us the utility of one species alone, and also that the amount of good done by the entire bird-world must be incalculable. It is, if not striking, still worthy of remark, that the most noxious creatures of all classes are principally destroyed by birds. In support of this assertion I will call the attention of my readers to several species of insects which are especially destructive, and then enumerate those birds which are their direst enemies.

My readers have assuredly heard, or read, of the depredations committed by locusts, as well as of their insatiable appetites. I have often observed this creature, which the Arabs call the "leaf stripper," while devastating the fields or forests of Central Africa. With the exception of the feathered tribe the enemies of the locust are limited to a few species of monkeys, mice, squirrels, hedgehogs, lizards, snakes, and frogs. The numbers devoured by these creatures, when taken altogether, is but "a drop in the ocean," when compared to the wholesale raid made on the locust swarm by birds. No sooner have these insects established themselves in a forest, and commenced their depredations, than their feathered pursuers immediately arrive from all sides, and the chase commences. Those Storks (*Ciconia*) and Ibises *(Tantalus falcinellus),* which are breeding during the locust season, arrive in countless numbers, often indeed from great distances, and support themselves and their young exclusively on these insects. Such birds as Kestrels, Lesser Kestrels, Buzzards, Harriers *(C. pallidus),* Crows, Rollers, Lamprotornis, Guinea-fowls, and Francolins, now in winter-quarters, approach the swarm and commence the work of destruction; Herons, even, if there happens to be water in the forest, as also Terns *(Sterna anglica)* take part in the raid. Hovering over the tops of the trees one sees hundreds of busy little Falcons, which seem to swoop down almost every second, and, actively seizing a flying locust, rise and devour it on the wing. The wings and branches, weighed down with the insect-plague, are sought by other birds. The Crows, stalking and hopping hither and thither, assiduously gleaning some, and shaking still more to the ground, are ably assisted by the Lamprotornis, Cuckoos, and Hornbills *(Buceros);* while the remaining members of the feathered crowd assiduously turn their attention to those locusts which have fallen to the ground. If the forests stand in inundated districts, localities generally attacked by the locust on account of the foliage being fresher and greener than elsewhere, their arrival in such places is the signal for the approach of a whole tribe of Ducks, Gulls, and other aquatic birds, who aid in their destruction by feeding on those which fall in the water. All the birds remain as long as do the locusts; some even follow the mighty army in its migrations. Thousands of greedy birds must be satiated! Hundreds of thousands of locusts are required to supply this demand; and should they number even billions, their ranks are yet in the end consumed!

It is not necessary to go out of our native land in order to observe a similar instance; for in Germany, even, some species of insects appear in countless thousands. A wood infested by the caterpillar of the Pine Lappet, or the Gypsy Moth, is a terrible scene of devastation. Visiting the plagued spot, one crushes them under foot by dozens at every step. Their excreta fall from the trees like rain, and the odor of their decomposing bodies taints the very air for some distance around. The unfortunate forester clamors in vain; each day shows a loss of some thousands of thalers. He tries every means to arrest the enemy; but, alas, without avail! Man is powerless, without the assistance of birds, to extricate him from his difficulty, and cries to heaven for help! His feathered friends, however, perform their part with untiring energy. Cuckoos, alone, can prey on hairy caterpillars with impunity; but these birds are, unfortunately, nowhere very numerous. The eggs and pupæ, however, of butterflies give ample occupation to thousands of active hunters. All the climbing birds, Tits, and Goldcrests, are unremittingly employed in seeking out and devouring them. It is a recognized fact that the winter following a plague of caterpillars, such as I have described, finds the forest inundated with countless numbers of Titmice and Goldcrests, as well as Woodpeckers of every kind. The forester who is well acquainted with his business knows their worth, *and affords them all the protection that lies in his power;* while the stupid, ignorant bird-catcher erects a *Titmouse trap on the borders of the wood, because it pays, forsooth!* Cuckoos, as before mentioned, also do their best to destroy the pest. Homeyer remarked, that in the case of a certain forest suffering under the inflictions of the Pine Lappet caterpillar, over a hundred Cuckoos, in the act of migrating, arrested their flight; and, in spite of their usually roving and solitary habits, remained for several weeks engaged in devouring these creatures. "A single bird," says he, "would often swallow as many as ten of these caterpillars in a minute. If we, however, only calculate at the rate of two per minute to each bird during a day of sixteen hours (which are well utilized by the Cuckoo), 100 birds would have destroyed 192,000 caterpillars daily, or close upon *three millions* in the space of a fortnight! A palpable decrease of numbers among these pests was unmistakable; and, indeed, one was tempted to believe that the Cuckoos finished by consuming them all, for, after the last straggler had taken its departure, not a vestige of a caterpillar was to be seen."

"To give a proof of the services rendered by Titmice, Goldcrests, and small climbing birds," says Count Wodzicki, "I will relate some of my experiences on the subject. In the year 1848, every leaf in my garden was devoured by numberless caterpillars of that most destructive moth, *Bombyx dispar,* so that the trees looked as though they had been blighted. In the autumn I found millions of eggs attached to the stems and branches of my trees, contained in a hairy envelope. I had them removed by hand at a very great expense; but soon finding that human means were insufficient to rid me of the plague, I made up my mind that I must inevitably lose all my trees. Toward winter, however, numerous flocks of Titmice and Goldcrests made their appearance day after day; and, to my intense delight, I perceived a daily decrease in the ranks of the enemy. In the spring no less than twenty pairs of Titmice selected my garden as their breeding place; whereas in other years I rarely ever found more than two or three nests. In 1849 the pest had sensibly diminished; and in 1850 I had the pleasure of seeing my trees so thoroughly purified by my little feathered gardeners, that through their instrumentality I again saw my orchard in full leaf the whole summer long. In the year 1842, I counted no less than two thousand plant-lice *(Aphidœ)* on three large rose-stocks in my green-house. I immediately introduced a Marsh Tit into the building; and in the course of a few hours every insect had disappeared."

My father always called the Woodpeckers, and other climbing birds, the "benefactors of the forest"; and strongly opposed the erroneous idea that these birds injure the timber by their operations. This is in nowise the case, for Woodpeckers never, by any chance, attack sound wood, but, on the contrary, seek out the sickly and decayed places, in which numerous insects breed. All well-informed foresters are agreed on this point. Ratzeburg, in his work on the "Spoilers of Forests and their Enemies," says distinctly: "Old hollow trees, as well as those covered with ivy and other creepers, should be allowed to stand, so as to afford nesting-places for birds."

Undoubtedly, the equilibrium between the plant- and animal-world is maintained principally by the *Scansores:* Titmice, Gold-crests, and other insectivorous birds, are not the sole agents employed in this matter, for the *Corvidœ* are scarcely less useful, especially one member of the family,—the common Rook. This bird is the chief enemy of the cockchaffer, and in destroying untold numbers of this insect, as also snails, etc., does us no small service. Buzzards, Kestrels, and Owls, are not less instrumental in preserving to man those plants which are most necessary to his existence. These three creatures ought to be as sacred to us as the Ibis was to the Egyptians, for they are the most active and untiring adversaries of the universally destructive fieldmouse. They all, in some way or another, contribute to the general service! A single Buzzard can devour some twenty field-mice in a forenoon, without any fear of an attack of indigestion; and a pair of these birds will, in the breeding-season, carry over a hundred of these little mammals to their young in a day. Owls and Kestrels are quite as useful in proportion to their size. One may rest assured that these birds will not be long before they find out and frequent a field over-run by these pests, and there carry out the work for which they were created. It is a veritable sin, a crime committed against agricultural interests, when the ignorant boor destroys them, and nails to his barn-door a crushing evidence of his folly and stupidity. In seasons when plagues of field-mice occur, these useful birds—they might almost be called angels—arrive, from whence no one can tell, and destroy them so long as one is to be found. The Snowy Owl has been known, from observation, to follow the Lemming, in its migration, for miles.

Of late years our attention has been attracted to another work, in which birds prove their utility to man. Not a few of them contribute greatly to keep down the over-growth of weeds. The farmer, who looks with distrustful eye upon Woodpigeons, or, in the autumn, upon Buntings and Finches, when feeding in his fields, does them the greatest injustice. They more than counterbalance the little mischief they commit during the few days' seed time. All Pigeons nourish both themselves and their young almost exclusively on the seeds of different weeds, namely, wild vetches, cornflower, charlock, millet-grass, and others equally abhorred by the farmer. These birds cleanse the fields from noxious plants, in the same manner as those mentioned in the preceding paragraph keep the land clear of destructive animals.

It is not necessary to enumerate further examples to convince any reflecting individual that birds are indispensable directors of the balance of Nature; we need not recall to mind the utility of the various reptile- and carrion-feeding birds of southern lands. Their whole lives are passed in heaping benefits upon us, and all the other higher orders of animated Nature; everywhere, and at all times, they appear to be employed in destroying what is hurtful, or in checking or removing its influence. They are the real guardians of order and the highest natural laws; they faithfully fulfill their most important duty.

And how rarely is the work they accomplish recognized by man! Only too often, unfortunately, he ruthlessly, and I may say criminally, seeks to disturb Nature's equilibrium, which they are engaged in preserving. And what is the result? Inevitable ruin! The "Sparrow war," which was carried on in Prussia by the government of our great king, was fearfully revenged. It cost the state, in the space of two years, many thousand thalers; and insect-vermin got the upper hand! "Frederick then wisely withdrew his hand from the tiller of Creation's harmonious work, where he thought he might meddle with impunity. He countermanded his orders, and was, moreover, obliged to *import* Sparrows, which were now preserved."

Today, war is no longer waged against the Sparrow, though a number of other highly useful birds are still subject to persecution. Without any reflection we destroy their breeding places by wholesale; and the birds themselves are pursued, harried, and destroyed, in the most wicked manner possible, thus driving them to emigrate to happier regions. The result of such conduct is only too easily to be seen in the works written by the forest authorities, or may, without difficulty, be recogized in many other ways. Plagues of caterpillars are more frequent, and their devastations are more felt; mice are the victors in their wars with us. Why? Because both *had* ruthless enemies, which *we* have despised, and either destroyed or banished; and this brings its own punishment. Do not, however, let us despair! Matters are not quite so bad as they used to be; voices, both numerous and influential, are beginning to make themselves heard, begging, aye, even demanding, protection for birds. Ratzeburg's demands will be satisfied; and breeding-places will be constructed for our feathered friends. And every sensible person will at last concur in the call of all students of Nature: *"Protection for birds!"*

Translated by H. M. Labouchere
and W. Jesse

Rudolf Virchow

The Task of the Natural Sciences

When the German scientists convened for the first time, all that could go by the name of German science was, to be honest, in such an early stage of its infancy that the contemporary scholarship, the textbook science, and the textbooks themselves were almost exclusively French. If one peruses the scientific and medical literature of that period, one will find only isolated, albeit brilliant, exceptions of purely German work; the actual textbook wisdom, the source of thought for all, upon which the entire scholarly community drew, was French. And that is more or less the way the situation remained until the 1830s. But in the small circle that Oken assembled about himself, however, and in the circle of his friends, a new notion was to be found, a singularly German notion that our nation can take pride in having nurtured to fruition, the notion that has become the foundation for the modern development of most of the natural sciences, and that, I hope, will become the foundation for even greater works; the notion I am referring to is the genetic notion.

It was in the final years of the last century when, from humble beginnings, the habit of treating things in the old, trite fashion was abandoned and the practice of apprehending them directly, not regarding them as simply given, but inquiring into their history and genesis, was established. Such an approach, of course, is not without great difficulties.

It is indeed much more convenient to imagine a certain thing as immutable, with definite, given properties that simply exist once and for all, and that, once one has become familiar with them, need only be retained in one's memory. From this concept originates that much-lauded method of memorizing, which in spite of all assurances to the contrary made by the regulative scholastics remains the foundation of our entire elementary educational system. The notion of the mutability of things in time, of their development, the notion that, strictly speaking, nothing immutable exists, that everything is subject to constant change—this notion has, to be sure, repeatedly cropped up throughout the course of the history of civilization. But a universally accepted decision between the seemingly irreconcilable antitheses of universal mutability and universal immutability was never reached. This conflict gave rise, initially in the field of the organic sciences, if I am not mistaken, and proceeding from the experience gleaned in the fields of botanical history, the metamorphosis of insects, and ultimately, biogenetics proper (i.e., embryology), to the notion that natural objects on the whole are to be regarded in light of their changes throughout the course of history, and that one must investigate them in terms of their variable properties, in spite of their individual persistence throughout the various times of their existence. One must not forget the speed with which this notion developed, from the end of the last century until Oken's day, into the precursor that gave rise in more recent times, hesitantly at first, then with ever-increasing clarity, to the theses of Darwin. For the step from the immutability of species to the mutability of species is indeed no greater than the step just mentioned, the step from seeing things not as given, but as nascent and evolving. If this notion initially asserted itself in the contemplation of organic nature, we are now seeing it gain more and more acceptance in the contemplation of the universe: modern astronomy is ceasing to be a mere physics of the stars; it is becoming a physiology of the stars.

Now if such significant advances have occurred in the past fifty years, if we may say that in the course of this period not a single area of science has been left untouched by the greatest revolutions, then one could conceivably conclude that by now practically everything that the sciences are capable of bringing about has been accomplished. The sciences are said to have gained a certain unshakability in their foundations; even in the schools, most of what is taught is the result of these experiences. It is deemed sufficient that the nation participate therein. There are also more than a few who maintain that the significance of the natural sciences lies in their utility, in the material achievements they bring about. It is acknowledged that medicine can repair afflicted limbs, and can even provide a positive foundation for physical education. It is emphasized that commerce and trade, mining and agriculture, shipping and transportation, the culinary and winemaking arts are influenced in the most significant way by the progress of science and are being in many respects fully transformed by this progress. By no means do I underestimate these material accomplishments. I should like to point out, however, that as valuable as all such material accomplishments in and of themselves may be, one might still perhaps hope that this very area of material accomplishments could well represent an incomparably greater source of benefit, perhaps immeasurable benefit, for mankind. No one who has studied the history of mechanical engineering in the century that has passed since the introduction of improved machines can escape the thought that machines replace human labor; no one who keeps abreast of this process by which human labor is replaced by mechanical labor can deny within himself the hope that the man-hours that have been saved by the advances in mechanical productivity might one day be made useful in the field of intellectual activity—the better, the more noble labor. If the workers begin, even in a crude and uncouth manner, to formulate their demands to this end, so shall then the topic of the normal working day be broached, in an analogous manner to which thousands of years ago the demand was made that the seventh day be made a holiday, a day of spiritual recuperation and elevation. It is not uncommon for an intelligent worker to suggest in all seriousness that the savings in time brought about by the introduction of the normal working day be dedicated to intellectual education; not simply to "elevation," but to progress in knowledge, which should then be employed as the point of departure for new technical and intellectual progress.

One may well retain, at this point in time, a cool opposition to such demands, but I imagine no one who brings to mind the entire history of mankind will be able to deny that justified demands do indeed exist in this respect, and that if one day success is attained not merely in finding the formula, but in paving the way to a general agreement on such a normal workday, with the subsequent savings in time as well as the purposeful utilization of the time thus saved, so that the nation and humanity in general would be in this way supplied with great energy towards new ends, then undreamed-of opportunities shall be brought about. It is becoming immediately apparent that the potential for progress in a nation does not lie in its ability to produce isolated eminent intellects. The achievements of certain periods, however, do indeed tend to cluster about certain names, and the tendency develops to use these very names to designate the past. When we look about ourselves in the history of science, however, getting back to the subject at hand, we must admit that the greater part of the work that in the memory of the masses is bound up with a single name does in fact emanate from the participation of many.

Many people are involved in the process of bringing to light the idea by stripping it of its various shrouds. One person tears away this shroud, another removes that one. The choice kernel becomes more and more tangible, until at last the final scientist grasps it and presents it to the delighted multitudes. It is, however, more the exception than the rule that a single scientist overcomes from the start all difficulties by himself, that he pulls a question out of the primeval darkness, as it were, and in the end answers it as well, working all by himself in the quiet of his study. Ordinarily the solutions are arrived at by the concerted effort of a multitude of minds, and their number is indeed great. Hence the phenomenon that as the number of those working on such problems grows, more and more international controversies of priority arise, because the same paths are trodden, the same problems are tackled, the same matters are debated almost simultaneously, or at least in rapid succession, in the most far-flung localities, and because in this way the truth comes at many different points so close to the surface that when the one lucky scientist finally comes along, he can immediately interpret it. For nearly every great discovery of the modern age, every civilized nation has its particular set of names that it tries to thrust into the foreground. If one reads the history of a wonderful discovery in Germany, it sounds completely different from an account written in England; not simply because of the jealousy, justifiable to a certain extent, that arises between nations, but to a much greater extent, in my opinion, because the various nations reduplicate each other's work in striving toward the solutions to such problems. . . . It must be realized that to the same extent that each individual in the various nations participates in the propagation of new knowledge, the whole progresses in wealth and well-being.

I admittedly place a higher value on the ideal aspect of the progress being made by the natural sciences than on this more material aspect, and I ask myself time and again, as a scientist and as a politician, whether science will, or indeed must, in the future exert a decisive influence upon the ideal life of the nation. In answering this question, at any rate, we run into the greatest of difficulties.

It has become increasingly popular to acknowledge the importance of school in all its various departments. But I must contend that only very few people have given sufficient thought to the extent to which the school of the future, the school from which future generations shall emerge, should be influenced by the new knowledge, and the extent to which we can hope that from this new knowledge a new interior life for the nation might indeed emerge. Everyone tells himself or herself that the nation, seen from without, has achieved such great things that this should suffice for a time. There are certainly not many who would want our outward development to progress in a similar fashion. It is thus a question of inward development, and if this inward development is not to consist merely in an improved structuring of the material life, if the conservative and orthodox circles rightfully insist that the inward life is not merely material, but has a more ideal content, then we will indeed have to ask ourselves: On which foundation should this new life, this new thought of the nation be placed? It is the task of the most immediate future, in a similar way to which the outward unity of the empire has been established, to likewise establish an inward unity—not merely to bring about an inward unification by force, by the suppression of political differences, but rather to establish a true unification of minds, to place the many members of the nation upon a common intellectual ground, where one truly feels part of a whole; where one is not merely aware of having a common ancestry, or even perhaps of lacking one, where one does not merely live together and share certain traditional customs, where one does not merely carry on a piece of banal, conventional society, but rather where people live together in intellectual unity and become aware of a common inner being, so that one can say: When I meet a German, I can presuppose a basis for mutual understanding and speak with him not only about common territorial borders, but about common interests of the intellectual life as well. . . .

If our further endeavors are to retain some bearing on the nation, if science is to make any specific contribution to the inward life of our nation, then it must make the attempt to imbue the populace with shared knowledge, to give the people with this knowledge a universally recognized foundation for thought, so that we might also reach an inward accord, and so that the most glaring contradiction with us and with our thinking does not persist among many of our fellow citizens in their first attempts to think, in the initial prerequisites to and indeed in the very methods of thought. If obligatory schooling exists among a people, if each person is compelled to submit to the education prescribed by the state, when the minimum amount to be learned by each person is determined through legislation, then, I hold, the first consequence to be demanded is that a sufficient measure of knowledge, a sufficient quantum of positive information about nature and about things natural be made accessible to each and every person, so that such absurd discrepancies between the knowledgeable and the ignorant can no longer persist, such discrepancies as do indeed exist at this time in most civilized nations. . . .

We must employ all of our energies to insure that science be made the property of all; not only by means of that which goes under the name of popularization, an approach that is certainly beneficial and that has indeed been pursued to a considerable extent, but rather by means of rational education. All merely popular education suffers from the fundamental shortcoming of being patchwork in nature. Incongruous fragments integrate themselves into the wholeness of an already closed consciousness. A dyed-in-the-wool orthodox thinker can be convinced that combustion of hydrogen takes place in the sun, and that this combustion is the prerequisite for our very existence upon the earth. This idea, however, has no connection whatsoever with the rest of his thinking; he harbors it as an organism would harbor some foreign body; if I may use a comparison from the field of medicine, in a similar manner to which an intestinal worm dwells within the body of an animal. We are dealing here with two different things; they can develop, one within the other, in a simultaneous and parallel manner, yet they remain two distinct entities: each is a thing unto itself. Such a person, in his attempt to develop himself further intellectually, gets caught in an inner disunion; the unreconciled conflict of his ideas brings about a loss of belief within him, and he may well come to doubt the correctness of the facts as well. Thus he becomes in the end an unfortunate skeptic. This result of popularization has shown itself in my experience to be a common one. Knowledge in the majority of educated people consists of nothing more than a mere conglomeration; it is somewhat porphyritic in nature.

Our task must be to make sure that knowledge becomes once again something uniform, something homogeneous, something flowing from one and the same source. To this end, a universally practiced method of thinking is necessary, as well as certain orderly forms of apprehension and interpretation of natural phenomena. Unfortunately, I still encounter scientists, and not infrequently, I might add, who in their specialized fields work in quite strict and conscientious adherence to the scientific method, but who, as soon as they leave their specialized field and embark upon another, take up a quite different method that clearly reveals the porphyritic construction of their psychological nature. Scientific thinking admittedly has its limits, and it does not suffice to explain the universe in its entirety. But it is making incessant progress. The work being done in physics today is gradually approaching such a degree of subtlety in its investigations that the question of the true constitution of the atom is becoming nothing short of an object of research. Consequently, it is impossible to keep silent when someone from the so-called philosophical standpoint says: "Atom, that is an absurdity; how can anyone speak of atoms? It is unthinkable that atoms could exist!," and tries to prove by philosophical means that all such suppositions are "nonsense." In my opinion, each person should receive enough education to be able to see that the problems pursued by physics are correctly posited. He may well cling to the opinion that atoms do not represent the ultimate solution to the question of the nature of matter, but he must allow that the path being taken by physics is a fully justified one, up to the limits of what is currently possible, and that one cannot, for the sake of "ultimate" problems, doubt the truth and the reality of those things that we with our methods are able to pursue in an ordered fashion.

We, who are faced with the more difficult task of tracing in the biological sciences the process of life on the basis of its individual phenomena, are quickly confronted with the problem of the soul or the spirit. When I conduct an investigation into what is subsumed under the concept of soul, I come upon a series of organic activities that are connected with certain parts of the body and that are quite specifically localized, whereby it is thoroughly impossible for the energy to go away, to leave the organ, and whereby nothing whatsoever of its activity can be found or detected in the absence of this organ. Strangely enough, the whole world agrees with this view in the assessment of mentally ill persons. It is generally conceded that a mentally ill person has a mind or a soul—it is also conceded that the body of the mentally ill person is in a bad condition, by virtue of which condition the mental activities cannot be carried out in a normal fashion—and when one then inquires into the location of this bad condition, one finds it an easy matter to come to the conclusion that in this case the brain is afflicted, in that case the spinal cord, etc. This point of departure is so commonly accepted that even our legal system subscribes to it. The only exceptions are those few people who even in this day and age still believe that the devil incarnate enters the human body and brings about the condition of demonic possession. This is yet another example of the relationship I characterized previously with the comparison involving the intestinal worm. Otherwise, in the assessment and interpretation of mental illness, there is essentially a general consensus that the organs are affected, and no one would believe that it is the immortal soul that is directly affected by the mental illness. As soon as one takes one step from the field of mental illness into everyday life, however, the fruits of this experience are at once completely lost. At this point the greatest resistance is encountered; at this point the vast majority of people say: "We cannot put up with the physiological view any longer." When the subject turns to the normal mental life, the mind is at once something quite special, and when the scientist proceeds to analyze the brain, to localize the individual mental activities in its various parts, and to break up the proposed unity of the soul according to the topography of the nervous system, the scientist is then a "materialist."

I mention this example only briefly, since the task at hand cannot be to discuss in detail such a difficult question. I emphasize it in order to attach to it the demand that what is legitimate in one field likewise be considered as such in the other. It is inadmissible to apply two different yardsticks of mental judgment to two analogous processes of nature. We must get into the habit of always thinking methodically, and methodical thinking is only possible when we study each individual process on the basis of that material which constitutes its sphere of action. We may then find that the movement we perceive as process is an imparted movement, that it has been transmitted from without, or that it rests in the characteristic activeness of the part itself that constitutes the object of our investigation. We simply do not have a third possibility; we must order our thoughts within the two possibilities mentioned. It is in my opinion in the long run impossible for humanity to escape the conclusion that the laws that can be inferred from everything that surrounds us, and whose validity proves true as far as the eye can see, simply must be valid for all judgment and for every attainable thing. Whether or not there are any other things beyond these attainable things, beyond the things that we can apprehend with our senses and with the methods available to us, can only be determined when our senses are given additional aid by new methods of research. Hence, to touch upon a case near at hand, a problem that has cropped up in recent research: namely, whether in addition to those elements that are found on our earth, another new, special substance exists within the sun: the new, oft-mentioned helium. No chemist can deny from the start the possibility that yet-unknown chemical bodies exist, nor particularly that on other heavenly bodies new substances might be discovered, but however many new substances are discovered, they will always be substances capable of being incorporated into the already existing spheres of thought and experience; substances essentially similar to the substances with which we are already familiar. They may well possess very peculiar properties, but they must be capable of being assessed on the basis of the positive experiences we have gleaned in our study of earthly substances. Should it ever happen that living beings are discovered on another heavenly body, these living beings may well be different from those that live on this earth. No scientist would ever contend that the circle of organisms with which we are acquainted represented the entire range of possibilities for organization. Just as we find within the various subterranean strata a multitude of organic forms that no longer exist, it is conceivable that other organic forms exist that have not developed on this earth, and it is in my opinion not necessary to assume that the developments with which we are familiar on this earth have taken place on other heavenly bodies. No one may contend that the limits of our knowledge will never stretch, that new problems of research will never crop up. No one may contend that all continuing research on the nature of matter will stop with the atom. But wanting to solve problems before one is able to formulate them I hold indeed to be an absolutely unfulfillable desire, and yet that is the way in which many people construe the entirety of the universe. One should not deceive oneself. Every postulation of a plan of the universe is a precipitate travesty of our earth, our existence, or our thought.

Translated by Daniel Theisen

Paul Ehrlich

On Immunity with Special
Reference to Cell Life

Nobel Lecture, Stockholm 1908

The history of our knowledge of vital phenomena and of the organic world can be divided into two parts. For a long time anatomy, especially the anatomy of the human body, constituted the beginning and the end of scientific knowledge. Further progress was only made possible by the invention of the microscope. Many years, however, passed by before Schwann demonstrated the cell as the final biologic unit. It would be like carrying wisdom to Athens to sketch for you the immeasurable progress which we owe to the introduction of the cell concept, the concept about which the entire modern science of life turns.

I take it to be generally accepted that everything which goes on within the body, assimilation and disassimilation, is referable, in the final analysis, to the cell; that the cells of different organs are differentiated from each other in a specific manner, and that this differentiation makes it possible for them to fulfill their various functions.

The results mentioned were achieved principally by histological examinations of dead and living tissues, though the allied sciences, physiology, toxicology, and especially comparative anatomy and biology, made most valuable contributions. Nevertheless I am inclined to believe that the aid which the microscope has given and can still give us is approaching a limit, and that in a deeper analysis of the all-important problem of cell life the application of optical contrivances, no matter how delicate, will fail us. The time has come for a further study of the minute chemistry of cell life; the concept *cell* must be resolved into a large number of distinct *partial functions*. The activities of a cell, however, are essentially chemical in nature, and since the formation of chemical structure is beyond the pale of visibility, it follows that we must cast about for other methods of study. This is important not only for a real understanding of vital phenomena, but because it constitutes the basis of a truly rational use of drugs.

The first step in this complicated domain was taken, as is often the case, quite indirectly. Following Behring's great discovery of the antitoxins, I sought to gain a deeper insight into the nature of their action, and after considerable study succeeded in finding the key to the mystery.

You all know that the power to excite the production of antibodies is confined to a distinct group of poisonous substances, the so-called toxins. These are products of the metabolism of animal or vegetable cells: diphtheria and tetanus toxins, abrin, ricin, snake venom, and many others. None of these substances can be crystallized; all seem to belong to the class of substances spoken of as albuminoid. In general the toxin is characterized by two properties, first, its toxicity, second, its power to excite the production of a specific antitoxin in the animal body.

In my quantitative investigations concerning this process I found that the toxins, especially solutions of diphtheria toxin, underwent a peculiar transformation, either spontaneously on standing, or through the action of thermic or chemic influences. While their toxicity was lost to a greater or less extent, their power to excite antibody production in the animal body remained intact. Furthermore, it was found that these transformation products, which I term toxoids and which my esteemed friend, Professor Arrhenius, has encountered in his numerous experiments, these toxoids still retained the power to specifically neutralize the antitoxin. In fact, in favorable cases it was possible to demonstrate that the transformation of toxin into toxoid is quantitative, i.e., a certain poison solution would neutralize exactly the same amount of antitoxin before as after the transformation into toxoid.

These facts permit of but one explanation, namely, that the toxin possesses two groups having different functions. One of these which remains intact in the "toxoid" and which therefore is to be regarded as the more stable, must possess the property of exciting the production of antibodies when injected into an animal, and must also be able to neutralize the antibody both in a test tube and in vivo. Since, however, the relations existing between toxin and its antitoxin are strictly specific (tetanus antitoxin neutralizes only tetanus poison, diphtheria serum only diphtheria poison, snake antivenin only snake venom, etc., etc.) it is necessary to assume that a chemical union occurs between the two opposing substances. In view of the strict specificity this binding is best explained by assuming the existence of two groups having definite configuration, of two groups fitting one another like a lock to a key, to use Emil Fischer's apt comparison. Considering the firmness of the union on the one hand, and the fact that neutralization takes place even in very high dilutions without the aid of chemical agents, we must assume that the binding is due to a close chemical relationship, in all probability analogous to a true chemical synthesis.

Recent investigations, in fact, have shown that it is possible, by chemical interference, to disrupt the combination, to split the toxin-antitoxin union into its components. Morgenroth, for example, has shown this with a number of poisons. Thus with snake venom and diphtheria poison he found that the action of hydrochloric acid caused the toxin-antitoxin combination to resolve into its original components, just as in pure chemistry stable combinations such as the glucosides, when acted on by acids, are resolved into their two components, sugar and the constituent aromatic group. These investigations showed that the more stable group of the toxin molecule, the group to which I have given the name "haptophore," is able to exhibit marked chemical activity of specific character, and it was therefore very natural to assume that just this group effected the anchoring of the toxin to the cell. We see, for example, how many species of bacterial poisons take weeks before they produce disturbances, and how they confine their injurious action to heart, kidney, or nerve. We see animals ill of tetanus infection exhibiting spasms and contractures for months. All this compels us to admit that these phenomena can only be caused by the anchoring of the poison by certain definite cell complexes.

I therefore assumed that tetanus poison, for example, united with certain definite chemical groups of the cell protoplasm, particularly of the protoplasm of the motor ganglion cells, and I further believed that this chemical union was the prerequisite and the cause of the disease. These groups I termed "poison receptors," or simply "receptors." Wassermann, through his well-known experiments, was able to demonstrate the correctness of this view, by showing that normal brain substance is able to neutralize definite quantities of tetanus toxin. A number of objections were made against these experiments, but they proved to carry no weight. I am convinced that it has been proven conclusively that the cells contain definite chemical groups which bind the poison. And that these groups, receptors, react with the haptophore portion of the toxin, is shown by the fact that it is possible to immunize with toxoids, in which, of course, only the haptophore group is present. We know that this haptophore group of the toxins must possess a peculiar, highly complex stereochemical structure, and since it reacts in exactly the same manner both with the antitoxin and with the cell receptors, we conclude that the group contained in the protoplasm, the cell receptor, must be identical with the "antitoxin" present in solution in the serum of the immunized animals. In view of the fact that the cell receptor constitutes the preformed element, while the artificially produced antitoxin represents the result, i.e., the secondary element, it is most natural to believe that the antitoxin is nothing else than thrust-off constituents of the cell, in fact surplus receptors which have been thrust off. The explanation for this is very simple. It is merely necessary to assume that the various specific cell receptors which bind, for example, snake venom, diphtheria poison, tetanus poison, botulism poison, etc., are not intended to serve as *poison catchers* for poisons with which the animal perhaps never comes into contact under ordinary conditions, but that they are really designed to chemically bind *normal metabolic products,* i.e., that they are intended primarily to effect assimilation. These receptors are therefore to be thought of as side chains of the protoplasm possessing the power of assimilation. When laid hold of by a toxin molecule, the particular normal function of this group is lost, put out of action. Thereupon, following the principle discovered by Weigert, the protoplasm not only repairs the injury, but even over-compensates the defect, i.e., there is superregeneration. Finally, with the accumulation and repetition of the injections, so many of these regenerated groups are formed in the body of the cell that they hinder, as it were, the normal cell functions, whereupon the cell rids itself of the burden by thrusting the groups off into the blood.

The most striking thing about this process is the enormous difference between the amount of poison injected and the antitoxin produced. Some idea of this disproportion can be gained from the statement made by Knorr that one part of toxin produces a quantity of antitoxin sufficient to neutralize one million times the quantity of toxin injected.

There are those, to be sure, who believe the process is much simpler than this. Straub, for example, thinks it is essentially analogous to simple detoxicating phenomena occurring in the body, comparing it, for example, with the formation of an ethereal sulphuric acid from injected phenol. The only difference, Straub believes, is that phenol sulphuric acid is stable in the organism, while the toxin-antitoxin combination is unstable, being partially destroyed in the organism. This destruction, however, affects only one component, the injected toxin, the other, the reaction product of the organism (being related to the organism and therefore not a foreign biological substance) escapes elimination and remains in the blood and body fluids. By systematically repeating the poisoning it is thus possible to increase the protective power of the blood, so that when this blood is injected into other animals the protective power is transformed, and the injected animals become resistant to the toxic infection.

This is Straub's idea. With so simple an explanation, one will wonder why this question has engaged the attention of so many investigators in immunity these many years. As a matter of fact, however, it seems entirely to have escaped the author that according to his theory a certain quantity of toxin can only produce an equivalent amount of antitoxin. Fortunately, however, in immunization this is not the case. It can be shown, as has already been said, that one part of toxin can produce an amount of antitoxin a million times more than the equivalent. This alone is enough to show how untenable Straub's conception is.

Of far greater importance is the fact that the demonstration of this hyperregeneration proves the preformation and the chemical individuality of the corresponding toxin receptors. That which the cell constantly produces and which can be given off to the blood after the manner of a secretion must have a chemical "individuality." This constitutes the first step toward resolving the cell concept into a large number of separate individual functions. From the beginning I had assumed that the toxin represented nothing more than an assimilable food stuff to which in addition, by chance as it were, was attached a side group, very labile in character, which really exerted the toxic action.

This view was very quickly confirmed in a number of ways. The actual independence of haptophore and toxophore groups was conclusively demonstrated by the discovery of substances which had the power to excite the production of antibodies, and which, therefore, were antigens, without possessing any toxic action. I may remind you of the precipitins first observed by Kraus, Tschistovitsch and Bordet. These authors showed that albuminous bodies derived from either animal or vegetable organisms were able to excite the production of specifically reacting antibodies, and this whether they possessed toxic properties or not. The demonstration of their antigen nature was thus extended to true food stuffs, a result to be expected on the basis of my theory. Moreover, even among the poisons found in nature, some have been encountered in which the independence of the haptophore and of the toxophore apparatus is at once recognized. I refer to cytotoxins which are found normally in the blood serum of certain higher animals, or which can be artificially produced by immunization with any particular species of cell. These cytotoxins differ from all other poisons known to us by the extraordinary specificity of their action by a degree of monotropism possessed, so far as we know, only by the poisons derived from the living animal body. Owing to their complex constitution it is easy to differentiate the haptophore and the toxophore apparatus, and to show that the function of the distributive component, the amboceptor, is to concentrate the really active substance on the affected cell. This is effected by an increase in the affinity of the amboceptor after union with the cell has taken place. The fact that animal cells act as antigens without possessing any toxic action, and the fact that it is possible to immunize with dissolved albuminous substances, demonstrates that only the haptophore group is responsible for the formation of antibodies.

The recognition and the careful analysis of the specific relations existing between the haptophore groups of antibodies and of receptors, has proven of the highest theoretical and practical importance in serum diagnosis. To cite only a few examples, let me call your attention to the determination of the agglutinating titer in its application to the Widal reaction in typhoid fever, to the method of differentiating albumins introduced by Wassermann and Uhlenhuth, and its significance in the forensic diagnosis of blood, to the measurement of the opsonic index introduced by Wright, and to numerous applications which have been made of the method of complement binding, a method whose scientific basis also rests on the principle of anchoring the antibody to the haptophore group.

Without going further into this subject, I wish merely to emphasize the fact that there are a number of foodstuffs, mostly probably albuminous in character, which find *specific* receptors on the cells, and that we are thus enabled by means of immunization to draw these receptors into the blood. Here they present themselves in various forms as agglutinins, precipitins, amboceptors, and opsonins, and as antitoxins and antiferments. By causing them to accumulate in the blood we can subject these substances to minute analysis, a procedure entirely out of the question so long as they remained part of the cell. The extent to which the analysis of these reactions can be pursued is well illustrated by the study of the toxin-antitoxin combination and by the recognition of the complex character of the amboceptor action.

This, of course, does not by itself solve the mystery of life. Comparing the latter to the complex structure of a mechanical apparatus, we might say that we are at least able to take out some of the wheels and study them minutely. This is certainly a great advance over the former method—to smash the entire apparatus and then hope to learn something from the mass of fragments.

I term all the receptors which are enabled and designed to assimilate foodstuffs for the cell "nutri-receptors." I consider that these nutri-receptors constitute the source of the antibodies mentioned above. From a pluralistic standpoint it is, of course, necessary to assume that there are a large number of nutri-receptors of various kinds. In view of the complexity of the organism, and of the multiplicity and specificity of the cell functions, a standpoint other than this appears out of the question. In immunizing we can distinguish three classes of nutri-receptors, namely:

(1) Those which do *not* pass into the blood in the form of antibodies. We may assume that this is the case with nutri-receptors serving the very simplest functions, as, for example, the absorption of simple fats and sugars.

(2) Those which pass into the blood in the manner described above, forming characteristic antibodies. The production of these corresponds to a superregeneration.

(3) The third form contrasts with the preceding, in that instead of a regeneration, there is a *disappearance* of receptors. Experimental evidence of the occurrence of this form, to be sure, has thus far been very meagre. The one example which may be familiar to the reader is the fact demonstrated by H. Kossel that on long-continued immunization of rabbits with the hemotoxic eel serum, the blood cells finally became insusceptible to this serum, as though they had lost their specific receptors.

Recently, aided by my colleagues, Dr. Röhl and Miss Gulbransen, I succeeded in gaining an insight into the nature of the disappearance of receptors. While the work will be made the subject of a special paper, I may here say that our experiments were made on trypanosomes. Working in my laboratory, Franke, after infecting a monkey with a particular species of trypanosome, had cured the disease by means of chemo-therapeutic agents, and had tested the immunity of the animal by again infecting it with the original strain. Contrary to expectations, it was found that the monkey was not immune, so that after a very prolonged incubation, the disease reappeared. If mice were inoculated with blood from the diseased animal, i.e., with blood containing trypanosomes, they became infected and died. Curiously, however, if the trypanosomes were first removed from this monkey blood, it was found that the serum was able to kill the *original* strain of trypanosomes. This showed that the trypanosomes had undergone some change in the body of the monkey, and that the variety thus produced differed from the original strain in its behavior toward the serum; it had become serum-fast. Similar observations were made at the same time by Kleine, and recently also by Mesnil.

We found that when animals which had been infected with a particular strain of trypanosome were treated with less than the complete sterilizing dose of suitable substance (arsanil, arsazetin, arsenophenylglycin) the trypanosomes disappear from the blood for a time. It can easily be shown that in this case also antibody has been produced. The few parasites which escape destruction lie dormant in the body for a time and gradually adapt themselves to the antibodies present in the serum. Then they again pass into the blood, where they rapidly multiply and bring about the death of the animal. We inoculated the trypanosomes so obtained into two series of mice. One series consisted of mice which had been infected with the original strain and then cured with suitable doses. These animals, therefore, possessed specific antibodies. The other series consisted of normal mice. Infection resulted equally rapidly in both series. This shows that the parasites of the strain producing the relapse have undergone a biological alteration, in that they have become serum-fast.* The alteration in these parasites is not superficial in character. On the contrary it may persist for many months and through repeated passage through normal animals. The relapse strain maintains its resistance to the antibodies produced by the original strain, and can thus be positively identified.

It was necessary to attempt to gain an insight into the nature of this alteration. After varying the experiments in many ways we reached the following conclusion: The original strain is plentifully supplied with a certain uniform type of nutri-receptor, which we may term group A. If the parasites are now killed and dissolved in the mouse's body, group A acts as antigen and gives rise to antibodies having definite relationship to group A. When living parasites are brought into contact with this antibody, either in vitro or in vivo, the antibody is anchored by the parasites. As a result of this occupation of its receptors, the parasites undergo the biological alteration which leads to the relapse strain. The alteration consists in the disappearance of the original group A, and its replacement by a new group, B. The following experiment shows that the relapse strain contains a new group. Two mice are infected with the relapse strain, which possesses group B, and are then completely healed. On infecting one mouse with the original strain, the other with the relapse strain, it will be found that infection with the original strain, carrier of group A, is successful, while reinfection with the relapse strain is at first unsuccessful. This shows that the original strain and the relapse strain are not identical, that they must be carriers of two different functional groups. We are dealing, therefore, with a typical case of disappearance of receptors following immunization, and accompanied by the formation of an entirely new variety of receptor.

It is probably of little consequence whether this alteration is regarded as a mutation or a variation. The important thing is that

*Exactly the same strain can be produced in much simpler fashion, by infecting mice with the original strain, and healing the animals on the second day with a full healing dose. After two or three days they are then again infected with the same strain. After a time parasites will appear in the blood, and these will be found to correspond to those of a relapse strain.

it can be artificially produced at will, and that it is hereditary. In view of the great interest attaching to this problem in biology and embryology, we have attempted a further analysis of the phenomenon.

To begin, it was necessary to determine in what manner the trypanosome antibodies affected the parasites. Corresponding to our previous knowledge of immunity we could assume that these antibodies exert a direct poisonous action, i.e., that they therefore probably contained toxophore or trypanolytic groups, so that the anchoring of the antibody by the parasite is followed by an injury or even the destruction of the latter. This, however, is not the case. In contrast to the ordinary strains of trypanosomes, which possess only a uniform group, A, B, or C, and which may therefore be termed "Unios," one meets with other strains which possess two groups in their protoplasm, A and B, and which may therefore be termed "Binios." If such a binio "A–B" is acted on by the isolated antibody A or B, growth will not be injured in the least. Not until both antibodies act at once does this occur. From this it follows that the presence of antibodies does not produce a direct toxic effect on the parasites. To us it seems that this three-fold experiment demonstrates that the antibody acts merely by blocking the food supply by occupying the corresponding receptors. It thus comes to pass that when in the binio A–B the group A is occupied by an antibody, the parasite can continue to vegetate by means of the group B. From this it also follows that groups A and B are essentially nutri-receptors.

If the amount of antibody is very large, the parasite finds it impossible to obtain nourishment, and consequently dies off. This can easily be demonstrated by mixing the parasite in a test tube with varying amounts of antiserum; the parasite is killed in the high concentrations which completely shut off the food supply, while in the weaker concentrations, which permit a vita minima, the parasites undergo the alteration already discussed, and give rise to a relapse strain. This mutation is therefore referable entirely to a hunger of the protoplasm, and under this influence the trypanosome develops new potentialities. I have given the name "atrepsins" to antibodies of the type just discussed, i.e., those whose action is purely *antinutritive,* and I believe that they play an important role not only with bacteria but in biology in general.

In view of the fact that the presence of antibodies demonstrates the existence of definite chemical groupings, most of the workers in immunity will have no difficulty in accepting the idea that there are definite chemical groups in the cell designed for the taking up of nutritive material. A much more difficult question is as to the existence of analogous groups for the assimilation of less complex substances. So far as the simplest additional function is concerned, namely, the absorption of oxygen, I believe this question is already partly answered. It is well established that in the hemoglobin molecule it is exclusively the organically bound iron residue which effects the loose union with the oxygen on the one hand, and the carbon dioxide and hydrocyanic acid on the other. It will therefore be necessary to assume that the red blood corpuscles contain definite groupings which possess a maximum affinity for iron and with that form a complex combination having the characteristic functional properties. The protoplasm of the red blood corpuscles would thus be characterized by a plentiful supply of "ferro-receptors," the completing of which receptors with iron leads to the finished hemoglobin molecule. Similarly we shall have to assume the existence of "cupri-receptors" in the blue respiratory pigment of crabs, and perhaps of "mangano-receptors" in other animals. The localization of iodine in certain glands, especially in the thyroid gland, and also the fact that the iodine is associated with certain aromatic side chains, will also be interpreted according to this conception.

The question as to whether the cell contains preformed chemo-receptors for the great host of true therapeutic substances is one of great difficulty. This leads us into the important domain governing the relation between chemical constitution and pharmacological action, which in turn constitutes the basis for the rational development of therapeutics. Not until we have really learned the site of attack of the parasites, when we have come to know what I term the therapeutic biology of the parasites, will we wage successful warfare against the producers of infection.

For this reason I have begun studying the existence of particular chemo-receptors on unicellular organisms, because here the conditions are much more favorable for gaining a clear insight than is the case in the extremely complex mechanism of the higher organisms. The problem I undertook to solve was this: Do trypanosomes possess, in their protoplasm, definite groupings which bring about the anchoring of certain particular chemical substances?

If any particular substance possesses the power to kill trypano-somes or other parasites in a test tube or in the animal body, it is obvious that this can only be due to the fact that the substance is taken up by the parasite. This bald fact, however, does not by itself give us an insight into the way in which this is brought about. A large number of different explanations can be brought forward. Not until we can prove that we are dealing with a function which is capable of being altered and varied in a specific manner is it possible to regard the existence of preformed groups as demonstrated.

Unfortunately it seems to be impossible to utilize the method employed in demonstrating the preformed existence of nutri-receptors, namely, by causing the liberated receptors to be thrust off into the blood. The chemo-receptors appear to be much more simply constituted, and remain attached to the cell, so that no thrusting-off occurs.

By indirect means, however, we succeeded in getting light on this phase of the subject. With the aid of my esteemed collaborators, Franke, Browning and Röhl, I was able to show that it is possible, by systematic treatment, to produce strains of trypanosomes pos-sessing immunity against the three trypanocidal poisons now known to us. These poisons, it will be remembered are (a) sub-stances of the arsenic group, (b) fuchsin, and (c) the acid azo dye known as trypanred belonging to the benzoburpurin series. The immune strains are marked by two characteristics:

(1) A stability of the acquired character. This is very great. Thus our arsenic strain, after having been passed some 380 times through mice in the course of two and one-half years, still possesses the same drug immunity as the original strain.

(2) An essential feature of the immunity to drugs is the strict specificity. This manifests itself by the fact that the immunity is related not against a certain definite elementary combination, but against the entire chemical group of which this combination is a part. Thus the strain made immune against fuchsin is resistant not only to that substance but also against a large number of related triphenylmethane dyes, e.g., malachite green, ethyl green, hexethyl violet. In contrast to this, however, the strain has remained suscep-tible to the action of the two other types, i.e., against trypanred and against an arsenical. A corresponding specific resistance is ex-hibited by the strain made fast against trypanred and by the one

made fast against arsenic preparations. That we are here dealing with three different functions is further shown by the fact that by successive treatment of a given strain with the three substances mentioned above we can produce a strain which is resistant against all three classes of substances, i.e., one which is triple fast. Provided that the resistance thus produced is of maximum intensity, such a strain is extremely useful in identifying new types of trypanocidal agents. If, for example, a new substance is encountered which is able to kill ordinary trypanosomes, we have merely to test its action on this triple-fast strain in order to determine whether the substance really represents a new type of trypanocidal agent. If it does not, we shall find that treatment with this substance does not cause the parasites to disappear; on the contrary they multiply. If they disappear, however, we can conclude that the substance does not correspond to any of the three types mentioned, but represents a new type of trypanocidal agent. The triple-fast strain thus acts as a kind of cribrum therapeuticum, by the aid of which it is possible to recognize substances belonging together and to separate unrelated substances.

It was now necessary to determine in what manner this specific drug resistance is brought about, and for this purpose I undertook a series of experiments with the atoxyl strain. In order to gain a clear insight into the question it seemed advisable to study the behavior of the arsenic-fast strains, also in a test tube, away from all disturbances and complications of the animal organisms. This method very soon encountered a great obstacle, for it was found that the drug mostly used therapeutically, namely, atoxyl (paramidophenylarsinic acid), does not exert the least destructive action on trypanosomes *in test-tube experiments*. Even solutions containing several per cent. of the substance proved insufficient for this purpose. This phenomenon was all the more remarkable because in the human body, according to Koch, injections of 0.5 gatoxyl suffice to cause the disappearance of the parasites within a few hours. In this case, therefore, destruction is effected in a concentration of 1 to 120,000.

We are here dealing with a phenomenon which is usually spoken of as "indirect action." It was not difficult for me to discover the reason for this peculiar behavior, as I had for years busied myself with reducing power of the animal organism. We know that in the body arsenic acid is transformed into arsenious acid; that cacodylic acid is reduced to the ill-smelling cacodyl. It was natural, therefore, to think first of reductions. In atoxyl, paramidophenylarsinic acid, the arsenic is pentavalent, whereas in the two products obtained from atoxyl by reduction the arsenic is trivalent. In this way we obtained two different products: (1) The monomolecular *p*-amino-phenylarsenoxid and (2) The further product, obtained from the latter by reduction, the yellow diamidoarsenobenzol.

In contrast to atoxyl, these substances exhibited marked trypanocidal properties not only in the animal body but also in the test tube. Thus a solution of the arsenoxid combination of a strength of 1 to 1,000,000 killed the tryponasomes in an hour. The closely related *p*-oxyphenylarsenoxid was still stronger killing in 1 to 10,000,000.

This proved that the pentavalent arsenic residue possesses no trypanocidal properties whatever; these are bound exclusively to the trivalent, unsaturated form.

As long as sixty years ago, Bunsen, with extraordinary insight, pointed out that cacodyl, the reduction product, is extremely poisonous, while cacodylic acid is almost nontoxic. This gave him the clue to the chemical character of the cacodyl combination. In striking agreement with this is the fact that the unsaturated carbon oxid, for example, and a number of other unsaturated combinations are so much more toxic that the corresponding saturated combinations. We shall, therefore, have to assume that the arseno-receptor of the cells is able to take up only the unsaturated arsenic residue, i.e., the group possessing the greater combining affinity.

With the aid of such reduced combinations it was simply a matter to test the atoxyl strain in test-tube experiments. These showed that the organisms could be killed with a suitable concentration of the chemical substances, and that we were not dealing with a loss of receptors as in the case of the relapse strain. A comparison, however, of the lethal dose with the dose sufficient to kill the ordinary strain, showed that the resistant strain required a much higher concentration. Amounts which effected immediate destruction of the ordinary strain did not in the least affect the vitality of the resistant parasites, even after one hour.

These test tube experiments seemed to indicate that the arseno-receptor, while still preserved in the atoxyl-fast strain, had undergone some modification so that its affinity had become lessened. This manifests itself by the fact that it required much stronger solutions to produce the poison concentration necessary to effect destruction of the parasites; the normal arseno-receptor of the original strain, by virtue of its higher affinity, takes up the same amount even from more dilute solutions.

We have succeeded in clearly demonstrating by biological methods that the arseno-receptor actually represents a distinct function whose affinity can be systematically decreased step by step by immunization. Thus far we have obtained three degrees of affinity. Grade I was produced by subjecting the parasites systematically to the action of *p*-amidophenylarsinic acid and its acetyl combination. We carried out this treatment *ad maximum* for years, until finally no further increase in resistance was produced. The resistant strain thus obtained proved to be resistant at the same time to a number of other arsenicals, among them particularly, the *p*-oxy-combination, the combination with urea, and with benzyliden, and a number of acid derivatives.

In practical therapeutics in man and animals, it is, of course, possible that arsenic-fast strains develop; and these, naturally, will absolutely hinder therapeutic success. In animal experiments this is a common occurrence. In view of this it is important to discover substances able still to attack these resistant strains, substances able to combine with their receptors. After long search we found altogether three combinations, of which the most important is arsenophenylglycin. With the aid of this combination it is possible to heal infections produced by the arsenic-fast strain I, which was described above. This can only be explained by assuming that the arsenophenylglycin lays hold on what is left of the arseno-receptor, somewhat as a stump is grasped by a pair of pliers. The anchoring of this substance, however, furnishes a possibility for still further increasing the arsenic-resistance of the strain. After considerable effort we succeeded in producing, out of arsenic strain I, a more resistant strain, arsenic strain II, which was entirely unaffected by arsenophenylglycin.

Plimmer has recently called attention to tartar emetic as a substance which kills trypanosomes, even in high dilutions. Tartar emetic is the salt of an antimony combination, and antimony, it is well known, is closely related to arsenic. On testing arsenic strain II with tartar emetic, we found that the parasites were destroyed by the tartar emetic. By treating arsenic strain II with arsenious acid we were able to produce a still further increase in resistance, so that arsenic strain III was resistant even against tartar emetic. I want to call particular attention to the fact that this arsenic strain III, produced only under the influence of arsenious acid, was resistant to tartar emetic *but not against arsenious acid.* This can only be explained by assuming that of all conceivable arsenicals, arsenious acid is the one possessing the greatest affinity to the arsenic receptor, and that only by the greatest effort, if at all, will it be possible to produce a strain (which would be arsenic strain IV) resistant also against arsenious acid.

I can adduce many other interesting facts to support my view that under the influence and attack of selected combinations, there is a successive decrease in the affinity of the receptor for that combination. Thus, we have found that we can at once employ one of the stronger agents producing resistant strains, using, for example, arsenophenylglycin. Corresponding entirely to our expectations, the strain thus produced proved resistant also against the less powerful substances, such as atoxyl, arsacetin, etc. A pan-resistant strain would, therefore, be obtained if from the outset we employed the most powerful agents, namely, tartar emetic and arsenious acid. Unfortunately, it appears from our work that it is impossible, at least in small laboratory animals, to directly use these substances for this purpose: it is necessary to proceed indirectly, by treating the organisms first with phenylarsinic acid derivatives.

The loss of affinity is, of course, a chemical phenomenon, and evidently to be interpreted by assuming that in the neighborhood of the arsenic receptor group other groups arise or disappear and thus cause the affinity to be reduced. The following chemical example will serve to illustrate the point. Benzylcyanid reacts with nitrosodimethylanilin. In order that the reaction take place, however, heat and a strong condensing agent, free alkali, are required. However, on introducing a nitro group into the benzole nucleus, the reactivity of the methylen group is markedly increased, so that the two substances, nitro-benzylcyanid and nitrosodimethylanilin, react even in the cold. In this case, therefore, the introduction of the nitro group has exercised a quickening influence on the reaction. If, however, the nitro combination is reduced to *p*-amidobenzylcyanid, we find that the latter is less active than the original material. The amido group has suffered a reduction of affinity. The acetyl product of the amido combination, on the other hand, reacts to about the same degree as the original material.

This simple illustration shows that three different groups attaching to the benzole nucleus in the para position either *increase* the affinity of the methylen group, or *decrease* it, or leave it *unchanged*. The reduction of affinity here observed would correspond to the affinity which we have described above.

According to my view, then, we should consider protoplasm as made up of a large number of individual functions, which, in the form of different chemo-receptors are scattered among the nutri-receptors. I believe that these two main groups cannot but be closely related, and for the following reason.

Trypanosomes of different origin, as they are cultivated in different laboratories, usually from the outset behave differently toward a particular therapeutic substance. The first strain of trypanosome with which I worked, Mal de Caderas, had no resistance whatever against trypan red, and this substance could be employed to effect a cure. This still holds true. Similar favorable results were obtained by Jakimoff in Russia, while Uhlenhuth obtained absolutely no result with this substance on the strains which he used. We are therefore dealing with natural differences in the various strains. Despite the fact that my strain has now been passed through normal mice for many years, it can still be cured by trypan red just as well as ever. This shows that the difference is not entirely artificial. On the other hand, my Nagana strain could formerly not be healed by trypan red, and cannot be healed by that substance now. However, on transforming this Nagana strain into a relapse strain, we were surprised to find that this property, which had persisted for many years, become altered within 14 days. This proves that the chemo-receptors really are related to the constitution of the protoplasm, and undergo alterations when we alter the constitution of the protoplasm.

Whether the reverse holds true, that is, whether, by influencing the chemo-receptors we can alter the cell substance, particularly the nutri-receptors, has not yet been definitely decided. Browning, to be sure, has observed that by means of serum reactions one can differentiate the fuchsin strain from the atoxyl strain, and both from the original strain. Careful investigation subsequently showed, however, that the changes in question were not specific alterations related to the fuchsin or to the arsenic, but alterations which correspond to the relapse mutation described above. These are due to the fact that during the treatment it often happens that the mice suffer relapses, which in turn lead to the formation of relapse strains.

I am well aware that what I have offered you has been quite fragmentary, but this could hardly be otherwise, for the adequate discussion of this theme would mean the recapitulation of an almost endless amount of work. My object in presenting this subject has been to show you that we are gradually approaching the problem of securing an insight into the nature of the action of drugs. I hope, too, that a systematic application of the views I have here presented will facilitate a rational development of the science of drug synthesis. In this connection I may say that thus far arseno-phenylglycin has proven in animal experiments to be a truly ideal therapeutic agent. By the aid of this substance it is possible to completely cure every kind of trypanosome infection in any kind of animal, and that by means of but a single injection. Truly, such a result may be termed *therapia sterilisans magna*.

Translated by Charles Bolduan

Hermann von Helmholtz

The Physiological Causes
of Harmony in Music

Music has hitherto withdrawn itself from scientific treatment more than any other art. Poetry, painting, and sculpture borrow at least the material for their delineations from the world of experience. They portray nature and man. Not only can their material be critically investigated in respect to its correctness and truth to nature, but scientific art criticism, however much enthusiasts may have disputed its right to do so, has actually succeeded in making some progress in investigating the causes of that aesthetic pleasure which it is the intention of these arts to excite. In music, on the other hand, it seems at first sight as if those were still in the right who reject all "anatomization of pleasurable sensations." This art, borrowing no part of its material from the experience of our senses, not attempting to describe, and only exceptionally to imitate the outer world, necessarily withdraws from scientific consideration the chief points of attack which other arts present, and hence seems to be as incomprehensible and wonderful as it is certainly powerful in its effects.

We are therefore obliged, and we propose, to confine ourselves primarily to a consideration of the material of the art: musical sounds or sensations. It always struck me as a wonderful and peculiarly interesting mystery that in the theory of musical sounds, in the physical and technical foundations of music, which above all other arts seems in its action on the mind the most immaterial, evanescent, and tender creator of incalculable, indescribable states of consciousness—that here especially the science of purest and strictest thought, mathematics, should prove preeminently fertile. Thorough bass is a kind of applied mathematics. In considering musical intervals, divisions of time, and so forth, numerical fractions and sometimes even logarithms play a prominent part. Mathematics and music! the most glaring possible opposites of human thought! and yet connected, mutually sustained! It is as if they would demonstrate the hidden consensus of all the actions of our mind, which in the revelations of genius gives us a feeling of unconscious utterances of a mysteriously active intelligence.

When I considered physical acoustics from a physiological point of view and thus more closely followed up the part which the ear plays in the perception of musical sounds, much became clear whose connection had not been previously evident. I shall attempt to inspire you with some of the interest these questions have awakened in my own mind by endeavoring to exhibit a few of the results of physical and physiological acoustics.

The short time at my disposal obliges me to confine my attention to one particular point, but I shall select the most important of all, which will best show you the significance and results of scientific investigation in this field; I mean the foundation of harmony. It is an acknowledged fact that the numbers of the vibrations of concordant tones bear to one another ratios expressible by small whole numbers. But why? What have the ratios of small whole numbers to do with harmony? This is an old riddle, propounded by Pythagoras and hitherto unsolved. Let us see whether the means at command of modern science will furnish the answer.

First of all, what is a musical tone? Common experience teaches us that all sounding bodies are in a state of vibration. This vibration can be seen and felt; in the case of loud sounds we feel the trembling of the air even without touching the sounding bodies. Physical science has ascertained that any series of impulses which produces a vibration of the air will, if repeated with sufficient rapidity, generate sound. This sound becomes a *musical* tone when such rapid impulses recur with perfect regularity and in precisely equal times. Irregular agitation of the air generates only noise. The *pitch* of a musical tone depends on the number of impulses which take place in a given time; the more there are in the same time, the higher or sharper is the tone. And, as we have observed, there is found to be a close relationship between the well-known harmonious musical intervals and the number of the vibrations of the air. If twice as many vibrations are performed in the same time for one tone as for another, the first is the octave above the second. If the numbers of vibrations in the same time are as 2 to 3, the two tones form a fifth; if they are as 4 to 5, the two tones form a major third.

If you observe that the numbers of the vibrations which generate the tones of the major chord *c e g c* are in the ratio of the numbers 4:5:6:8, you can deduce from these all other relations of musical tones by imagining a new major chord, having the same relations of the numbers of vibrations, to be formed upon each of the above-named tones. The numbers of vibrations within the limits of audible tones which would be obtained by executing the calculation thus indicated are extraordinarily different. Since the octave above any tone has twice as many vibrations as the tone itself, the second octave above will have four times, the third eight times as many. Our modern pianofortes have seven octaves. Their highest tones, therefore, perform 128 vibrations in the time that their lowest tone makes one single vibration.

The deepest *c* which our pianos usually possess answers to the sixteen-foot open pipe of the organ—musicians call it the contra-C—and makes thirty-three vibrations in one second of time. This is very nearly the limit of audibility. You will have observed that these tones have a dull, bad quality of sound on the piano and that it is difficult to determine their pitch and the accuracy of their tuning. On the organ the contra-C is somewhat more powerful than on the piano, but even here some uncertainty is felt in judging of its pitch. On larger organs there is a whole octave of tones below the contra-C, reaching to the next lower *c*, with sixteen-and-a-half vibrations in a second. But the ear can scarcely separate these tones from an obscure drone; and the deeper they are, the more plainly can it distinguish the separate impulses of the air to which they are due. Hence they are used solely in conjunction with the next higher octaves, to strengthen their notes and produce an impression of greater depth.

With the exception of the organ, all musical instruments, however diverse the methods in which their sounds are produced, have their limit of depth at about the same point in the scale as the piano, not because it would be impossible to produce slower impulses of the air of sufficient power, but because the *ear* refuses its office and hears slower impulses separately without gathering them up into single tones. (The oft-repeated assertion of the French physicist Savart that he heard tones of eight vibrations in a second upon a peculiarly constructed instrument seems due to an error.)

Ascending the scale from the contra-C, pianofortes usually have a compass of seven octaves, up to the so-called five-accented *c,* which has 4,224 vibrations in a second. Among orchestral instruments only the piccolo flute can reach as high; it will even give one tone higher. The violin usually mounts no higher than the *e* below, which has 2,640 vibrations. Of course we exclude the gymnastics of heaven-scaling virtuosi, who are ever striving to excruciate their audience by some new impossibility. Such performers may aspire to three whole octaves lying above the five-accented *c* and very painful to the ear, for the existence of such tones has been established by Despretz, who, by exciting small tuning forks with a violin bow, obtained and heard the eight-accented *c,* having 32,770 vibrations in a second. Here the sensation of tone seemed to have reached its upper limit, and the intervals were really indistinguishable in the later octaves.

The musical pitch of a tone depends entirely on the number of vibrations of the air in a second, not at all upon the mode in which they are produced. It is quite different whether they are generated by the vibrating strings of a piano or violin, the vocal chords of the human larynx, the metal tongues of the harmonium, the reeds of the clarinet, oboe, or bassoon, the trembling lips of the trumpeter, or the air cut by a sharp edge in organ pipes or flutes. A tone of the same number of vibrations has always the same pitch, by whichever one of these instruments it is produced. That which distinguishes the note *a* of a piano, for example, from the equally high *a* of the violin, flute, clarinet, or trumpet, is called the *quality of the tone,* to which we shall have to return presently. . . .

The human ear is affected by vibrations of the air within certain degrees of rapidity—from about 20 to about 32,000 in a second—and that the sensation of musical tone arises from this effect. That the sensation thus excited is a sensation of musical tone does not depend in any way upon the peculiar manner in which the air is agitated, but solely on the peculiar powers of sensation possessed by our ears and auditory nerves. I remarked a little while ago that when the tones are loud, the agitation of the air is perceptible to the skin. In this way deaf mutes can perceive the motion of the air which we call sound. But they do not hear, that is, they have no sensation of tone in the ear. They feel the motion by the nerves of the skin, producing that peculiar description of sensation called whirring. The limits of the rapidity of vibration within which the ear feels an agitation of the air to be sound depend also wholly upon the peculiar constitution of the ear. When the siren is turned slowly and the puffs of air succeed each other slowly, you hear no musical sound. By the continually increasing rapidity of its revolution, no essential change is produced in the kind of vibration of the air. Nothing new happens externally to the ear. The only new result is the sensation experienced by the ear, which then for the first time begins to be affected by the agitation of the air. Hence the more rapid vibrations receive a new name and are called *sound*. If you admire paradoxes, you may say that aerial vibrations do not become sound until they fall upon a hearing ear.

I must now describe the propagation of sound through the atmosphere. The motion of a mass of air through which a tone passes belongs to the so-called wave motions—a class of motions of great importance in physics. Light, as well as sound, is one of these motions.

The name is derived from the analogy of waves on the surface of water, and these will best illustrate the peculiarity of this description of motion. When a point in a surface of still water is agitated—as by throwing in a stone—the motion thus caused is propagated in the form of waves, which spread in rings over the surface of the water. The circles of waves continue to increase even after rest has been restored at the point first affected. At the same time, the waves become continually lower, the farther they are removed from the center of motion, and gradually disappear. On each wave ring we distinguish ridges, or crests, and hollows, or troughs. Crest and trough together form a wave, and we measure its length from one crest to the next.

While the wave passes over the surface of the fluid, the particles of the water which form it do not move on with it. This is easily seen by floating a chip of straw on the water. When the waves reach the chip, they raise or depress it, but when they have passed over it, the position of the chip is not perceptibly changed. Now a light, floating chip has no motion different from that of the adjacent particles of water. Hence we conclude that these particles do not follow the wave but, after some pitching up and down, remain in their original positions. That which really advances as a wave is, consequently, not the particles of water themselves but only a superficial form, which continues to be built up by fresh particles of water. The paths of the separate particles of water are more nearly vertical circles, in which they revolve with a tolerably uniform velocity as long as the waves pass over them. . . .

To return from waves of water to waves of sound. Imagine that an elastic fluid like air replaces the water and that the waves of this replaced water are compressed by an inflexible plate laid on their surface, the fluid being prevented from escaping laterally from the pressure. On the waves being thus flattened out, the ridges where the fluid had been heaped up will produce much greater density than the hollows, from which the fluid had been removed to form the ridges. Hence the ridges are replaced by condensed strata of air and the hollows by rarefied strata. Now further imagine that these compressed waves are propagated by the same law as before and also that the vertical circular orbits of the several particles of water are compressed into horizontal straight lines. Then the waves of sound will retain the peculiarity of having the particles of air oscillating backwards and forwards in a straight line, while the wave itself remains merely a progressive form of motion, continually composed of fresh particles of air. The immediate result then would be waves of sound spreading out horizontally from their origin.

But the expansion of waves of sound is not limited, like those of water, to a horizontal surface. They can spread out in any direction whatsoever. Suppose the circles generated by a stone thrown into the water to extend in all directions of space, and you will have the spherical waves by which sound is propagated. Hence we can continue to illustrate the peculiarities of the motion of sound by the well-known visible motions of waves of water.

The lengths of various waves of water, measured from crest to crest, are extremely difficult. A falling drop or a breath of air curls the surface of the water gently. The waves in the wake of a steamboat toss the swimmer or skiff severely. The waves of a stormy ocean can find room in their hollows for the keel of a ship of the line, and their ridges can scarcely be looked down upon from a masthead. The waves of sound present similar differences. The little curls of water with short lengths of wave correspond to high tones, the giant ocean billows to deep tones. Thus the contrabass C has a wave thirty-five feet long and its higher octave a wave of half the length, while the highest tones of a piano have waves only three inches in length. You perceive that the pitch of the tone corresponds to the length of the wave. To this we should add that the height of the ridges, or (transferred to air) the degree of alternate condensation and rarefaction, corresponds to the loudness and intensity of the tone. But waves of the same height may have different forms; the crest of the ridge, for example, may be rounded or pointed. Corresponding varieties occur in waves of sound of the same pitch and loudness, and the so-called *timbre* or quality of tone corresponds to the *form* of the waves of water.

The conception of form is transferred from waves of water to waves of sound. Supposing waves of water of different forms to be pressed flat as before, the surface, having been leveled, will of course display no differences of form; but in the interior of the mass of water we shall have different distributions of pressure, and hence of density, which exactly correspond to the differences of form in the uncompressed surface. In this sense we can continue to speak of the form of waves of sound and can represent it geometrically. We make the curve rise where the pressure, and hence density, increases and fall where it diminishes—just as if we had a compressed fluid beneath the curve, which would expand to the height of the curve in order to regain its natural density.

Unfortunately, the form of waves of sound, on which depends the quality of the tones produced by various sounding bodies, can at present be assigned in only a very few cases. Among those which we are able to determine with some exactness is one of great importance, here termed the *simple* or *pure* wave form. It can be seen in waves of water only when their height is small in comparison with their length and when they run over a smooth surface without external disturbance and without any action of wind. Ridge and hollow are gently rounded, equally broad and symmetrical, so that, if we inverted the curve, the ridges would exactly fit into the hollows, and conversely. This form of wave would be more precisely defined by saying that the particles of water describe exactly circular orbits of small diameters with exactly uniform velocities. To this simple wave form corresponds a peculiar species of tone which, for reasons to be hereafter assigned, depending upon its relation to quality, we shall term a *simple* tone. Such a tone is produced by striking a tuning fork and holding it before the opening of a properly tuned resonance tube. The tone of tuneful human voices, singing the vowel *oo* in *too*, in the middle positions of their register, appears not to differ materially from this form of wave.

We also know the laws of the motion of strings with sufficient accuracy to assign in some cases the form of motion which they impart to the air. . . .

It is to such differences in the forms of the waves of sound that the variety of quality in musical tones is due. We may carry the analogy even further. The more uniformly rounded the form of wave, the softer and milder is the quality of tone. The more jerking and angular the wave form, the more piercing the quality. Tuning forks, with their rounded forms of wave, have an extraordinarily soft quality, and the qualities of tone generated by the zither and violin resemble in harshness the angularity of their wave forms.

Finally, I would direct your attention to an instructive spectacle which I have never been able to view without a certain degree of physico-scientific delight because it displays to the bodily eye, on the surface of water, what otherwise could only be recognized by the mind's eye of the mathematical thinker in a mass of air traversed in all directions by waves of sound. I allude to the composition of many different systems of waves, as they pass over one another, each undisturbedly pursuing its own path. We can watch it from the parapet of any bridge spanning a river, but it is most complete and sublime when viewed from a cliff beside the sea. It is then rare not to see innumerable systems of waves of various length propagated in various directions. The longest come from the deep sea and dash against the shore. Where the boiling breakers burst, shorter waves arise and run back again towards the sea. Perhaps a bird of prey darting after a fish gives rise to a system of circular waves, which, rocking over the undulating surface, are propagated with the same regularity as on the mirror of an inland lake. And thus from the distant horizon, where white lines of foam on the steel blue surface betray the coming trains of wave, down to the sand beneath our feet, where the impression of their arcs remains, there is unfolded before our eyes a sublime image of immeasurable power and unceasing variety, which, as the eye at once recognizes its pervading order and law, enchains and exalts without confusing the mind.

Just in the same way you must conceive the air of a concert hall or ballroom traversed in every direction, not merely on the surface, by a variegated crowd of intersecting wave systems. From the mouths of the male singers proceed waves of six to twelve feet in length; from the lips of the female singers dart shorter waves, from eighteen- to thirty-six-inches long. The rustling of silken skirts excites little curls in the air, each instrument in the orchestra emits its peculiar waves, and all these systems expand spherically from their respective centers, dart through one another, are reflected from the walls of the room and thus rush backwards and forwards, until they succumb to the greater force of newly generated tones.

Although this spectacle is veiled from the material eye, we have another bodily organ, the ear, specially adapted to reveal it to us. This analyzes the interdigitation of the waves (which in such cases would be far more confused than the intersection of the water undulations), separates the several tones which compose it, and distinguishes the voices of men and women—even of individuals— the peculiar qualities of tone given out by each instrument, the rustling of the dresses, the footfalls of the walkers, and so on.

It is necessary to examine the circumstances with greater minuteness. When a bird of prey dips into the sea, rings of waves arise, which are propagated as slowly and regularly upon the moving surface as upon a surface at rest. These rings are cut into the curved surface of the waves in precisely the same way they would have been cut into the still surface of a lake. The form of the external surface of the water is determined in this, as in other more complicated cases, by taking the height of each point to be the height of all the ridges of waves which coincide at this point at one time, after deducting the sum of all similarly simultaneously coincident hollows. Such a sum of positive magnitudes (the ridges) and negative magnitudes (the hollows), where the latter have to be subtracted instead of being added, is called an algebraic sum. Using this term, we may say that *the height of every point of the surface of the water is equal to the algebraic sum of all the portions of the waves which at that moment there concur.*

It is the same with the waves of sound. They too are added together at every point of the mass of air, as well as in contact with the listener's ear. For them also the degree of condensation and the velocity of the particles of air in the passages of the organ of hearing are equal to the algebraic sums of the separate degrees of condensation and of the velocities of the waves of sound, considered apart. This single motion of the air produced by the simultaneous action of various sounding bodies has now to be analyzed by the ear into the separate parts which correspond to their separate effects. For doing this the ear is much more unfavorably situated than the eye. The latter surveys the whole undulating surface at a glance; the ear can, of course, only perceive the motion of the particles of air which impinge upon it. Yet the ear solves its problem with the greatest accuracy, certainty, and specificity. This power of the ear is of supreme importance for hearing. Were it not present, it would be impossible to distinguish different tones.

Some recent anatomical discoveries appear to give a clue to the explanation of this important power of the ear.

You will all have observed the phenomenon of the sympathetic production of tones in musical instruments, especially stringed instruments. The string of a pianoforte, when the damper is raised, begins to vibrate as soon as its proper tone is produced in its neighborhood with sufficient force by some other means. When this foreign tone ceases, the tone of the string will be heard to continue some little time longer. If we put little paper riders on the string, they will be jerked off when its tone is produced in the neighborhood. This sympathetic action of the string depends on the impact of the vibrating particles of air against the string and its sounding board.

Each separate wave crest (or condensation) of air which passes by the string is, of course, too weak to produce a sensible motion in it. But when a long series of wave crests (or condensations) strike the string in such a manner that each succeeding one increases the slight tremor which resulted from the action of its predecessors, the effect finally becomes sensible. It is a process of exactly the same nature as the swinging of a heavy bell. A powerful man can scarcely move it sensibly by a single impulse. A boy, by pulling the rope at regular intervals corresponding to the time of its oscillations, can gradually bring it into violent motion.

This peculiar reinforcement of vibration depends entirely on the rhythmical application of the impulse. When the bell has been once made to vibrate as a pendulum in a very small arc, if the boy always pulls the rope as it falls and at a time when his pull augments the existing velocity of the bell, this velocity, increasing slightly at each pull, will gradually become considerable. But if the boy applies his power at irregular intervals, sometimes increasing and sometimes diminishing the motion of the bell, he will produce no sensible effect.

In the same way that a mere boy is thus enabled to swing a heavy bell, the tremors of light and mobile air suffice to set in motion the heavy, solid mass of steel contained in a tuning fork, provided that the tone which is excited in the air is exactly in unison with that of the fork. In this case also, every impact of a wave of air against the fork increases the motions excited by the like previous blows.

This experiment is most conveniently performed on a fork which is fastened to a sounding board, the air being excited by a similar fork of precisely the same pitch. If one is struck, the other will be found after a few seconds to be sounding also. Damp the first fork, by touching it for a moment with a finger, and the second will continue the tone. The second will then bring the first into vibration, and so on. But if a very small piece of wax be attached to the end of one of the forks, rendering its pitch scarcely perceptibly lower than the other, the sympathetic vibration of the second fork ceases, because the times of oscillation are no longer the same. The blows which the waves of air excited by the first fork inflict upon the sounding board of the second fork are indeed, for a time, in the same direction as the motions of the second fork and consequently increase the latter, but after a very short time they cease to be so and consequently destroy the slight motion which they had excited.

Lighter and more mobile elastic bodies, such as strings, can be set in motion by a much smaller number of aerial impulses. Hence they can be set in sympathetic motion much more easily than tuning forks and by means of musical tones which are far less accurately in unison with themselves. If several tones are sounded in the neighborhood of a pianoforte, no string can be set in sympathetic vibration unless it is in unison with one of those tones. To test this, depress the forte pedal (thus raising the dampers), and put paper riders on all the strings. They will of course leap off when their strings are put in vibration. Then let several voices or instruments sound tones simultaneously in the neighborhood. All those riders, and only those, will leap off which are placed upon strings that correspond to tones of the same pitch as those sounded. You perceive that a pianoforte is also capable of analyzing the wave confusion of the air into its elementary constituents.

The process which actually goes on in our ear is probably very like that just described. Deep in the petrous bone out of which the internal ear is hollowed lies a peculiar organ, the cochlea or snail shell—a cavity filled with water and so called from its resemblance to the shell of a common garden snail. This spiral passage is divided throughout its length into three sections, upper, middle, and lower, by two membranes stretched across it. The Marchese Corti discovered some very remarkable formations in the middle section, consisting of innumerable plates, microscopically small and arranged side by side in an orderly manner, like the keys of a piano. They are connected at one end with the fibers of the auditory nerve and at the other with the stretched membrane. . . .

In the so-called vestibule also, where the nerves expand upon little membranous bags swimming in water, elastic appendages, similar to stiff hairs, have been lately discovered at the ends of the nerves. The anatomical arrangement of these appendages leaves scarcely any room to doubt that they are set into sympathetic vibration by the waves of sound which are conducted through the ear. Now if we venture to conjecture—it is at present only a conjecture, but after careful consideration I am led to think it very probable—that every such appendage is tuned to a certain tone like the strings of a piano, then the recent experiment with a piano shows you that when (and only when) that tone is sounded, the corresponding hairlike appendage may vibrate and the corresponding nerve fiber experience a sensation, so that the presence of each single such tone in the midst of a whole confusion of tones must be indicated by the corresponding sensation.

Experience shows us that the ear really possesses the power of analyzing waves of air into their elementary forms. Up to this point we have been considering those compound motions of the air which have been caused by the simultaneous vibration of several elastic bodies. Since the forms of the waves of sound of different musical instruments are different, there is room to suppose that the kind of vibration excited in the passages of the ear by one such tone will be exactly the same as the kind of vibration which in another case is there excited by two or more instruments sounded together. If the ear analyzes the motion into its elements in the latter case, it cannot well avoid doing so in the former, where the tone is due to a single source. And this is found to be really the case.

I have previously mentioned the form of wave with gently rounded crests and hollows, and termed it simple or pure. In reference to this form the French mathematician Fourier has established a celebrated and important theorem which may be translated from mathematical into ordinary language thus: *Any form of wave whatever can be compounded of a number of simple waves of different lengths.* The longest of these simple waves has the same length as that of the given form of wave, the others have lengths one-half, one-third, one-fourth, etc., as great.

By the different modes of uniting the crests and hollows of these simple waves, an endless multiplicity of wave forms may be produced. . . .

When various simple waves concur on the surface of water, the compound wave form has only a momentary existence. The longer waves move faster than the shorter, and consequently the two kinds of wave immediately separate, giving the eye an opportunity to recognize the presence of several systems of waves. But when waves of sound are similarly compounded, they never separate, because long and short waves traverse air with the same velocity. The compound wave is permanent and continues its course unchanged, so that when it strikes the ear there is nothing to indicate whether it originally left a musical instrument in this form or was compounded on the way out of two or more undulations.

What does the ear do? Does it analyze this compound wave, or does it grasp it as a whole? The answer to these questions depends upon the sense in which we take them. We must distinguish two different points—the audible *sensation,* as it is developed without any intellectual interference, and the idea, which we form in consequence of that sensation. We have, as it were, to distinguish between the material ear of the body and the spiritual ear of the mind. The material ear does precisely what the mathematician effects by means of Fourier's theorem and what the pianoforte accomplishes when a confused mass of tones is presented to it. It analyzes those wave forms which were not originally due to simple undulations, such as those furnished by tuning forks, into a sum of simple tones and feels the tone due to each separate simple wave separately, whether the compound wave originally proceeded from a source capable of generating it or became compounded on the way.

For example, when a string is struck, it gives a tone corresponding, as we have seen, to a wave form widely different from that of a simple tone. When the ear analyzes this wave form into a sum of simple waves, it hears at the same time a series of simple tones corresponding to these waves. . . .

Not only strings, but almost all kinds of musical instruments, produce waves of sound which are more or less different from those of simple tones and are therefore capable of being compounded out of a greater or less number of simple waves. The ear analyzes them all by means of Fourier's theorem better than the best mathematician, and on paying sufficient attention can distinguish the separate simple tones due to the corresponding simple waves. This corresponds precisely to our theory of the sympathetic vibration of the organs described by Corti. Experiments with the piano, as well as the mathematical theory of sympathetic vibrations, show that any upper partials which may be present will also produce sympathetic vibrations. It follows, therefore, that in the cochlea of the ear every external tone will set in sympathetic vibration, not merely the little plates with their accompanying nerve fibers, corresponding to its fundamental tone, but also those corresponding to all the upper partials, and consequently that the latter must be heard as well as the former.

A simple tone is one excited by a succession of simple wave forms. All other wave forms, such as those produced by the greater number of musical instruments, excite sensations of a variety of simple tones. Consequently, every tone of every musical instrument must be strictly regarded, so far as the sensation of musical tone is concerned, as a chord with a predominant fundamental tone.

This whole theory of upper partials, or harmonic overtones, will perhaps seem new and singular. Probably few or none of those present, however frequently they may have heard or performed music and however fine may be their musical ear, have perceived the existence of any such tones, although, according to my representations, they must be always and continuously present. A special act of attention is requisite in order to hear them, and unless we know how to perform this act, the tones remain concealed. As you are aware, no perceptions obtained by the senses are merely sensations impressed on our nervous systems. A distinct intellectual activity is required to pass from a nervous sensation to the conception of an external object, which the sensation has aroused. The sensations of our nerves of sense are mere signs indicating certain external objects, and it is usually only after considerable practice that we acquire the power of drawing correct conclusions from our sensations respecting the corresponding objects.

It is a universal law of the perceptions obtained through the senses that we pay only so much attention to the sensations actually experienced as is sufficient for us to recognize external objects. In this respect we are very one-sided, inconsiderate partisans of practical utility—far more so, indeed, than we suspect. All sensations which have no direct reference to external objects we are accustomed, as a matter of course, entirely to ignore. We do not become aware of them until we make a scientific investigation of the action of the senses or have our attention directed by illness to the phenomena of our own bodies. Thus we often find patients, when suffering from a slight inflammation of the eyes, become aware for the first time of those beads and fibers known as muscae volitantes *(mouches volantes)* swimming about within the vitreous humor of the eye; then they often hypochondriacally imagine all sorts of coming evils because they fancy that these appearances are new, whereas they have generally existed all their lives.

Who can easily discover that there is an absolutely blind point, the so-called punctum cecum, within the retina of every healthy eye? How many people know that the only objects they see single are those at which they are looking and that all other objects behind or before these appear double? I could adduce a long list of similar examples, which have not been brought to light until the actions of the senses were scientifically investigated and which remain obstinately concealed until attention is drawn to them by appropriate means, often an extremely difficult task to accomplish.

To this class of phenomena belong the upper partial tones. It is not enough for the auditory nerve to have a sensation. The intellect must reflect upon it. Hence my former distinction of a material and a spiritual ear.

We always hear the tone of a string accompanied by a certain combination of upper partial tones. A different combination of such tones belongs to the tone of a flute, or of the human voice, or of a dog's howl. Whether a violin or a flute, a man or a dog, is close by us is a matter of interest for us to know, and our ear takes care to distinguish the peculiarities of their tones with accuracy. The *means* by which we can distinguish them, however, is a matter of perfect indifference. Whether the cry of the dog contains the higher octave or the twelfth of the fundamental tone has no practical interest for us and never occupies our attention. The upper partials are consequently thrown into that unanalyzed mass of peculiarities of a tone which we call its *quality*. As the existence of upper partial tones depends on the wave form, we see, as I stated previously, that the quality of tone corresponds to the form of wave.

The upper partial tones are most easily heard when they are not in harmony with the fundamental tone, as in the case of bells. The art of the bell-founder consists precisely in giving bells such a form that the deeper and stronger partial tones shall be in harmony with the fundamental tone, as otherwise the bell would be unmusical, tinkling like a kettle. But the higher partials are always out of harmony, and hence bells are unfitted for artistic music. On the other hand, it follows, from what has been said, that the upper partial tones are all the more difficult to hear, the more accustomed we are to the compound tones of which they form a part. This is especially the case with the human voice, and many skillful observers have consequently failed to discover them there.

The preceding theory was wonderfully corroborated by a method which enabled not only myself but other persons to hear the upper partial tones of the human voice. No particularly fine musical ear is required for this purpose, as was formerly supposed, but only proper means for directing the observer's attention. Let a powerful male voice sing the note e♭ to the vowel O in *ore*, close to a good piano. Then lightly touch on the piano the note *b′* in the next octave above, and listen attentively to the sound of the piano as it dies away. If this *b′♭* is a real upper partial in the compound tone uttered by the singer, the sound of the piano will apparently not die away at all, but the corresponding upper partial of the voice will be heard as if the note of the piano continued. By properly varying the experiment, it will be found possible to distinguish the vowels from one another by their upper partial tones. . . .

The following easy experiment clearly shows that it is indifferent whether the several simple tones contained in a compound tone like a vowel uttered by the human voice come from one source or several. If the dampers of a pianoforte are raised, not only do the sympathetic vibrations of the strings furnish tones of the same *pitch* as those uttered beside it; but if we sing A (*a* in *father*) to any note of the piano, we hear an A quite clearly returned from the strings; and if E (*a* in *fare* or *fate*), O (*o* in *hole* or *ore*), and U (*oo* in *cool*), be similarly sung to the note, E, O, and U will be echoed back. It is only necessary to hit the note of the piano with great exactness. The sound of the vowel is produced solely by the sympathetic vibration of the higher strings, which correspond with the upper partial tones of the tone sung. In this experiment the tones of numerous strings are excited by a tone proceeding from a single source, the human voice, which produces a motion of the air, equivalent in form, and therefore in quality, to that of this single tone itself.

We have hitherto spoken only of compositions of waves of different lengths. We shall now compound waves of the same lengths which are moving in the same direction. The result will be entirely different, according as the elevations of one coincide with those of the other (in which case elevations of double the height and depressions of double the depth are produced), or the elevations of one fall on the depressions of the other. If both waves have the same height, so that the elevations of one exactly fit into the depressions of the other, both elevations and depressions will vanish in the second case, and the two waves will mutually destroy each other. Similarly two waves of sound, as well as two waves of water, may mutually destroy each other, when the condensations of one coincide with the rarefactions of the other. This remarkable phenomenon, wherein sound is silenced by a precisely similar sound, is called the interference of sounds.

This is easily proved by means of the siren already described. When the upper box is place so that the puffs of air may proceed simultaneously from the rows of twelve holes in each wind chest, their effect is reinforced, and we obtain the fundamental tone of the corresponding tone of the siren very full and strong. But if the boxes are arranged so that the upper puffs escape when the lower series of holes is covered and the fundamental tone vanishes, we only hear a faint sound of the first upper partial, which is an octave higher and which is not destroyed by interference under these circumstances.

Interference leads us to the so-called musical beats. If two tones of exactly the same pitch are produced simultaneously and their elevations coincide at first, they will never cease to coincide; and if they did not coincide at first, they never will coincide. The two tones will either perpetually reinforce, or perpetually destroy each other. But if the two tones have only approximately equal pitches and their elevations at first coincide, so that they mutually reinforce each other, the elevations of one will gradually outstrip the elevations of the other. Times will come when the elevations of the one fall upon the depressions of the other, and then other times when the more rapidly advancing elevations of the one will have again reached the elevations of the other. These alternations become sensible by that alternate increase and decrease of loudness which we call a beat.

These beats may often be heard when two instruments which are not exactly in unison play a note of the same name. When the two or three strings which are struck by the same hammer on a piano are out of tune, the beats may be distinctly heard. Very slow and regular beats often produce a fine effect in sostenuto passages, as in sacred part-songs, by pealing through the lofty aisles like majestic waves, or by a gentle tremor giving the tone a character of enthusiasm and emotion. The greater the difference of the pitches, the quicker the beats. As long as no more than four to six beats occur in a second, the ear readily distinguishes the alternate reinforcements of the tone. If the beats are more rapid, the tone grates on the ear or, if it is high, becomes cutting. A grating tone is one interrupted by rapid breaks, like that of the letter R, which is produced by interrupting the tone of the voice by a tremor of the tongue or uvula. When the beats become more rapid, the ear finds a continually increasing difficulty when attempting to hear them separately, even though there is a sensible roughness of the tone. At last they become entirely undistinguishable and, like the separate puffs which compose a tone, dissolve as it were into a continuous sensation of tone.

Hence, while every separate musical tone excites in the auditory nerve a uniform sustained sensation, two tones of different pitches mutually disturb each other and split up into separable beats, which excite a feeling of discontinuity as disagreeable to the ear as similar intermittent but rapidly repeated sources of excitement are unpleasant to the other organs of sense—for example, flickering and glittering light to the eye, scratching with a brush to the skin. This roughness of tone is the essential character of dissonance. It is most unpleasant to the ear when the two tones differ by about a semitone, in which case, in the middle portions of the scale, from twenty to forty beats ensue in a second. When the difference is a whole tone, the roughness is less; and when it reaches a third, it usually disappears, at least in the higher parts of the scale. The (minor or major) third may in consequence pass as a consonance. Even when the fundamental tones have such widely different pitches that they cannot produce audible beats, the upper partial tones may beat and make the tone rough. Thus, if two tones form a fifth (that is, one makes two vibrations in the same time as the other makes three), there is one upper partial in each tone which makes six vibrations in the same time. If the ratio of the pitches of the fundamental tones is exactly as two to three, the two upper partial tones of six vibrations are precisely alike and do not destroy the harmony of the fundamental tones. But if this ratio is only approximately as two to three, then these two upper partials are not exactly alike and hence will beat and roughen the tone.

It is very easy to hear the beats of such imperfect fifths because, as our pianos and organs are now tuned, all the fifths are impure, although the beats are very slow. By properly directed attention, or still better with the help of a properly tuned resonator, it is easy to hear that it is the particular upper partials here spoken of that are beating together. The beat are necessarily weaker than those of the fundamental tones because the beating upper partials are themselves weaker. Although we are not usually clearly conscious of these beating upper partials, the ear feels their effect as a want of uniformity or a roughness in the mass of tone, whereas a perfectly pure fifth, with pitches precisely in the ratio of two to three, continues to sound with perfect smoothness, without any alterations, reinforcements, diminutions, or roughnesses of tone. As has already been mentioned, the siren proves in the simplest manner that the most perfect consonance of the fifth precisely corresponds to this ratio between the pitches. We have now learned the reason of the roughness experienced when any deviation from that ratio has been produced.

In the same way, two tones which have their pitches exactly in the ratios of three to four, or four to five, and consequently form a perfect fourth or a perfect major third, sound much better when sounded together, than two others whose pitches slightly deviate from this exact ratio. In this manner, any given tone being assumed as fundamental, there is a precisely determinate number of other degrees of tone which can be sounded at the same time without producing any want of uniformity or any roughness of tone, or which will at least produce less roughness than any slightly greater or smaller intervals of tone under the same circumstances.

This is the reason why modern music, which is essentially based on the harmonious consonance of tones, has been compelled to limit its scale to certain determinate degrees. But even in ancient music, which allowed only one part to be sung at a time and hence had no harmony in the modern sense of the word, it can be shown that the upper partial tones contained in all musical tones sufficed to determine a preference in favor of progressions through certain determinate intervals. When an upper partial tone is common to two successive tones in a melody, the ear recognizes a certain relationship between them, serving as an artistic bond of union. Time is, however, too short for me to enlarge on this topic, as we should be obliged to go far back into the history of music.

I shall but mention that there exists another kind of secondary tone, which is only heard when two or more loudish tones of different pitch are sounded together and is hence termed *combinational*. These secondary tones are likewise capable of beating and hence producing roughness in the chords. Suppose a perfectly just major third, *c′ e′* (ratio of pitches, four to five), is sounded on the siren, or with properly tuned organ pipes, or on a violin; then a faint *c* two octaves deeper than the *c′* will be heard as a combinational tone. The same *c* is also heard when the tones *e′ g′* (ratio of pitches five to six) are sounded together.

If the three tones *c′*, *e′*, *g′*, having their pitches precisely in the ratios four, five, six, are struck together, the combinational tone *c* is produced twice in perfect unison and without beats. But if the three notes are not exactly thus tuned, the two *c* combinational tones will have different pitches and produce faint beats.

The combinational tones are usually much weaker than the upper partial tones, hence their beats are much less rough and sensible than those of the latter. They are consequently but little observable, except in tones which have scarcely any upper partials, as those produced by flutes or the closed pipes of organs. But it is indisputable that on such instruments part music scarcely presents any line of demarcation between harmony and disharmony and is consequently deficient both in strength and character. On the contrary, all good musical qualities of tones are comparatively rich in upper partials, possessing the five first, which form the octaves, fifths, and major thirds of the fundamental tone. Hence, in the mixture stops of the organ, additional pipes are used, giving the series of upper partial tones corresponding to the pipe producing the fundamental tone, in order to generate a penetrating, powerful quality of tone to accompany congregational singing. The important part played by the upper partial tones in all artistic musical effects is here also indisputable.

We have now reached the heart of the theory of harmony. Harmony and disharmony are distinguished by the undisturbed current of the tones in the former, which are as flowing as when produced separately, and by the disturbances created in the latter, in which the tones split up into separate beats. All that we have considered tends to this end. In the first place the phenomenon of beats depends on the interference of waves. Hence they could only occur if sound were due to undulations. Next, the determination of consonant intervals necessitated a capability in the ear of feeling the upper partial tones and analyzing the compound systems of waves into simple undulations, according to Fourier's theorem. It is entirely in accord with this theorem that the pitches of the upper partial tones of all serviceable musical tones must stand to the pitch of their fundamental tones in the ratios of the whole numbers to one, and that consequently the ratios of the pitches of concordant intervals must correspond with the smallest possible whole numbers.

How essential is the physiological constitution of the ear which we have just considered, becomes clear by comparing it with that of the eye. Light is also an undulation of a peculiar medium, the luminous ether, diffused through the universe; and light, as well as sound, exhibits phenomena of interference. Light, too, has waves of various periodic times of vibration, which produce in the eye the sensation of color, red having the greatest periodic time, then orange, yellow, green, blue, violet—the periodic time of violet being about half that of the outermost red. But the eye is unable to decompose compound systems of luminous waves, that is, to distinguish compound colors from one another. It experiences from them a single, unanalyzable, simple sensation, that of a mixed color. It is indifferent to the eye whether this mixed color results from a union of fundamental colors with simple or with non-simple ratios of periodic times. The eye has no sense of harmony in the same meaning as the ear. There is no music to the eye.

Aesthetics endeavors to find the principle of artistic beauty in its unconscious conformity to law. Today I have endeavored to lay

bare the hidden law on which depends the agreeableness of consonant combinations. It is in the truest sense of the word unconsciously obeyed, so far as it depends on the upper partial tones,
which, though felt by the nerves, are not usually consciously present to the mind. Their compatibility or incompatibility, however,
is felt without the hearer knowing the cause of the feeling he
experiences.

These phenomena of agreeableness of tone, as determined solely
by the senses, are of course merely the first step toward the beautiful in music. For the attainment of that higher beauty which appeals to the intellect, harmony and disharmony are only means,
although essential and powerful means. In disharmony the auditory
nerve feels hurt by the beats of incompatible tones. It longs for the
pure efflux of the tones into harmony. It hastens toward that harmony for satisfaction and rest. Thus both harmony and disharmony alternately urge and moderate the flow of tones, while
the mind sees in their immaterial motion an image of its own perpetually streaming thoughts and moods. Just as in the rolling
ocean, this movement, rhythmically repeated and yet every varying,
rivets our attention and hurries us along. But whereas in the sea,
blind physical forces alone are at work and the final impression on
the spectator's mind is nothing but solitude, in a musical work of
art the movement follows the outflow of the artist's own emotions.
Now gently gliding, now gracefully leaping, now violently stirred,
penetrated by or laboriously contending with the natural expression of passion, the stream of sound, in primitive vivacity, bears
over into the hearer's soul unimagined moods which the artist has
overheard from his own, and finally raises him to that repose of
everlasting beauty of which God has allowed but few of his elect
favorites to be the heralds.

But I have reached the confines of physical science and must
close.

Translated by Russell Kahl

Adam Müller

On the Art of Listening

There is an art of *listening* as well as an art of speaking. And, according to my precept, the orator must, in addition to himself, also allow his adversary's personality to speak. Thus, it is clear that, to the same degree as the art of penetrating unknown natures by means of his speech, he must possess the art of listening, the art of becoming conscious of the character and individuality of unknown natures. These two arts depend on each other; nobody can be a greater orator than listener.

In music the world will agree with my demand. Whoever wants to learn how to sing must have a musical ear. And whoever wants to feel music as an art and not as a mere flattery of the ear should have trained his ear for music, just as he who produces it must have trained his voice or his instrumental skill. In general, people believe of all arts that one has to practice them himself in order to enjoy to the full what they afford. Only in rhetoric people believe it is sufficient that the receiving sense, the ear, be open and experience passively. One presupposes, perhaps vaguely, that a sense which is trained daily by means of an art, such as the art of speaking (which we cannot do without entirely in any situation in life) needs no intentional assistance and that the soul, this artist of all art, certainly would be automatically a prudent and eager door-keeper of the main entrance which leads to it.

To begin with, however, one overlooks the fact that the whole world is expressed by means of speech. And for everything which the world gives to man—goods, wealth, pleasures, knowledge— man returns, in general, only a single worthy equivalent to it, namely, speech—that is, the world represented in a human form. One overlooks, therefore, that through this sense of the ear both great and small, powerful and weak, immeasurable and trivial things are received, so that things must be received in very different ways, sometimes in a grand, sometimes in a light and cursory manner. Therefore, the ear, which is only accustomed to perceiving "Good morning," or "How do you do?" or "What's the price?" is not for that reason alone qualified to listen appreciatively to a speech by Johannes Müller to the Swiss, or by Gentz for the European balance of power, or to listen to some other popular spokesman. It is not, perhaps, because the knowledge, the scholarly preparations are lacking which are necessary for the understanding of these orators, but because the ear is not accustomed to the grand phrases of speech. In reality no transition takes place from the over used, crumbling tones of common life (in which no law governs other than the law of necessity, no rhythm other than the rhythm of laziness) to the harmonic whole which a deliberating mind has arranged rhythmically and with freedom.

Further, one overlooks men's vanity by giving the ear in itself credit for its necessary cultivation. To be inactive, to experience passively is no art; but to be receptive, to *receive* with understanding and dignity, is everywhere just as great an art as to act, or to *give* with intelligence, with taste, and with power. But the art of doing and, likewise, the art of speaking are observable. An effect seems to emanate from them and they seem to do pleasant violence to entire bodies of men and forces. On the other hand, the art of being receptive and of listening is less striking. It finally follows that in every given society many more people want to speak than to listen. Nature, however, seems to want the complete opposite by having arranged that many can listen to what one person says, yet it is impossible that one person can listen to what many people say at the same time. Men's vanity causes the speech organ to be much more trained than the ear and causes one to withdraw more and more from the soul, which, if anywhere, lies between both of those sublime organs; and one wants to produce by mechanical means the highest effect which mind can ever accomplish over mind.

The eye receives all pictures, all colors, all characteristics of the world. What does it give the world in return besides its expressive, but quiet gleam? What do taste, the sense of smell, for which nature seems to mix the most delicate proportions of the material world,

return to nature? With which faculty does man respond to all benefits and flatterings of his feelings and of all these senses? He pays
all his debt, he requites all this infinite receiving, he responds to
all of nature's questions with the faculty of speech. Out of all these
pictures, this splendor, this fragrance, this pleasant taste, these
thousand-fold stimulations of the feelings, is prepared a single,
simple-infinite substance—*the word*. Therefore, the ear, to which
nature has attached the faculty of response and which is not just
destined to be receptive as the others, has a higher function than
the other senses. The truth of this assertion also appears more
closely in the fact that our ear, entirely alone and almost without
aid of the other senses, can feel the law of the world. In music one
can note, and most of the musical virtuosi confirm it, that this
sense is the most independent of all. I might even say that the whole
man can withdraw into the ear and, with this one organ, live, think,
and write poetry and leave all other organs in an animal condition.
The ancients aimed at a great concept when they spoke of a harmony of the spheres, as if only the ear could really sense the wonderful arrangement of the world's structure!

Man's vanity prefers to effect this sense rather than receive impressions from it; in the meantime, the faculty of receiving higher
impressions of this kind and, naturally, also the art of causing them
by means of speech gradually are lost. And granted even that nature
provided for the ear's training, nevertheless, man spoils it by his
vain and unfortunate striving to have a more reactive effect upon
the world than the world affects him.

Finally, by giving credit automatically to our present, cultivated
Europeans' ear for the necessary training, people overlook the confusion and inversion in the realm of minds which the art of printing
has produced. In the times before this beneficial, but also pernicious
invention, the art of writing was only employed for those absent
and for posterity. Living speech, however, was dominant for the
contemporaries, for everyone whom one could reach with his
breast and his voice. It was the same as in money matters; where
one could reach each other, there everyone repaid each other with
the strength of his hands and with services. One paid those present
and contemporary with one's own person; only for those far off,
for those absent, for the future, did one make use of gold and
silver. Gold and silver are to the living deed exactly as writing is
to the living word. Thus all of man's practical relations dissolved

into money relations. All of man's talk in life's higher matters, namely, in the control of the state and the scholarly realm, dissolved into written transactions. In the whole area of civil life, except perhaps between parents and children, there remained no unpaid personal assistance. Living speech maintained its right only in the altogether common and everyday conditions of life. It is not surprising, then, that from that time on, the energy of this race was paralyzed; the power of the divine organ of speech was broken and humbled; and the ear was closed for all higher impressions, which one assigned in a most unnatural manner to the deciphering eye.

This great transformation took place approximately in the middle of the sixteenth century. Did this race suddenly become so frail, powerless, or filled with the thought of its own transitoriness, that it wanted to cling to gold and to letters, to the permanent qualities of those things? Or did this change as to action and word happen only because of the misuse of both of those gifts—i.e., the misuse of money, to which America misled it, and the misuse of letters, to which the art of printing misled it? I do not want to decide this question, but I know that every sound mind must feel and deplore with me this inversion of nature.

Since the art of printing became common, the Bad, False, and Unimportant do not immediately disappear as they formerly did after they were spoken. They do not dissolve into the common air to which they belonged more than to the mind. They stay, they advance in full squadrons on our unfortunate successors, growing in accelerated proportions as the *libraries* of our time show. To illustrate this: an economic misfortune, in former times, was borne directly by the generation which it befell and was shaken off and then died away with its sufferers. Now, since all action is expressed in gold, it rolls toward posterity in heavy and always heavier *masses of debts*.

The speech and hearing organs are robbed of their noblest functions; they do nothing; they execute useless matters or at least only the most common domestic service. As I have recently shown, only in the highest stratum of European life—in French private life and in British public life—do the two best fruits which the last past centuries produced continue in their old significance. How can one presuppose, therefore, that the ear is already automatically sufficiently trained? This is a time when, from all sounds of speech, from all of life's fullness, from all of civil actions' impetuosity, from all of poetry's singing of earlier centuries, nothing has remained but a monotonous rustling of book leaves in lonely chambers. In the same way, a similar dead rustling of the leaves in autumn remains behind instead of all merry tumult of the more beautiful season.

After speech has been transferred most unnaturally from the ear's area to that of the reading eye and from the voice's area to the sphere of action of writing hands, consequently it now also dies, shrinks, and withers more and more. The word dwindles into itself and becomes more and more a number. All sciences, all civil occupations count on and hold onto the beloved number. They pupate like voracious insects into cocoons of numbers and formulas. The popularity of card games, after all, parodies in a very graceful way this quite strange condition. This entire era is reflected in this plain entertainment—a combination of certain numerical proportions instead of social conversation and a petty monetary commerce instead of personal contact.

You see, I am going rather far in the rhetorical strategy with which I have opened these lectures—namely, in the accusation of that which it is my duty and my intention to defend. At first it was Germany in whose language and in whose sense I really spoke. Now it is even the entire age, which, after all, I really cannot drop for the simple reason that I cannot just leave it and seek or create another one for myself. But is it, then, so small a thing to defend and save a forgotten, shabbily neglected human sense since only four other senses would not even have to come to an end, but, merely like this one, to become deadened in order that from the deeds of a whole race nothing noteworthy would remain? Is is possible to restore the cultivator of this noblest sense and, together with it, eloquence by means of mere lectures and rules on demonstration, on arousing of the passions, etc., in the manner of Blair, Priestley, and Batteux? All Greece had to speak for centuries; at first the humblest peasant woman in Athens' market place had to be able to discriminate by means of a mere training of the ear what was Attic and beautiful Greek and what was not, before the time was ripe for Demosthenes to come. The nation must be conducive, the world's conditions must be conducive, as well as he who teaches eloquence, so that a single person can speak as is proper. Because I want to learn a single science, a single art, the world is not, therefore, isolated from me for this time. Neither does it stand still meanwhile. But I cannot speak when my people do not participate in the dialogue. And the world, by continuing to move, can disturb my work and my study. Because it finally must, after all, refresh and enliven all my study and because my work should be for the benefit of the world, therefore, I got accustomed early to interweaving the living world with science and art from the beginning. In reality, it is the bond of things we seek. The secret of eloquence lies in that which binds the word and action, the thought and living life with one another. If it lay in the little hooks and threads which bind words to words and phrases to phrases, then it would have been discovered long ago by our century's hairsplitters. So much for an apology when I often speak of something besides eloquence.

There is, therefore, an art of listening. I am firmly convinced that he who possessed it to the proper degree could make someone else an orator by the mere practice of this art, by means of mere ingenious and lively listening. One can notice in every theater how many degrees of increased attention there are in an assembly of men and how many degrees of silence, which reaches at certain moments that breathlessness of nature which one experiences on the peaks of very high mountains. One can notice innumerable kinds of attention and interest; and one will become aware that man, because and as long as he listens, is not also mute. The great actor knows what he has to think of the fixed and traditional kinds of response on the part of the audience, on the clapping of the hands, and of the really screaming and roaring applause. But a large assembly may be overwhelmed by the power of speech in such a way that it forgets the conventional response, that it listens as with one single ear and every breath is concerned only with how to fit in the speech's occasional pauses. Single low, short sounds of admiration emerge with unagreed and, nevertheless, surprising uniformity from the deeper and deeper silence. And the whole assembly leans against one another, invisibly, but quite clearly, when each one feels that he is only a part of a greater man who is addressed. Then something unexpected by him, greater than humanness, also seizes the artist on the stage. It is not, perhaps, a common transformation into that which he portrays, not a drunkenness of rapture, but a certain divine calm. The whole framework of preparatory exercise and study on his part disappears; his effort becomes useless; his very talent recedes. It is as if a higher mind, the poet or somebody else, has removed this art's whole earthly apparatus, as if he spoke through the artist's mouth. It is also as if the same mind again listened, through the ear of the assembly, in blissful perception of his own work. Seemingly, that happy commonness of ground and sky, of which we spoke in our last conversation, seized all, and the boundary of the proscenium between pit and stage disappears. Art, in reality, always should abolish this boundary, as the ancients indicated by locating the statue of the god Dionysus, and the moderns by locating the music, at this boundary.

Those are the moments when everybody feels, while listening, that he too could speak. In such a moment Schiller may have recognized himself and, aside from himself, felt in his breast something divine and, accordingly, his entire calling. But we remember that this state of the union in the word (which only seldom happens to us during our life's present miserable conditions and then accidentally and temporarily) is really man's natural state. Man's element is the living, the spoken, the felt language, as the fish's element is the water, and the bird's, the air. We remember, moreover, that we have driven out of all higher life the present, immediate power of the tones and, accordingly, the essential element of our existence. We want to *see* in signs and characters this element, which can only be heard. Even the French during their most splendid period have only but tasted it. We must admit, then, that our author's lament is valid not only for Germany in particular, but also for the whole era: When the soul *speaks,* etc. This lament is the truer since it is also completely valid when one inverts it and says: When the soul *listens,* etc.

Man learns only during great suffering how to act with greatness. Only by obedience does he learn how to rule. And only by listening does he learn how to speak. The acting, the commanding, in itself, one cannot learn—for example, by being shown how to act and being shown how to command. Just as little can one learn speaking by being shown how to speak and repeating another's words, as our whole era believes. A noble pupil was brought to a great and eloquent writer of the last century in order that he might acquire the art of eloquence by the example of an ever-present model—of the writer's language and of his writing. The master said to the prospective pupil, "Write! then I will tell you if you can write; more influence I do not have over you." This author felt that in this noble art no common transferring takes place. But, even more significantly, he could have said, "Read! then I will tell you if you can write. Listen to me and I will tell you definitely if you can speak."

But, I hear you objecting, is listening, and even quite artistic listening, more than a mental repeating of another's words? Is listening not just for that reason the school of the orator because it is a silent manner of becoming accustomed to speaking? When I speak, am I satisfied when each of my words impresses and molds itself on the listener like a seal on wax and when each phrase of my speech makes him senseless and turns and trims him as the wind trims the weather-vane by means of cold necessity? I do demand an answer. I do want freedom facing me and self-determination—not a machine. There are mechanical forces in the world to govern machines; and the word's magic power ought not to be misused for this purpose in a ridiculous way. You should not become silent, but you should listen! I want to attain something specific by means of my speech because I am a human being! But, more eagerly, I desire that my speech would arouse other speakers, that it would inflame the discourse of my people and my time, that it would give courage to others to say and utter the sufferings, the hopes, and the pride of this century. Why? Because there is, in addition to the human being, something *divine* in me, something which I do not silence even by the fulfillment of all my wishes and by the persuasion of all my adversaries!

Listening is a kind of answering. Nature allows at each given moment only a single individual to speak, like the Speaker in the British Parliament, who allows only he, who happens to have stood up first to have the floor. It has, on the other hand, endowed those who must be inferior, be silent and listen for this moment, with an invisible eloquence, with signs, with a quiet reluctance against any rhetorical act of violence, with very noticeable hints, with very uncompromising rewards. And, what is more than all this, in the moments of true contact with the orator, or of complete success of his purpose, nature endows them with the proud, radiant feeling of being filled with the same divine spirit which speaks through the orator's mouth. Also here nature gently necessitates justice (exactly at the moment of human success, where the idolizing of he who has succeeded could begin). Generally it is thus when man becomes greatest. Then he becomes an obedient instrument of a higher spirit. One cannot respect him without worshipping, at the same time, something higher; and in himself, the more there are external causes for pride, the more inner reasons for humility. As I have shown above, the love for an earthly subject rises highest if it becomes pious and just.

For the moment, kindly, forget us—the reading and writing orators—and all learned barbarism and all bookishness of our time. Imagine a living, improvising orator, who has not given his own speech on paper in advance, whom libraries, printing types, and the tinsel of literary fame, and, furthermore, silent nature with its so-called beauties do not inspire to speak. He is one who must have human facial features in front of him and who is, likewise, impelled to speak by what impels the true hero to be victorious— the ability of answering, the invicibility, the freedom, the heroism of his enemy. This orator, like the Iliad's heroes, only speaks when he is asked, or when somebody speaks to him, or at least when someone smiles at him, or is at least one who is motivated by nothing short of a god. Facing such an orator one can recognize that the listener, when he is silent, is not dumb. He incessantly intervenes and helps support the flow of speech. He governs the most powerful orator with the gentle sweep of his look, or movement of his eyebrows, with a soft twitch of his muscles, with an imperceptible smile, with emotions which scarcely cloud the crystal of his eyes, or, I might say, with pulse beats, with breaths, and with all the light gestures which are drowned by life's common tumult. Believe me, every great eighteenth-century "paper orator" or true writer became what he was chiefly by the power of his fantasy with which he interwove in the intervals of his speeches those quiet gestures of an attentively listening people. With his fantasy he assembled around himself in his mind everything beloved, respected, revered, everything which had ever listened to his requests or answered his questions. He became an orator only insofar as he possessed the art of listening to himself in a thousand-fold ways and in the free manner of the most various natures. His was not the miserable art of repeating his own words in his mind with learned, lonely complacency. It was the art of listening to himself like a third person—with protestation, with opposition, with other opinions, and not merely with another ear, but almost with a heart other than his own.

Therefore, eloquence flourishes in republics, not only because everyone is allowed to say something, but because everyone will be accustomed early to enter into the free opinions, into his neighbor's ear. Whoever wants to govern must tolerate so much independence around him, so many individual ways of listening and feeling, and must obey so many. Usually, therefore, in our time one is more eloquent towards women than towards men because one must listen to what one says with a more sensitive ear, with a certain sensibility of decorum and of manners, in short, with another ear—to which one cannot do violence.

The art of listening, therefore, consists in the independent mastery which one maintains over this sense, in the ability to listen in the same way as the other and, nevertheless, to listen to oneself at the same time. In short, it consists, like all art, and particularly like musical art, in the ability to feel chords and harmonies. This ability is not innate in everybody or is, perhaps, not trained simply because the ear is open and is passive. The savage discriminates more clearly the tone from the non-tone and one tone from another. Even the animal is more adroit than man in the skill of decomposing coldly, without additional pleasure, the material world's impressions. But cultured man arranges a euphony, a chord, for what happens at the same time; he arranges symmetry, rhythm, and melody for that which succeeds one another; he reconciles the power, the hostile, the seemingly incompatible by means of a law of harmony in his breast. Out of this earth's fighting forces he develops the art of preparing for himself a feeling of eternal calm. He develops the art of taking the burden of two embittered parties upon his shoulders like two heavy wings and of raising himself more freely by means of symmetry with just that which heavily presses down to the ground earth's other species by its weight. Man's noble nature consists in all this. All of man's senses are susceptible to this most beautiful peculiarity. But their teachers are the organs of hearing and of the voice, which, themselves, I would like to say, receive this great law directly from God and must cultivate and improve it above all others. The Mosaic revelation wisely is silent about all other instruction from God; the first man is taught nothing more than the language, the world's whole harmonic law. With language true dominion over the world is handed to him and the creation of man is now perfected.

That human hearing is, by nature, already in the proper condition, and, by the ears merely being open, it is already as cultivated as it could become, therefore, does not apply to human hearing, but only to the perceiving, discriminating instinct of the savage and the animal. But how, we ask, should the ear cultivate itself artistically when there is no speaking, when the era writes when it should speak? Now then, let us practice this important art along with justice to the great dead and to those ornaments of our nation still living to our joy. They are lonely, without contact with the people to whom they spoke and for whom they lived, without answer other than that which they called back to themselves by obediently entering into the heart and the way of thinking of their fellow citizens. They are without reward except the ambiguous, much envied, and much embittered praise of remote contemporaries (whom they have never looked in the eye) and except the newspaper fame, which they had to share with the most unworthy of their time. They, nevertheless, have uttered—without any favor of circumstances, without any scent of luck—this German language in such a way, so filled up and animated, that it sounds quite pleasing today, that it can place itself quite courageously beside the other much favored languages of Europe. Let us be just to the poets and orators of the nation *by learning how to read them,* which we are not yet able to do. I mean read them with a lively articulate voice by (in order to repeat myself where it is appropriate) begrudging the paper on which this literature is written, by tearing it out of the dead letters, and, in defiance of the art of printing, by handing it down orally to German posterity, as France and Italy have done long since with their national literatures. German posterity, being trained early and accustomed early to a national harmony, then may surpass us in the art of listening and, therefore, also in eloquence.

Translated by Dennis R. Bormann
and Elisabeth Leinfellner

Georg Christoph Lichtenberg

On Physiognomy

To elude all old misunderstandings and to prevent new ones, let us issue here a reminder once and for all that we arc using the term "physiognomy" in a more limited sense, and are taking it to mean the art of determining the characteristics of the mind and heart from the form and characteristics of the external parts of the human body, primarily of the face, exclusive of all transitory signs produced by the emotions. The entire semiotics of the passions—i.e., the knowledge of the natural signs of the emotions in all their gradations and mixtures—shall be known as "pathognomy." It has already been suggested that the latter word be used for this very purpose. It shall not be necessary here to create a new word that would encompass the meanings of the two other words, or what would be even better, to search for one to replace the former, and then to elevate the word "physiognomy" to a term of general scope, as commensurate with current usage, and as it has for this very reason been taken up in the title of this essay.

No one will deny that in a world in which everything is related by cause and effect, and in which nothing comes about by miracles, each part is a mirror of the whole. If a pea is shot into the Mediterranean, an eye sharper than our own, but infinitely weaker than the eye of Him who sees all, would be able to discern the effect upon the coast of China. And how is a light corpuscle that strikes the retina of the eye, compared with the mass of the brain and all its branches, any different? Cases like this often enable us to make inferences from what is near to what is distant, from the visible to the invisible, from the present to the past and to the future. Thus do the scratches on a pewter plate tell the story of all the meals in which it took part, and likewise does the form of each tract of land, the form of its dunes and that of its rocks, contain the story of the earth, written in the script of nature. Indeed, each rounded pebble tossed out by the ocean would tell this story if it had a soul linked to it the way ours is to our brain. It is even conceivable that the history of Rome lay in the entrails of the slaughtered animal, but the swindler who pretended to read it certainly did not see it there. So then is the inner person indeed imprinted upon the outer? On the face, which shall be the primary subject of our investigation here, are certainly to be found signs and traces of our thoughts, inclinations, and capabilities. How distinct are the signs that climate and occupation impress upon the body! And what are climate and occupation in comparison with an ever-active soul, which lives and creates in every fiber of our being? No one doubts this absolute readability of everything in everything. Nor would it be necessary, if one wanted to prove that there was such a thing as physiognomy, to come up with numerous examples of cases where one does draw inferences from the exterior of something and apply them to its interior, as a number of authors have done. The proof will be quite succinct if one says: Our senses present to us nothing but surfaces; everything else is inference. Nothing particularly comforting for physiognomy results from any of this without further qualification, since this very life at the surface is the source of our errors, and in some matters that of our entire ignorance. If the inner is imprinted upon the outer, does that mean it is necessarily there for our eyes to see? And is it not possible that traces of effects we are not looking for obscure and confuse those which we are looking for? Thus, when order is not understood, it becomes in the end disorder; effects of unidentified causes become coincidence; where there is too much to see, we see nothing. "The present," says one of the world's great minds, "having been impregnated by the past, gives birth to the future." Very nice. But what vain, wretched piecework is our meteorological wisdom! And now our prophetic art! In spite of the volumes of meteorological observations assembled by entire academies, it is still just as difficult to predict whether the sun will shine the day after tomorrow as it must have been a few centuries ago to predict the splendor of the house of Hohenzollern. And yet the object of the science of meteorology, as far as I know, is a mere machine, with whose driving mechanism we can in time become more and more acquainted. There is no free-willed being behind the changes in our weather, no capricious, jealous, enamored creature, which, for the sake of a loved one, might lead the sun back into the Tropic of Cancer in winter. If our bodies developed in the purest celestial air, modified only by the movements of their souls and disturbed by no external forces, and if the soul likewise, with analogous pliancy, conformed back to the laws to which the body is subject, then the dominating passion and the superior talent would, I will not deny it, with varying degrees and admixtures bring forth varying facial forms, just as different salts crystallize into different forms when they are not disturbed. But does our body belong to the soul alone, or is it not a joint member of series that intersect themselves within him, series whose every law he must obey and comply with? Each simple mineral type has, in its state of greatest purity, its own characteristic form. The anomalies, however, brought about by the combination with other minerals, and the accidents to which they are subject causes often even the most skilled to err when they try to classify them on the basis of their appearance. Our body, then, stands in the middle, between the soul and the rest of the world, a mirror of the effects of both. It registers not only our inclinations and capabilities, but the whip scars of fate, climate, illness, nutrition, and the thousand tribulations to which we are subjected not only by our own evil resolutions, but often by accident, often by duty as well. Are the imperfections I notice in a wax sculpture all mistakes of the artist, or could they not just as well be the effects of clumsy handling, the heat of the sun, or a warm room? Extreme suppleness of the body, its perfectibility and its corruptibility, the limits of which one does not know, operate here to the advantage of chance. The wrinkle, which appears in one person only after a thousandfold repetition of the same movement, appears even less distinctly in another person. That which in one person causes distortion and deformity noticeable even by dogs, passes over another without leaving a trace, at least no trace detectable with the human eye. This demonstrates just how pliant everything is, and how a little spark can cause one person to erupt all over without leaving behind so much as a pockmark in another. Does everything in the face relate to the head and the heart? Why don't you divine the month of birth, a cold winter, messy diapers, careless nursemaids, damp sleeping chambers, childhood illnesses from the nose? That which has an effect on a man's color, has an effect on a child's form; the fire that warps green wood merely turns seasoned wood brown. This is most likely the reason for the more regular facial features of the aristocratic classes, who certainly do not possess any superiority in mind or heart to which we could not also attain. Or is an oversight on the part of the soul the same as an oversight on the part of the wet nurse, and will the former, after some distortion has been inflicted upon its body, become likewise distorted, so that it would afterwards build for itself again just such a body, if it were to get a new body to build? How? Or does the soul perhaps fill the body like an elastic fluid, which at all times assumes the form of its vessel, so that if a flattened nose signified the characteristic of taking pleasure in another's misfortune, would anyone then assume this characteristic when you flattened his nose? A coarse example, but one chosen with care. In our body itself and its various humors lie a hundred sources of equally perceptible, but less violent changes. Furthermore, you do not deny that long after the formation of the immutable parts of the body a betterment or a worsening is possible. But does the smooth forehead cover itself with flesh, or does the convex collapse when the memory fails? Many a clever fellow has fallen on his head and become a fool, and I remember having read in the memoirs of the Parisian Academy about a fool there who once fell on his head and became clever. In both cases I would like to see the silhouette of the antecessor placed side by side with that of his successor, and to compare the lips and eyebones of one with the other. The examples are admittedly far-fetched. But then would you perhaps like to determine where violence begins and illness ends? The bridge that links the two series of ideas can just as well collapse when I catch a cold, as when I fall on my head, and in the end one would have to equate being human with being ill. In my lifetime, I have observed approximately eight dissections of human brains, and out of at least five of them, the false conclusions were drawn like red threads and the *lapsus memoriae* like grains of sand. Thus even from these few examples (more will follow below), one can see how rash it is to infer from similarity of face similarity of character, even if this similarity were absolute; but who can judge such similarity? A frail sensory apparatus, whose impressions are so easily weakened and distorted by prejudiced conclusions and associated conceptions, that in cases far more simple than this one, into which no passions enter, and even after demonstrated error, it is nearly impossible to separate judgment from feeling. If the point had been reached when one could say with certainty that of ten villains, one actually looked like one, then one could determine characters as one determines mortality. But immediately, insurmountable difficulties appear, of the very same kind as those to which the art of prophecy owes its reliability. For although in everyday life, under the written law and before the human judge, the judgment of the character may be easy, it is very difficult, perhaps impossible, in cases where not the isolated deed is being judged but an entire character, to say in a particular case just what a villain is, and it would be presumption bordering on madness to say that someone who looks like the fellow considered a villain in this or that little town is himself a villain. It is a commonly accepted truth that there are few evil deeds that are not perpetrated out of passions which under a different set of circumstances could have formed the basis for great and praiseworthy ones. As absurd as such an excuse after the perpetrated misdeed would of course be, in the same measure does it deserve consideration in the case of a man of otherwise good reputation, or at least whose reputation is not known; whereby the latter would have a legitimate claim, justifiable before God and the law, to a judge who is a man of reason, a claim that in the case of the former would be justifiable on the grounds of human kindness. What then would you infer from similarity of face, particularly of the immutable parts thereof, if the same fellow who was hanged would under other circumstances have deserved, on the basis of his potential, not the rope but laurels? Opportunity creates not only thieves, it creates great men as well. Here the physiognomist comes to his own rescue with ease; he seeks a predicate that applies equally to the great man and to the rogue: they both had great potential. A splendid dodge! I will predict the outcome of the American War for anyone who gives me a hundred more such delphic words. What in all the world is the practical meaning of "a foiled good potential"? Nothing more than a straight line that has been bent crooked; a crooked line. No one knows all of his capacities for good and evil. It would be a kind of psychological chess, and an inexhaustible field of instructive occupation for the dramatic poets and novelists, to invent for certain given degrees of capabilities and passions circumstances and events to guide the boy who possesses these capabilities and passions after each given instance through probable steps. I believe that if we were thoroughly acquainted with the person, we would find that the resolution would rarely be impossible, and that if we wanted to avoid those that under a certain set of circumstances could lead to danger, we would have to avoid ninety-nine out of a hundred. And it is this very perfectibility or corruptibility (which is nothing more than the former working in the opposite direction) that constitutes the person, and that will exclude him forever from the domain of physiognomy. He stands alone upon this orb, like God, who created him in His image, alone in nature. Even if physiognomy were ever to lay hold of him, it would simply be a matter of making a bold resolution to make himself inapprehensible again for centuries. The trust in physiognomy, however, had to increase in a land such as Germany, a land in which, according to the writings it would be able to show itself, self-observation and knowledge of human nature is lying in an almost disgraceful state of decay, and is languishing in a state of enervation, out of which, one should think, only the reinvigorating hibernation of a new barbarity would be capable of pulling it. This is not the place to offer proof thereof. But I am convinced that the best minds of my fatherland will agree with me, and it is to be hoped that the long-awaited opportunity to make it clear to the weaker ones through examples from the writings of their idols will soon present itself.

An insufficient regard for a number of these truths, combined with an unusual ignorance of the world and of human nature and with a ruinous aspiration, springing from this very source, to bring salvation, an aspiration that a portion of our audience supports with pious fanaticism when it should at most forgive, have now, on top of everything, as though everything else were already beyond dispute, given rise to the utterly ill-considered and depressing thought that the most beautiful soul dwells in the most beautiful body, and the ugliest dwells in the ugliest body. Does that then mean, with a slight change in the metaphor, that perhaps the largest soul dwells within the largest body, and the most healthy soul in the most healthy body? Good heavens! What does beauty of the body, the entire measure of which perhaps was originally refined sensual lust, which hides its coarseness behind auxiliary ideas, and whose purpose is consummated in this very lust, have to do with beauty of the soul, which struggles so bitterly against this lust and which stretches into infinity? Is the flesh supposed to be the judge of the spirit? The author believes, and shall in the end lead his argument in this direction, that virtue, particularly saintly sincerity and the knowledge of one's innocence, can bestow upon a face, in the eyes of one who is a good judge of such things, great and unspeakable charms. But it is inexperience and antiquated pedantry to believe that this beauty is the same as that which Winckelmann refers to as beauty. The author has a measure of acquired sensitivity to the latter as well, but must confess in all honesty that he has seen in the faces of sincere persons, men and women, who were considered ugly by those not acquainted with their virtue, expressions that he would not have wanted to trade for all the charms we have been told to admire, nor for all the faces renowned, more out of obligingness than feeling, throughout the land where the bandits are beautiful. The above thought, which can receive no formal refutation here, and for that matter is hardly worthy of a serious one, has given rise to yet another one; namely, to lead the body, through beautification of the soul, to a state of final perfection, so that in the end it conforms to the ideals of the Greek artists. Virtue and sincerity, at least by themselves, may not be sufficient; otherwise, we could easily lose the way, and be rewarded for all our efforts with the simian faces of the inhabitants of Mallicolo, whom Captain Cook visited on his last journey, and whose honesty and ugliness were equally remarkable and nearly unprecedented. On the other hand, the most direct method for making our German faces similar to those of the Greeks (one, however, which perhaps will do little for our virtue) might well be the one by which the English enabled their sheep and horses to approach Spanish and Arabian ideals. Just how such a proposition, which has not been proven, but only exclaimed, which will never be proven, and can never be proven, has been able to find acceptance here and there, is nearly incomprehensible. Only in modern-day Germany is it comprehensible. For are not the history books and all large cities full of beautiful, depraved people? Of course, if one wants to see handsome scoundrels, smooth-faced swindlers, and charming orphan exploiters, one need not necessarily always look for them behind hedges and in village jails. One must go to where they eat from silver plates, where they command a knowledge of faces, and have power over their own muscles, where they can plunge families into despair with a shrug of the shoulders, and where they can ruin an honest man's credit or good name with a whisper, or, affecting indecisiveness, with a stutter. The potential was there, replies the physiognomist, but the corruptible human brought about his own depravity. The potential? For what? For what ensued, or for what did not ensue? If that is all you have to teach, I would like to answer then your book is not worth the trouble of opening. I don't want to know what someone could have become. What couldn't anybody have become? I want to know what he is. And yet, taken from *that* angle again, when (to reuse a worn-out example) Zopyrus saw the evil potential in Socrates' face, why did he not see the more powerful force of self-improvement, of Socrates' potential to become his own creator? For if the former had to dwell in the head of a faun, the latter would deserve no less than a family resemblance to Jupiter. As I write this, a criminal nefarious beyond compare (and that he is without a doubt), the supper poisoner, * is stalking unrecognized about Zurich, and thus indeed with a face that could have others like it. I know a man of sound intelligence who imagines the devil as the most beautiful person, as an angel without wings. I can think of no other reason for this than that he is an avid reader of Milton, and comes from the land in which most of those who end up with the beggar's staff or on the gallows are brought there by angels without wings. Of course we must not encounter the beautiful face often at its devilish deeds, otherwise it would soon become demonized in our eyes, and we would soon find some previously unnoticed feature repulsive. In this way, the face of an enemy makes a thousand other faces seem ugly, just as the face of a loved one lends it charm to a thousand others. Cartesius and Swift, and perhaps a thousand others, were charmed by crossed eyes; and a lisping tongue found repulsive in a Jew who does us out of our louis d'ors has perhaps soured the hearts of many of my readers. The association of ideas explains a host of phenomena in physiognomy, without it being necessary, to the detriment of the rights of reason, to assume new senses, with which false, complacent philosophy and modernism have always been very freehanded.

"But what?" asks the physiognomist. Newton's soul would be able to dwell in the head of a negro? An angelic soul in a hideous body? The creator should delineate virtue and merit accordingly? This is impossible. This shallow stream of youthful declamation

---

*Lavater

can be stemmed forever with a single "and why not?" Are you, O wretched one, the judge of God's works? First tell me why the virtuous so often spend their entire lives wasting away in infirm bodies, or is perpetual ailing perhaps more bearable than healthy ugliness? Do you presume to decide whether a distorted body, like an ailing one (and is not infirmity the same as an inner distortion?) is one of the afflictions to which the just, inexplicably to mere reason, are subjected here? Tell me why thousands are born with afflictions, to whimper through a few years and then die off. Why the promising child, a joy to its parents, dies when they start to need its help. Why others must leave this world immediately after their arrival into it, and are born only to die. Answer these questions for me, and I will answer yours. If you ever create or paint a world, then create and paint vice ugly, and all poisonous animals hideous, so that you can better survey it, but do not judge God's world on the basis of your own. Prune your boxwood as you will, and plant your flowers according to the shades understandable to you, but do not judge the garden of nature by the measure of your flower bed. On this basis can one refute the proofs offered for physiognomy that were derived from representations of Christ's head. And yet, to counter the physiognomist with something other than just reason, one could also easily show, if this were the proper place, how little hope for his system he could expect from the physiognomies of the savages. The ability to unmask antiquated prejudices with equanimity, the perspicacity enabling one to discern the straight trunk obscured by tangled underbrush, the philosophical self-denial to confess that one saw nothing wonderful where everything is supposed to be teeming with wonders, and impartiality without fear of other men, accompanied by the thirst for pure truth and love of mankind; all of these together constitute a precious apparatus rarely taken on board by explorers sailing to distant lands—in the realm of the body as well as in the realm of thoughts.

Yet the soul constructs its body, does it not, and can one not from the building make inferences concerning the architect? This useless adage of the physiognomists can be conceded without objection if one can come to a provisional agreement on the concept of building, and if one adds the minor stipulation that, to ensure that this judgment be passed correctly, one must also be acquainted with the overall intention of the building. Obviously we do not build our bodies the same way we build brick ovens, and without the stipulation, a Greenlander, upon seeing a graduation house, could conclude that whoever built the dwelling must have been a fool; the wind can blow right through the walls, and the construction is such that there is no lack of rain, even on sunny days. I would reply to this good simpleton: "If you became acquainted with the land in which this building stands, you would have no choice, if you ever get that far, but to admire the wisdom with which it was carried out."

If one looks around a bit, one will find that the physiognomist shares this particular inductive faculty with not a few others, who do him credit in all manner of different ways. The one who first linked an infinitely evil being to the infinitely good one, and the clever minds who even now worship the devil, have presumably drawn their similar conclusions as a result of having been led astray by pain, earthquakes, pestilence, and war—a deplorable example of where reason without revelation can lead, and the more deplorable, the more pardonable. Inferring from the works of nature an almighty, infinitely benevolent, and infinitely wise creator is more a leap of instructed devotion than a step of reason. Nature reveals to her limited observer nothing but an originator that infinitely surpasses him, but she does not tell him to what extent. Revelation asserts that it is an infinite extent, and judging from present appearances, not even thousands of centuries of observation will give the unlimited observer grounds to throw, with the help of reason, this assurance into doubt. It is indeed of no little credit to the human mind that it already gazes deeply enough into that wisdom to surmise that what it surveys is a mere nothing compared with the whole. So you, who believe that the soul creates its body, you too must listen to what the soul reveals to you by means other than its own creation: regard that person as wise, who acts wisely, that person as righteous, who practices righteousness, and do not let yourself be misled by irregularities in the surface, irregularities that belong to a plan you do not comprehend in its entirety, to the plan made by the one according to whose instructions at least the soul had to build its body, if indeed it did build it. "Speak," said Socrates to Charmides, "so that I might see you," and "Ye shall know them by their fruits," which is taken from a book read little more than the former, and which oddly enough appears twice in succession in the same passage, every word of which has been weighed before God.

"Yet in this way, one could throw physics in its entirety into doubt," one could answer. "We may not know how stupidity and thick lips fit together, and we do not need to know, either. We see them together, and that is sufficient." The answer to this has long since been given by all systems of logic: that is the very point about which we are arguing. We gladly concede to the physiognomist his right to number himself among the teachers of nature, but he may not claim for himself a rank any higher than that of a prophet among statesmen. The true physicist and the physiognomist are simply not to be placed in the same category. The former is often subject to human error; the latter has always proceeded from a state of eminent error. The former never leaves with his conclusions the machine with whose workings he wishes to become acquainted, whose wheels are uniform, whose driving forces are sharply defined and immutable. He observes not only the natural workings of the clockwork, but performs experiments as well, and forces phenomena to occur together in a single day that would have required a thousand years of close attention were he simply to have waited passively for them to occur. What could not have been taught in a hundred years of experimentation can be taught in an hour of calculation will perhaps one day be transformed into five minutes of leafing through a book. Every body, I should like to say, about which a physicist wraps his hand is for him a model of creation with which he can do as he pleases. It is then indeed no wonder when man, lifted by such machines, reaches a height that makes him dizzy.

Now consider for a moment the physiognomist; how helpless, and yet how audacious does he stand there. He induces from an elongated submental region not, for example, the form of the shin bones, or from attractive arms attractive calves; he does not, as the doctor does, make inductions from pulse and from face and tongue color concerning illness, but rather he leaps and stumbles from similar noses to similar mental capacities, and with inexcusable presumptuousness from certain deviations from the norm in exterior form to analogous changes in the soul. A leap, which in my opinion is no smaller than the one from comets' tails to war. If I shift the meaning of each word in a brief aphorism by only an inch, the meaning of the whole can be changed by miles. To what calamities have indefinite words not led? What in the household would not cause much damage would lead in science in exactly the opposite direction. Furthermore, it is already endlessly difficult for the physiognomist to find the first solid point from which to proceed: the first irrefutable experience. A fatuous wrinkle behind the corner of the mouth, or a tooth revealed only by the occasion of a rare laugh could make a liar out of Newton's nose, and so from two on into infinity. Not to mention the inner distortion, which, as imperceptible as it may be to the eye, can have consequences all too perceptible to the mind. If imperceptible changes in the brain can lead to death, then how much more easily changes in the mind? What is the relationship between instruction through the senses and illumination of the mind? An addition of one through the senses could bring about an illumination with the magnitude of a thousand. We are simply not inclined always to see the changes to the brain in the proportion to which the changes in the mind appear. We see only color and form, and these can differ from the accompanying thought in another mind just as easily by a factor of one as by a factor of a thousand. This makes no difference. A change to the brain massive to our eye might entail just a very small one for the soul that dwells therein, and vice versa. And you want to make inferences from the vault that arches over the brain? But I am trying to save words and am becoming unintelligible. What then is the consequence of the above observations? This: physiognomy will suffocate in its own fat. Man could not be presented with an iota more clarity outlined in a physiognomical atlas weighing a hundred pounds than he is now in his own body. It is terrible even to think of such a rambling work, and one at that whose very essence is ramblingness, since a thousandfold interest in the body and the soul entices and impels us to study man firsthand. The physiognomist has now become almost completely cut off from the path of arriving at truth through experimentation; all this taken together makes his situation desperate. The semiotician will soon find out after all whether his interpretations of signs have been deceiving him: on the one hand, infinitely more difficulty than in science, and on the other hand much less help. What can become of it? To shrug one's shoulders and to fall silent would be the only thing a healthy person could do; blinded pride is never at a loss for words. But would it be not good to try and see what one could do in this respect? Not quite, for the suffering of a single innocent soul in the course of the experiment deserves more consideration than the poor, empty fanaticism is worth. And has it not been tried in vain all along, without its ever having asked itself, in all seriousness, why? It may very well turn out to be good in the end, but it seems to me that planting oaks would be better.

But is physiognomy completely questionable? We interpret faces every day, everyone does so, even those who dispute physiognomy do so the minute after they finish disputing it, and violate their own principles. Let us illuminate these objections more carefully.

There exists unquestionably a universal, involuntary language of gestures that gives expression to the passions in all their gradations. A person generally learns to understand this language with great proficiency by the time he reaches his twenty-fifth year. Nature teaches him to speak this language, and in such a compelling manner, it might be added, that making mistakes in it has been elevated to an art form. It is such a rich language that the sweet and the sour faces alone would fill a book, and so clear that elephants and dogs learn to understand humans. This has never been denied, and the knowledge of this language is what we have referred to above as pathognomy. What would pantomime and all the arts of the actor be without it? The languages of all times and all peoples are full of pathognomic references, and are in part inseparably interwoven with them. No one has ever taken the trouble to classify these references and present them for home use, so to speak, for in the time it would take to understand such a book, the matter is generally grasped better than it can ever be taught. Such a work would be unnecessary as a work on the art of loving. To practice it according to rules that one's own observations have not yet inferred would in any case lead to error and to ridiculous situations. On the other hand, our languages are quite lacking in actual physiognomical observations. If any truth were contained therein, the peoples would certainly have likewise deposited it into the archives of their wisdom. Wherever one come upon traces thereof, they are always suspicious and seem to have been made from a single observation, such as the German word *spitzkopf* (pointed head, or person with a pointed head); even proper nouns can in the end be transformed into popular epithets. The word *laster* (vice) meant originally "mutilation," not "shortcoming." Neither does the word *häßlich* (ugly) have its origin in *hassen* (to hate). The nose figures in a hundred sayings and proverbs, but always pathognomically, as a symbol of temporary action, and never physiognomically, or as a symbol of enduring character or disposition. "He's lacking above the nose" is commonly said in everyday life of one lacking in intelligence; according to the newer physiognomy, one would have to say "He's lacking about the nose." There are admittedly sayings that lend support to physiognomy, but what can be proven with sayings? "Beware of those who have been marked" is an epithet to which the marked have always been subjected by a certain class of nonmarked in the world. The marked would therefore have even more of a right to say "beware of the nonmarked." "In a beautiful body dwells a beautiful soul" belongs here as well. The sayings exist in a state of eternal war, just as do all rules posited not by the spirit of inquiry but by caprice. Shakespeare, who could combine to serve his ends the most disparate concepts, concepts that had perhaps never before been placed together in a human head; who was able to call the world an "O," and even call the stage a wooden "O"; who furthermore possessed greater powers of observation and more talent in speaking perspicuously of clear things than perhaps any other writer; the writings of this Shakespeare are very poor in actual physiognomical observations. Something of the sort might turn up here and there in his works; the author has never read them through in their entirety with this end in mind, but in eight of his plays that the author read with a view to such references, he found not a thing worthy of mention. On the other hand, Shakespeare's works are full of the most splendid pathognomical observations, expressed in the most cogent manner. Among these are to be found even some that are not yet as well-known as they deserve to be, for example his ever-smiling, music-shy villains, and his liars of polished manner, if one may number such observations among these. His epithets that merely address the surface and whose sole purpose is to point out a lack of beauty do not belong here. Thick-lipped stupidity, horizontal and thin-lipped intelligence with its angular eye bones would certainly not have escaped his penetrating eye. But in the great stone "O" in which he lived and wrote, he wasted no time in coming to the conclusion that there is no physiognomy that holds true for two different peoples, for two different tribes, or for two different centuries.

Shakespeare's pathognomy deserves to be investigated in its own right by someone with a respectable background in philosophy, so that after completion of such a work he would not inadvertently posit the law he is supposed to be following; someone who would proceed with reason in such a way as not to spoil everything with the lack thereof. He would have to work with a heart full of love for mankind—full of love for mankind, for heaven's sake, which would serve to guide an intelligent mind. An active love for mankind without intelligence misses its mark, just as does misanthropy without power: just as the latter often does more good than harm, so does the former often do more harm than good. The unfortunate difference is that if someone with the intention of doing me harm promotes my welfare, I punish him in the end with a smile, whereas if someone acting out of love for mankind makes me unhappy, I cannot even reprimand him with a good conscience. Furthermore, the man who would investigate Shakespeare's pathognomy would have to possess a deep knowledge of the English language, of the English nation and people, and of himself. Without a significant command of all four of these, one might still be able to read Shakespeare with pleasure, but one would lose the very thing that makes him such an unusual man. This explains the variation in opinions on this author, and of such opinions we have in recent times again seen some peculiar examples. This does not surprise me. People are wont to believe that they can read any book that does not contain squiggly lines and algebraic formulae, as long as they understand the language in which it is written. This, however, is patently wrong. A reader might be so lacking in the above-mentioned requirements for reading Shakespeare and in any desire to awaken within himself that in the end he would understand nothing but his ribaldries, his curses, and a few of his more licentious metaphors. But that will be, until that day, the fate of all great minds who write with deep insight about mankind. Such works are mirrors; when a monkey peers into one, an apostle can never look out. So much for that small digression. I said above that Shakespeare's works were very poor in actual physiognomical observations, at least in the plays I read through with the intention of looking for such observations. Impartial readers will see that this does not mean that his works do not contain any at all. Shakespeare portrays people, and people have most likely always physiognomized and erred; Shakespeare's physiognomists err as well. I took them rather to mean such observations tossed out on equal terms with other simultaneously given explanations that designated the matter at hand and at the same time indicated the seriousness of his intention. An example would be if he had ascribed to people with whose hearts and minds he was acquainted on the basis of their places in history, but whose physical figures he did not know, a physical trait he would have felt to be in some way telling. His "broad-fronted Caesar" would be such an observation, but unfortunately other editions read "bald-fronted." The "foolish hanging netherlip" found in one of these plays proves even less. The physiognomist who attempts to clarify Shakespeare by means of dictionaries need not, led astray by a systematic spirit, believe that he has made a discovery here. The Englishman calls everything "foolish" that he cannot stand. Furthermore, when dealing with a writer who depicts people with such perception, one must carefully consider whose mouth it is in which he places the observation. The jealous Cleopatra asks the courier in Shakespeare's *Anthony and Cleopatra:* "Bear'st thou her face in mind? is't long or round?" "Round, even to faultiness" is the answer. "For the most part, too, they are foolish that are so," replies Cleopatra. Who cannot see here that this is a penetrating look into the soul of Cleopatra, which reveals to us that *nothing has changed* concerning the inner properties of Octavia's head?

Let us proceed. The pathognomic signs, when they reoccur often, do not always completely disappear, and they leave physiognomic impressions behind. From these develop sometimes the "folly wrinkles" that are caused by marveling at everything and understanding nothing, the sanctimonious beguiler wrinkles, the dimples in the cheeks, the stubbornness wrinkles, and heaven knows what other types of wrinkles. Pathognomical distortion that accompanies the perpetration of vice is often made additionally perceptible and hideous by diseases that result from this perpetration, and likewise can pathognomical expression of friendliness, tenderness, honesty, piety, and moral beauty in general become physical beauty in the eyes of those who recognize and honor moral beauty. This is the basis for Gellert's physiognomy (if this word can be used for a collection of observations that contain a basis for probable causal relationships of the character upon the facial features, but not the other way around), the only true physiognomy, if indeed a true one exists, which is indubitably of infinite benefit to the cause of virtue, and which can be summed up in a few words: virtue makes one more beautiful, vice makes one uglier. One should judge these traits, however, with the greatest caution; they lie astoundingly often, for the most part for the following reasons. It has already been pointed out above that one person will be immediately marked for something that another can do a thousand times unscathed. After a night of revelry, one person's cheek sinks into the gap in his teeth, while another is seen by the rising sun sitting just as youthfully behind his bottle and at his girl's side as he was by the setting sun the evening before. Thus, the meaning of each feature lies in the combined relationship between the brittleness of the tissue fibers and the number of repetitions. Furthermore (and this cannot be noted often enough by the hasty physiognomist), if someone's normal facial expression resembles my friend's or mine when we are sneering, does that necessarily make him a mocker? Is someone who when wide awake resembles me when I am sleepy necessarily a sleepy person? No judgments are baser than these, and none can be more erroneous. For one thing, those features could just as well have come about for reasons other than mockery, sleepiness, or culpability, and if perhaps indeed culpability, than not mockery or sleepiness. And in this, of course, human beings differ from all other known creatures. I contend that mimicry and the endeavor to bring about in one's own appearance features seen in famous, admired, or beloved persons, to imitate their imperfections and their ridiculous, even their pernicious mannerisms, bring forth astounding revolutions in the face, which by no means extend to the heart or the head. Thus do head hanging, sagacious furrowing of the brow, lisping, stammering, gait, voice, the hearkening tilt of the head, the erudite, myopic squint, the aristocratically dreary gaze, sentimental melancholy, frivolous vivacity, the suggestive winking of an eye, and the satyric countenance pass from one person to another with the contagion of yawning; sometimes through deliberate practice in front of the mirror, sometimes without the mimicker even being aware of it. There are people out of whose eyes the satyrs themselves seem to wink, out of whose lips they seem to sneer, yet who are as innocent as lambs, and every bit as dull-witted. The author once knew a splendid young man who had acquired in the company of a certain man of renown a decisive tossing of the head and a scornful drawing-down of the corners of the mouth whenever he spoke, gestures that by no means came from his heart, and of which he later divested himself. Not having done so would most certainly have been detrimental to his good fortune. It takes a good measure of worldly wisdom and virtue to excuse utterances made with the accompaniment of such a face, and not to transpose the face onto that which is spoken. Yet pathogenic facial expressions shall always remain a language for the eyes; one can just as easily say something sensible with inferior words disharmoniously combined as one can say something very foolish with the most well-chosen words and all the power of number. The former has been demonstrated by the example of a number of our oldest writers, and as for the latter, our day and age can boast more examples than Rome and Greece combined.

Well-nigh ridiculous is the proof for the reliability of physiognomy that its proponents believe they can infer from the daily, nearly hourly practice thereof. The moment we see a person, it is admittedly a law of our thinking, of our perception, that the most similar person we have ever known comes immediately to mind, and generally determines our judgment as well. We judge people's faces on an hourly basis, and err on an hourly basis. Thus does man prophesy on the times, hereditary princes, and the weather; the peasant has his days that determine the weather conditions for the whole year—these are usually feast days, because he is then idle enough to physiognomize. Everyone is a prophet once a day. Indeed, the would-be physiognomists even judge on the basis of names, with the Balthasars falling a bit behind the Friedrichs. I believe there are a few people who have not at one time or another done or thought something similar, as laughable as it may sound. The assumed names of satirical writers are composed according to such rules. If we were to take all the people we judge at first sight and test our judgments by spending years paying close attention to these people, then I believe that physiognomy would fare even worse than astrology. Imagination and wit are dangerously useful here, thus are the most profound thinkers commonly the worst physiognomists. They are not satisfied with a fleeting similarity, while the flighty physiognomist sees a face in every ink spot and a meaning in every face. All of this is understandable on the basis of idea association. These hypotheses provide amusement in any case. Anyone who has ever traveled overnight on a stagecoach, and made in the darkness the acquaintance of people he had never seen before, will in the course of the night have formed in his mind an image of them, and will on the following morning be every bit as disappointed as the physiognomist will on that great, solemn morning on which our souls will for the first time stand face to face with each other. The author himself ranged about for a long time in the field of physiognomy, before it had become fashionable, in a manner that he now, since experience has shown him the folly of those ways, can no longer conceal from his readers. He tried to draw a portrait of a night watchman, who had trumpeted and bawled him out of many a night of sound sleep for several years in order to tell him what time it was, solely on the basis of the sound of his voice. Now listen to the success of this endeavor. The watchman's voice evoked in the author the image of a tall, gaunt, but otherwise healthy man, with an elongated face, a downward-hooked nose, thick, unbound hair, and a slow, measured, stately gait. Having formed in his mind this image, the author was eager to see the man by the light of day, and he soon had the opportunity to do so. The discrepancy between the drawing and the original was inordinately great; the portrait had missed its mark in every detail. The man was of below-average stature, nimble and quick, even his hair was bound in a stiff plait that contained more string than hair. It is in this connection a pleasant pursuit, one that can prove significant to the psychologist, to dissociate such ideas. The author tried often to get to the bottom of the phenomenon of his night watchman, and found in the end that the tall stature he had imagined was due to the penetrating bass voice; two characteristics that he has seen together several times in his childhood. The tentativeness, the gauntness, the furtiveness, on the other hand, proved after careful deliberation to have come from far nobler origins, for these characteristics were fond to be traceable back to the obscurity of certain poetic ideas of the goddess of the night, and several ghosts of the masculine gender, with whom the author had in his youth been acquainted. In the school I attended in D., I had a classmate, a person of lively wit and no mean talent, who could have gone far in life, had he been forced at an early enough age to apply scholarly discipline to the raging fires of his wit, thus enabling him to apply their heat to some useful end. He prided himself in all seriousness on his ability to discern from a man's appearance whether his name was Kaspar. He erred not infrequently, one may take my word on this, yet apart from minor modifications (quite in the spirit of physiognomy), he stood on the whole by his conviction, and Kaspar was a name with which he designated an exceedingly composed character. Since I knew several of the people upon whom he had bestowed this name, I would gladly describe them to the best of my ability for the benefit of my readers, if only I were not afraid of subjecting myself thereby to annoying interpretations. Another, who was much older and who attended an institution of higher education, found it strange, and could, had his blood been thicker, have been caused thereby to waver in his faith, that of the three great Christian scholars whom he revered nearly to the point of veneration, one was named Abraham, the second Isaak, and the third Jacob. And yet he was a great admirer of Gellert. So when he once came to me with the lament of his observation, I replied that Gellert's middle name had been Fürchtegott [translator's note: "fear God"], and that he should do the same. There are, however, far more flattering and subtle enemies of physiognomy with whom one will become fully acquainted only after one has tilled a field that is as yet still quite choked with weeds—namely that of philosophy. A word can be transformed within us into a face, and a face into a word, through association. We see the heroes of the novels we read as though they stood before us, and the layouts of the cities as well. Long before I ever saw the portrait of the general of the American rebels, Lee, I had formed within myself an image of him, an image so wonderfully composed of deserter and double "e" that I can never think about it without a feeling of pleasure. Anyone who has ever thought about the origins of words will not find this observation unimportant, and will be able to link it with ease to others that have been more sufficiently clarified. These subtle enemies of truth, a countless number of which dwell within us, escape all observation, one by one in the case of most people, with the bright dawning of reason. But as soon as that day sinks into twilight, in the interstices of a fitful sleep, in a delirium of fever, or an enraptured prospect of restorational honor, they often emerge, enlarged to a high degree of clarity. I have, to my delight, managed to capture several of them, and have deposited them for future psychological use into my collection. That woman who believed the pope to be dragon, or a mountain, or a cannon, deserves more interest than derision. The same thing happens to all of us when we dream; and who, I ask, can say for certain where the border lies between waking and dreaming? Not everyone who sleeps dreams; likewise, not everyone who dreams necessarily sleeps.

Because no one can apprehend the entire face, everyone creates for himself, according to his situation in the world, to the ideas in his head, his interests, moods, and wit, an abridged version thereof, which, according to his system, contains the most noteworthy features, and that is what he judges. Thus, everyone sees in four dots arranged so   a face, and not everyone sees the same face. And thence as well the disputes over the similarity of portraits and the similarity between two people. Two people viewing a half-length portrait will infer the height of the man portrayed; one will say he is tall, the other will say he is short, and neither can say why. It would work for a horse or an ox, if one knew the scale of the picture, but it simply does not work with people, and yet from forehead, nose, and mouth we still draw conclusions, the audacity of which is infinite compared the ones drawn when judging the size of the animals. I could just cry when I see the treatment accorded the masterpiece of creation, which has already learned to accept the fact that it knows next to nothing of the reasons for its existence. It rains every time there is a public market, says the vendor, and every time I want to dry my laundry, says the housewife.

The firmness and immutability of certain parts of the body, particularly the forms of the bones, deceives. First, because this immutability persists alongside any type of improvement upon the perceptible creature, improvement for which there is still room long after such immutable parts have reached their final state of stability. Second, for the reason that, since their form so little depends upon our will, the influence of exterior causes is unavoidable as well, and a single pressure or impact can bring about changes, the progress of which can be no longer checked by any countermeasures one might think to undertake. Even if something could be inferred from them, the immovable parts would still constitute but one constant quantity, a single, in countless cases insignificant member of the infinite series of quantities that determine the character of a person. Mr. Lavater considers the nose the most significant member, since no dissimulation has any effect on it. That would all be well and good if the transition from truth to dissimulation and from dissimulation to truth were the only change to be seen in people. In the case of a being, however, which can be truly changed not only by moral forces, but by physical ones as well, without the nose necessarily being subject to this change, such an immutable member would not only be insignificant to the question of truth, but would indeed serve to lead one astray from the truth. The finer and more pliant the clay, the more faithful and truthful the impression. The movable parts of the face, which show and enumerate not only the pathognomical, involuntary movements, but also the deliberate movements of pretense, therefore deserve far more in my opinion pride of place. Even regression in character can cause here an analogical regression in the indicator. The indicator can deceive, unfortunately. But anything meaningful the forms of the immovable parts may possess was impressed upon them by similar causes under similar conditions. I freely admit that even the face at rest, with all of what has been pathognomically impressed upon it, by no means determines the person. It is primarily the series of changes therein, which no portrait, much less so the abstract silhouette, can depict, that expresses the character, even if it is often believed that what the latter have taught us we learned from the former. The pathognomic transformations in a face are a language for the eye, a language in which, as the great physiogist says, one cannot lie. And ten words in the language of a people are worth more than a hundred of their speech organs preserved in alcohol. Just as we hear better here than we see, so do we see more than we depict. The movable parts and the various results in movement are not corollaries that follow from the theorem given by the immovable parts. They are necessary conditions, without which the solution will always remain indefinite.

Indeed, the latter are even more important than the former, the closer they lie to real actions. Three heads that resemble each other to the point where they could have been cast from the same mold could lose all similarity when they start to smile or speak. Who can deny this but one who does not understand it?

One need not even attempt to counter this reasoning with the purported experiences of the physiognomists. They err when they make judgments on the basis of silhouettes or portraits of people they know not in the least, or err so grievously, that if one were to look at the ratio of hits to misses, the first notion to pop into one's mind would have to be that of gambling. But they do as the lottery players do; they publish leaflets full of lucky numbers, and keep the quarto volumes one could fill with the unlucky ones for themselves. Even the valid judgments they make are often couched in oracular words, with plenty of leeway as far as the meaning is concerned, and not uncommonly does the physiognomist see in a man's eye bones a keen scientific mind, or in his lips poetic genius, because for lack of knowledge or taste, or having been led astray by the journals, he thinks to have found these qualities in the man's writings. To the thinker who finds these writings empty, the whole art of physiognomy will be thrown into a suspicious light.

An alert, sober mind can easily see the source of this error, and does not waste its time with treatises not commensurate with it. Should such a mind ever venture aimlessly into such fields, as of course can sometimes happen even to great people, it does so generally only in the hours when, in the company of merry wit and piquant imagination, it receives a little nudge. So then if one takes a closer look at the physiognomists, one will find that they are more often than not people whose lively imagination provides them at the sight of most faces with the related features of other faces, and with them, entire courses of life and private histories; and who interpret these at every opportunity to those around them. They typically do so with a good measure of wit, for seeing in this mode and being able to speak in this mode both spring from one and the same source. Nor does society judge such observations as pure philosophy, but as wit, whose charm is doubtlessly increased by the touch of rakish levity that would have detracted from the former. Often they are innocent, and see in the people only what they already know about them. The verification of the observation is in most cases just as cursory as the observation itself. One need only eat, with the man upon whose head and heart one has passed such a cursory judgment, the bushel of salt that Aristotle in his day demanded, and one shall then find out what will become of the matter. But to err is human; but not always—it is sometimes . . . far less.

There is another way to investigate the character of a person, a way that could also perhaps be pursued in a scientific manner; namely, to proceed from a person's overt actions, ones that he believes he has no reason to conceal, and to try to deduce from these other actions to which he does not own up. This is a skill that people wise in the ways of the world possess to a higher degree than the wretched creatures who constitute their daily victims will ever know. In this way one can infer from an orderly parlor an orderly mind; from a good sense of proportion a sound faculty of judgment; from the colors and cut of one's clothes in certain years the entire character, with greater certainty than from a hundred silhouettes from a hundred different angles of one and the same head. Whoever says "I am a hothead when I get going" is a meek lamb; and the pious zealot who cries out time and again "I am but a weak instrument!" would believe himself to have been irreconcilably insulted if one was to answer him: "That's what we've thought all along." Discretion has inseparably kindred virtues. From the mistress one can tell a lot about the man, at least about many of the ways in which he relates to us. Whoever is good to his servants is usually fundamentally good: One does not generally put up a false front to people for whose services one pays, people one does not deem worthy of the honor of having such a false front put up to them, and whom one does not fear. The works of the good novelists and dramatists, Le Sage and Shakespeare, contain more such traits then one can shake a stick at. The latter in abundance, but without a trace of ostentatious self-reference, so that they are often overlooked. But what good does any of this do in the face of the sliest and most dangerous class of people? None at all. Every new attack produces a new art of defense that always succeeds in the hands of the most perfectible, the most corruptible creature.

But whatever objections sophistic sensuality may raise for a time, it is doubtlessly an inexorable proposition that no lasting charm is possible without unadulterated virtue, and the most spectacular ugliness, as long as it is not disgusting, is capable of bestowing upon itself charms that somebody will find irresistible. The examples of this type among persons of either gender are rare, to be sure, but no rarer than the virtues that produce such charm. What I am referring to here are primarily saintly sincerity, modest acquiescence without self-abnegation, general goodwill without an officious preoccupation with garnering thanks, careful consideration for the delicacy of feeling of other persons, even in small matters, the endeavor to give unobtrusively each person in one's company the opportunity to contribute to the conversation—furthermore, the love of order without a petty obsession with cleaning, and neatness without foppishness in one's dress. The author has encountered in women examples of these virtues, which, were he able to list them here, would fill even the ugliest of them with courage. What these virtues bring about when they are coupled with beauty, will be found by each reader more easily if he looks into the history of his own heart than I could ever describe here. Similarly, vice can

distort to a high degree if it finds pliable enough material on which
to work, particularly if, coupled with cases of coarse upbringing
and a total lack of acquaintance with virtuous wrinkles, or even a
lack of willingness to accept such wrinkles, it does not find time
to repair the cracks, not even once a day, in one or the other hour
of paid duty. These observations have long since awakened in the
author the desire to see portrayed by a born observer of people,
who possessed in addition a great skill at drawing and who had
lived in a large city, the same boys and the same girls on two
different paths through life. Their story would be best shown more
through facial features than through action. Even at that time the
author believed, and he was strengthened in his belief by the approbation he received from a number of men of learning, who had
given thought to these matters long before he had, that the execu-
tion of this thought would not be unworthy of the greatest artist.
The artist could show here everything he had ever perceived about
beauty and ugliness, and all the other observations he had made
about people, and at what a great advantage to the cause of virtue!
What Hogarth has accomplished in this respect is well known. He
was not as adept at embellishing beauty as he was at accentuating
ugliness. The reason for this is easy to grasp. Of all the artists alive
today with whom I am acquainted, Mr. Chodowiecki in Berlin
would be the only one capable of doing justice to this subject matter in such a manner as to satisfy even the most experienced observers of people. His small heads, particularly several that appeared
in the *Nothanker,* become in their genius, which makes one forget
that they are mere lines, more than simply entertainment; they
become society, at least as far as I am concerned.

Translated by Daniel Theisen

Humanities, Social Sciences and Law

Johann Heinrich Pestalozzi

The Art of Human Education

Every word spoken by a mother to her child, and every action of the child motivated by such maternal words exerts a joint influence upon the child's physical maturation, intellectual development, and emotional awakening. Even when the child responds to a gesture by his mother and merely carries a cup from one table to another, he is strengthening his b o d y through m o v e m e n t , sharpening his mind through practice in various types of a t t e n-t i o n , and experiencing in the more noble r e g i o n s of his heart beneficial stirrings when the eyes of his mother smile lovingly at him in the midst of such action.

The entire art of human education rests for this reason essentially and generally upon the instinctive concurrence in the mother and child of these three motives. These motives should for this reason be nothing more than a free and simple extension of what nature has instinctively begun; they are and should essentially be a straight, simple, but active and uninterrupted progression along the path that nature has drawn with the flaming stylus of her inextinguishable power as the only true path for the human race. Mere memory training, carried out separately from the development of the other intellectual faculties, is but a branch of the education of the intellect; a pedagogical program consisting exclusively of such memory training is sure to bring about the ruin of education with regard to the mind. For the same reason, I contend that the mere education of the mind, carried out separately from the development of the physical and moral faculties, is but a branch of a general education, a branch that when pursued to the exclusion of the others is sure to bring about the ruin of the totality of the human faculties.

Consequently, my method strives above all to preclude any separation of this tripartite criterion held together by nature in such fundamental unity, and for the very reason that this method must once and for all be envisaged c h i e f l y as intellectual education, it proceeds from a principle that bears within itself the highest guarantee for the unification of this tripartite criterion.

This principle is: perception is the foundation of all human knowledge.

When based upon this principle, the method as intellectual instruction is in essence nothing other than visual instruction. Visual instruction, as an essential element of the general art of human education, rests upon the tripartite criterion touched upon previously, and is, regardless of its particular relationship to intellectual education, nothing other than the simple continuation of what nature has instinctively begun, and even of the way in which she has begun it.

According to this method, visual instruction consists of two elements: (1) G e n e r a l instruction and (2) S p e c i f i c instruction in measurement and number.

G e n e r a l visual instruction is contained in the *Book of the Mother*. This book renders even a mother of modest education capable of enabling her child to express himself or herself with clarity in regard to the entire sphere of the objects he or she perceives. The instruction that leads to this goal begins with the person as such. By learning from and on the basis of the person to name the parts of the human body, in a general fashion at first, then according to their positions, shapes, colors, and other characteristics that might come to mind; by furthermore being able to express himself with equal clarity about the functions and activities of such parts, the child is informed and familiarized with a basic form in the simplest way possible. Once the child is in possession of this basic form, he can gradually progress to apprehending with equal clarity the objects of nature and art that constitute his immediate environment, and to expressing himself about these objects. The learning child's physical and mental faculties are always equally occupied in following the directives of this book. All objects with which the child freely occupies himself or herself raise his spirits, fill him or her with joy, and awaken the urge to expand his or her activity in all directions and to increase his or her development with each passing day.

S p e c i f i c visual instruction, or the science of the actual artistic perception of all objects, is included in the *Rudiments of Perception*. These "rudiments" proceed from the h o r i- z o n t a l and the v e r t i c a l line, and the square that results from their juxtaposition. Through diligent and diversified practice in freely perceiving and determining the measurements and the numerical properties of the various derivatives of this elementary form, as well as through equally diligent practice in copying and manipulating such derivative forms, the child is enabled to use the square and its derivatives as a general foundation for measurement, arithmetic, drawing, and handwriting skills.

All the elements of this twofold visual method of instruction are presented in sequences that generally proceed from simple points of departure and that in their power for the development of the child move forward only by additions, extremely small in and of themselves, to his previous knowledge—knowledge that by this point has been deeply impressed upon his mind. Additionally, it lies in the nature of these points of departure that this methodically guided progress admits of no gap, no leap over intermediate steps, and that consequently instruction by this method is the only type of instruction that can be employed and regarded as an extension of natural instruction, as an extension of the mother's instruction.

The truth of these views has been borne out by two years' experience. I have sixty-eight to seventy pupils ranging in age from five to eighteen living at my institute working at a level of quiet, tranquil, and nearly uninterrupted activity, a level that without the principles of this method would be unattainable. Likewise, a group of teachers with unbelievably diverse educational backgrounds, abilities, views, and principles has filled these pupils with the greatest enthusiasm and, with regard to the pupils themselves, united them in the most diligent activity for their advancement.

Regarding the moral effect of these principles, let me add I have them to thank for my success in bringing a number of children, who on account of unfortunate habits were standing with one foot in the grave, back to their true selves.

Translated by Daniel Theisen

Johann Jakob Bachofen

My Life in Retrospect

A review of my work over the last fifteen years is not to be undertaken lightly. The recollection of past occupations carries one back to the life one was leading at the time, and awakens memories that seemed to be buried forever. For inner and outward life are indivisible, and every literary endeavor inevitably takes its place in the general picture of one's past activities and state of mind. Inner experience and purely outward circumstances join to shape our work. It is impossible to think of one without the other. Consequently, when I began to think back on my work in this early period, images of my whole past life rose to mind, and the paper your Excellency asked me to write grew from a mere literary inventory to a kind of autobiography. I must own that it fills me with the sort of malaise that a man experiences at the sight of his own portrait—and there is no doubt that at many points it will call for the reader's indulgence and patience.

I was drawn to the study of law by philology. It is here that I started and hither that my legal studies led me back. In this respect my attitude toward my field has always remained unchanged. Roman law has always struck me as a branch of classical and particularly of Latin philology, hence as part of a vast field encompassing the whole of classical antiquity. What interested me was the ancient world itself and not the applicability of its lessons to present-day needs; it was ancient and not modern Roman law that I really wanted to study. With these attitudes taken over from philology, I often found myself in a painful opposition to the instructors and books I had chosen as my guides. More and more I came to disre-

172 · German Essays in Science in the 19th Century

gard the modern point of view and subordinate it to ancient crite-
ria. I felt an increasing distaste for all modern systems. I wanted
to see the material in its original form, and looked on all attempts
to adjust it to modern conceptions as mere misrepresentation of a
sort that was bound to frustrate any true understanding of ancient
life. It struck me as an unwarranted dogmatization that could only
result in error and perplexity. I was also dissatisfied with the current method of resolving controversies, which struck me as no better than Justinian's dream of a jurisprudence free from doubt and
contradiction. It seemed to me much more fruitful to investigate
the profound reasons why equally distinguished jurists could come
to entirely different conclusions. For strange as it may seem, it is
perfectly true that in questions of jurisprudence opposite views can
often be equally justified. I was glad that Justinian had not succeeded in effacing every trace of these disputes that always arise
where there is freedom of thought. I myself was convinced that the
golden age of Roman law must have brought forth the most abundant deviations and conflicts in all its branches. With this in mind,
I derived the greatest pleasure from reading our legal sources, and
if it had been up to me, I should have given the explanation of
Pandect titles precedence over all systematic lectures with their
dogmatic principles and the so-called proofs so painstakingly collected in support of them.

But this notion of mine had one great drawback, as I was soon
to discover. I memorized very few of the positive rules of jurisprudence and was always at a loss when called upon to recite rules
and exceptions. From an intellectual point of view it seemed to me
that I had not lost much. But my method of study had not been
calculated with a view to examinations. Of this I was well aware.
And in order to make good the deficiency, I was compelled to
abandon the source materials and memorize from textbooks for a
year. A *privatissimum* in Göttingen drilled me thoroughly, and a
few months in Basel completed the work. There was a brief period
in which I knew Mühlenbruch's *Doctrina* almost word for word,
and could have opened the tattered old tomes to any desired paragraph even in the dark. The ideal candidate for the doctorate was
held to be one who could find any reference in any book without
either a light or an index. My work was not in vain. I came through
both preliminary and final examinations with flying colors and
received the highest grades. Once again I was able to exchange my

textbooks for the *corpus juris,* the classics, and Cujacius. It was high time. For the breath of antiquity that I drew from its literary works was as refreshing to me as the Alpine air of the Engadin that I visited recently. I found Gaius and Cicero infinitely more enjoyable than Mühlenbruch, and my dissertation gave me several months of the most delightful and satisfying association with the sources. This work completed, I thought of devoting a small book to explaining the difference between *res mancipi* and *res nec ma-nicipi.** I abandoned the idea, partly because the reading of the significant literature made the subject utterly distasteful to me, and partly because the work would have delayed my departure for Paris, planned for the winter of 1839–40. The prospect of visiting a French university after those of Switzerland and Germany was very attractive to me, and although there was little to be learned about the classics in Paris, I spent a whole year at the École de droit. I had no objection to the subordinate position occupied by Roman law in France. I had always regarded it as a part of ancient rather than modern life, a fragment of classical philology, a product of conditions that had long sunk into oblivion, an outgrowth of ideas that had very little relation to those of the Christian Germanic peoples.

Hitherto I had been preoccupied with ancient law, totally disregarding its modern adaptation. Now for the first time I came into close contact with one of the most celebrated and widespread bodies of modern legislation and with the literature and jurisprudence based on it. Even though it did not give me the same intellectual pleasure as the study of Roman antiquity, I thoroughly enjoyed this introduction to a purely practical field and was glad to immerse myself in the juridical life of our time to the exclusion of ancient learning. From this period dates my belief that such a separation between the ancient and the modern in legal studies is far preferable to the fusion of the two then prevailing in Germany. If the classical and modern eras are each accorded their own independent rights, we shall have the most thorough scholars as well as the most capable practitioners. There are two means by which jurisprudence can preserve or recover its freshness; by direct association

---

**Res mancipi* are things in which, under Roman law, property was transferred by a formal process of seizing or taking in hand (mancipium); *res nec mancipi* are things in which property passed by simple delivery.

with the old wisdom and by occupying itself with practical life. Even if Paris does nothing for the appreciation of classical law, it is superior to the German schools when it comes to inculcating efficiency in modern legal practice. Thus I may say that Germany disclosed the ancient world to me, while France gave me access to that of modern law.

It was at this time that I met Pardessus, Count Pellegrino Rossi, and the aged Count Pastoret, then Chancellor of France, men who have all made significant contributions to our field, though in different branches. Rossi and Pastoret had preserved grateful memories of Switzerland from their early years, and it is perhaps to this circumstance that I owed my family reception in their homes. At this time Rossi enjoyed high favor among the students, who had thrown stones at him some years earlier. The two gendarmes who had escorted him for a long time had long since become superfluous. His often adroit and assuredly insincere pronouncements in favor of trial by jury, the constitutional charter, freedom of the press, Polish independence, and similar catchwords of the revolutionary journalism of the time had brought about this shift of mood. Otherwise his personality was unchanged. He had about him an insulting, Italian sort of arrogance which increased, or at least became more blatant, with the brilliance of his situation, and which was one of the reasons for his unexpected downfall in Rome. I believe that in his heart he particularly despised those qualities of the French people which he most warmly praised in public. He held the British nation in far higher esteem, and it is certain that the admiration for its great political qualities that he expressed on every possible occasion was no concession to the public mood in the most brilliant days of the July monarchy,* but rather the expression of a deep-seated conviction and an expressly chosen means of holding up a mirror to French vanity.

It was these frequent glances at England that chiefly decided me to spend some time in London after my stay in Paris. Blackstone and several French works had given me a general knowledge of English political and juridical institutions, and this added to my curiosity. My plan was carried out. No year in my life has been so rich in work, instruction, and enjoyment as the one spent in En-

---

*The Orléanist regime in France under Louis Philippe, lasting from July 1830 till 1848.

gland. It is seldom that one can fully estimate the value of such periods of life. The flexibility of youth makes one equally receptive to all manner of learning and the study of so many different fields gives one the sensation of a continuous triumphal march. When I established myself in London, I was still uncertain as to what I had particularly come to look for. Everything, I thought, or at least a little bit of everything, material and ideas for the future. I was at an age when everything still belonged to me, when even this everything was not enough, and I had no idea in what corner of this vast field my spirit would ultimately settle down. I was fascinated by the life of the law courts with all their patriarchal pomp, but there was also the British Museum with its treasures. Might it not be possible to combine the two aspects, to cultivate them both, side by side? My experience showed that far from being incompatible, the two occupations were mutually helpful.

I wrote nothing about English law. When I think of it now, I am amazed that I was able to gain even a general view of the most important material. Amid all these occupations the end of the winter approached, slowly, slowly, like old age. I wished to be gone out of the fog, the hustle and bustle of the big city. A quiet abode of the Muses—that was what I needed in order to glance back over all that I had experienced and learned, and translate it into ideas. Oxford did not live up to my expectations. Its glacial air of aristocracy, the hollow splendor, the immobility that lay over everything, the countryside, the people, and particularly men's minds, drove me away after a few days. I went to Cambridge and there found what I was looking for: scholarly activity, pleasant companionship, and above all peace and quiet. With a great sense of well-being I now continued my search for medieval processualists in the public library and in those of some of the colleges. The good people of Cambridge could not see what interest there could be in such works nowadays.

England's schools aim to educate the upper classes of the country, not to form scholars or officials. And scholarship is only a small part of education, particularly when it comes to teaching a British subject how to exercise the rights and duties which constitution and custom accord the privileged classes represented at the universities. This higher purpose would not be achieved by courses of lectures, and still less by leaving the student to his own resources, giving him full independence in the choice of his studies or of his extracurricular activities. In England, consequently, the young man is assigned a tutor. He lives in the tutor's college, and the association between them extends even to vacation periods and the customary tours of the Continent. In those days I was so close to my German student's life that the contrast with the English system made a strong impression on me. What is the situation of a twenty-year-old boy in Berlin or in Paris when his parents have trustingly sent him off to the university? The question surely deserves the most thorough consideration. I have given it a good deal of thought in connection with Basel, for in order to take a practical view of matters, one must live in the midst of them. And I have not abandoned the hope that something of the sort will come into existence here. The form, after all, is indifferent provided that the aim is achieved: general education on a foundation of humane sciences in place of mere specialized instruction. Besides, if present materialistic trends become dominant, learning is likely to become once more a priesthood which will lack state support, and must have recourse to private funds and private activity of all sorts. Only then will it be possible to realize the ideal of which I have spoken and to eradicate the literary proletariat with all its evil consequences. My visit to Cambridge marked my last protracted stay in England.

On my return home I took the words "Thy lot is Sparta"* very much to heart. In exchanging the broad perspectives of Paris and London for the petty circumstances that now surrounded me, I really had great need of this philosophical consolation. Yet even here I was soon to find not a little that was good and estimable. It is only in one's own native land that one can be firmly rooted. It is only here that one can know life's great experiences, for the destinies of families and states are fulfilled not in one life, but in the chain of successive generations.

Here, in Switzerland, no one who has studied can decline to take part in public affairs, least of all one who has acquired a doctorate in law and, as the shopkeepers say, has nothing to do. Study for the mere sake of study is something that is not understood by a people whose character is chiefly distinguished by practical con-

---

Spartam nactus es: the first part of a proverb quoted by Cicero (*Letters to Atticus* 4.6.2), meaning roughly, "Sparta is the place fate has chosen for you; be an ornament to it."

cern. But my plans were sharply opposed to the public opinion of
my native land. After all my digressions in France and England, I
wished to settle down quietly in my intellectual homeland, the field
of philology and jurisprudence. At this time I resumed my work
on the Voconian law and another on the ancient Roman law of
debt, both of which youthful ventures were published. I began my
course on the history of Roman law with a lecture on "Natural
Law and Historical Law," printed in manuscript form. This lecture
offended the philosophers by its recognition of all manner of historical phenomena and the political scientists by its emphasis on a
higher origin of legal systems, independent of human will. And yet
my superiors did not despair of me. Perhaps it would do no harm
to try me out. At all events I did not seem to be of a revolutionary
nature, perhaps on the contrary, too close to Savigny. In short, at
the next vacancy the Grand Council appointed me a regular member of the Basel criminal court, and a short time later I was advanced to the position of *Statthalter,* i.e., vice-president.

My hope of undivided scholarly activity had again been shattered. Yet, even so, I found considerable free time. I began to carry
out my plan of reading through all the classics, legal and nonlegal,
at least once, and in addition I studied the principal works of the
modern [juridical] literature.

My literary studies were limited to two works, Blume's *Iter Ital-
icum* and Wincklemann's *History of Art* with Fernow's notes.
From the former I gained a few learned notations which were later
useful to me in the libraries of Milan, Turin, and Rome. But to my
reading of Wincklemann's works I owe an enjoyment of a far
higher order—indeed, one of the greatest pleasures of my whole
life. Since then I have dwelt much in the regions that it opened,
especially at times when everything else seemed to lose interest
for me. Ancient art draws our heart to classical antiquity, and
jurisprudence our mind. Only together do the two confer a harmonious enjoyment and satisfy both halves of man's spirit. Philology
without concern for the works of art remains a lifeless skeleton.
The *id quod decet* (that which is fitting) that Cicero's Archias de-
clared to be the supreme element in all art and something that
cannot be taught or learned—this is what one acquires from association with ancient art, a sense of the measure and fullness in all
things, the supreme human harmony. The magic of Wincklemann's
history of art lies in these perfections, in the noble classical grace,

unrelated to that of the modern dancing master, that is diffused throughout the work. One cannot help seeing that it was written beneath the warmer sun of Italy, where one feels everything more deeply, pain and joy and the true meaning of things; it is no product of our smoky study rooms, with their rancid smell of tallow candles and oil lamps.

In my wanderings through the museums of Italy my attention was soon attracted to one aspect of all their vast treasures, namely mortuary art, a field in which antiquity shows us some of its greatest beauties. When I consider the profound feeling, the human warmth that distinguishes this realm of ancient life, I am ashamed of the poverty and barrenness of the modern world. The ancient tombs have given us a well-nigh inexhaustible wealth. At first we may regard the study of tombs as a specialized field of archaeology, but ultimately we find ourselves in the midst of a truly universal [religious] doctrine.

All the treasures that fill our museums of ancient art were taken from tombs, and in general human civilization owes them more than is usually supposed. In nomadic societies the tomb was the first and only stable edifice. Building was done more readily for the dead than for the living; perishable wood was held to be sufficient for the life span allotted to the living, but the eternity of man's ultimate dwelling place demanded the solid stone of the earth. In all essential things the earliest men thought soundly and correctly, as we may expect of those who were still so close to their eternal origin. The oldest cult is bound up with the stone that designates the burial place; the earliest temples were related to the burial site, while art and ornament originated in the decoration of tombs. It was the tombstone that gave rise to the concept of the *sanctum*, of the immovable and immutable. This concept also applies to boundary posts and walls, which along with tombstones constitute the *res sanctae*. In them ancient man saw an image of the primordial power which dwells in the earth, and consequently all three bear its symbol. The earth sends forth tombstones, boundary posts, and walls as though from its womb, where, as Plato says, they previously slumbered; the phallus is its mark. The altar cult is also related to the tomb, itself an altar among the most ancient peoples as well as in the Christian catacombs: sacrifices to the giver of life were made over the resting place of the corpse. The symbol came into being in the tombs and there it was longest preserved. The thoughts, feelings, silent prayers conceived over the tomb cannot be expressed in words, only intimated by the symbol with its eternally unchanging earnestness. Antiquity made full use of the symbolic, most enduringly and profoundly in its art.

Ought I, by way of explaining my interest in the ancient tombs, to speak of epigraphy and epigrammatics and many other related fields? I prefer to think of the enjoyment I have derived from my visits to tombs. There are two roads to knowledge—the longer, slower, more arduous road of rational combination and the shorter path of the imagination, traversed with the force and swiftness of electricity. Aroused by direct contact with the ancient remains, the imagination grasps the truth at one stroke, without intermediary links. The knowledge acquired in this second way is infinitely more living and colorful than the products of the understanding.

The cemeteries of southern Etruria are close to the great military highway leading from Florence to Rome, and yet are little visited. Castel d'Asso, Vorchia, Bieda, Toscanella, Corneto do not awaken depressing thoughts as do modern monuments to human transience. Like the ruins of Rome they suggest only that a necessary end is appointed to all things human. No painful feelings disturb our contemplation of the natural course of development, and these ruins recall the strength rather than the weakness of mankind. I love the peoples and the ages that do not work for the day, but have eternity in mind in all their activity. They deserve to have their tombs standing as they stood on the day they were built. We find no fault with the roof which has burst through the ceiling like an artificial wedge or split off a fragment of the portal and cast it into the depths. The stillness of nature is the most worthy setting for an eternal home. When all else has forsaken man, the earth with its vegetation still tenderly embraces his stone dwelling place. For the ancient mind this is no mere image but a truth. All those necropolises are situated beside streams. The lapping waters seem to intone the eternal praises of the dead, as an epigram in *The Greek Anthology* puts it, and according to Aeschylus in the *Prometheus* the flowing sources of the sacred streams murmur their grief. These again are no mere images but truths arising from the innermost content of the nature religions. For us, to be sure, such lines are only poetry, whose richest source would seem to lie in its disclosure of the intimate relation between the phenomena of lifeless nature and our own feelings.

All these impressions are made still more poignant by the utter remoteness and forlornness of the ancient burial sites. All who approach them have a sense of discovery. But this stillness strikes us as a homage of the living to the dead. Nothing intervenes between them and us. The sun warms and illuminates these resting places of the dead so wonderfully, and infuses the abodes of horror with the magic of joyous life. What beauty there must have been in an age whose very tombs can still arouse so much yearning for it! What a vast abundance of beautiful ethical ideas the ancients drew from their myths. The treasure house that encompasses their oldest memories of history serves also as a source of the oldest ethical truths, and provides consolation and hope for the dying. The wounded Penthesilea seems doubly beautiful to her conqueror Achilles in the moment of her death; it is only as she is dying that he discovers the fullness of her charms. It is Plato who discloses this meaning of the image.

Yes, there is something in the walls of Rome that arouses what is deepest in man. When you strike a bronze disk, it resounds until you set a finger on it to stop the vibrations. That is how Rome affects the spirit that lives with antiquity. One stroke follows another, until every corner of our soul is stirred and we finally become aware of all that was slumbering within us. I returned home from my stay in Rome with an enriched spirit, a new seriousness of soul with which to confront my future, and a more living, positive background for my studies. There the wheel of life hollowed out a deeper track. Among the favorite images that I carried away with me is that of the Campagna. Often I draw aside the curtain and follow with delight the long shadows cast by the evening sun over this broad green plain that is so incomparably important for the history of the world. Here, to speak with Plato, the feet of the immortals have left more than one trace. But instead of following these traces, human scholarship has intentionally effaced more than one of them. Everything was dissolved in mist and fog by the Hyperboreans, who believed in their self-conceit that the great epochs of the ancient world could permanently be reduced to the petty proportions of their own minds.

I went to Rome as a republican who wished to hear no more of the seven kings, as an unbeliever who respected no tradition, as an adventurer bent on entrusting his ship to the high seas instead of steering cautiously along the shore and keeping the solid ground in sight. All this I left behind in Italy. I should gladly have sacrificed this part of me to one of the old gods of the land as a parting gift. But wrathful over my past sacrilege, they all veiled their faces. Little by little everything took on an entirely different form in my mind. Italy stepped down from the remote pedestal to which the scholars had so long relegated it. Its Eastern lineage became clear to me, and I saw that no culture can properly be understood in isolation. The force of tradition came to seem more and more firmly grounded. History stretched further and further back, and assumed more and more grandiose proportions. The founder of Rome had been represented to me as a kind of Italic Adam, but now I saw him as an extremely modern figure; Rome became the fulfillment and end of a cultural era spanning a millennium.

There are moments when the public life of states and nations succumbs to fatalism. We now stand at such a moment. When we consider particulars, much that is good can still be saved, much that is new and worth while still remains to be done. My studies and past had prepared me for a bench in the provinces. In this position I followed the dictates of a truly historical sense, and I brought myself to subordinate the pardonable vanity of the scholar to the greater considerations of the public welfare. I learned to adjust myself with humility to given historical conditions.

The period whose endeavors and teachings I have been discussing extends up to 1848. Then I decided on a second stay in Rome. First my studies had inspired me with a yearning for Italy, and then Italy had awakened a desire for a new and more thorough association with the classics. This interchange began again, but now I had incomparably richer resources than before. I wished to round out my knowledge of various fields and I believed that Rome would give me new inspiration. But the peace of mind I should have required was soon shattered by the wild passions that had chosen Rome as their arena at this time. Rossi fell on the second day after my arrival. The storming of the Quirinal, the flight of the Pope, the Constituent Assembly, the proclamation of the Republic, followed in swift succession.

But for all the gruesome events, the atmosphere would have suggested a riotous but harmless carnival. And with the arrival of Garibaldi's band and the various patriotic legions from all over Italy, things became even more fantastic. Wherever Garibaldi appeared with his flaming red shirt and coal-black stallion, escorted by a Negro on a white horse, every hat in the quarter was tossed into the air. There was disorder of all sorts. Heaven had elected me to witness the first heroic deeds of the Italians against the advancing French; a little later in Tivoli I received a good deal of undesired attention from the populace, which suspected me of being a French spy; and finally, on my journey homeward, I beheld the breakdown of all order. Since then the storm has subsided. Once again Italy has become for me the land of antiquity and of tranquil studies. After such experiences I felt a redoubled need to rest among times and objects bathed in the stillness of the ages, in fields whence the floods of passion long ago subsided.

Despite the name he bears, a man is a highly anonymous being; the name remains identical however often its possessor may have changed his innermost being. I had known a period when the medieval processualists delighted me, and their long-forgotten names, that I had come across by chance, filled me with rejoicing. Later I was capable of forgetting the whole world for the sake of a fine passage in the Pandects, and regarded a successful interpretation as ample reward for protracted labors. But little by little all these pleasures forsook me. All my reading and studies, considered in the light of day, struck me as insignificant, as meager food for the soul, as irrelevant to the fulfillment of what is immortal in us. I found myself in a period of transition such as occurs in the life of every striving man. As to what brings it about—who can see so deeply into the human soul?

The transition was a painful one, but now I am thankful for it. A time inevitably comes when the scholar seriously examines his studies for their relation to the supreme truths. He becomes aware of a desire, an urgent need, to come a little closer to the eternal meaning of things. The husk no longer suffices. The thought of having struggled so long with mere worthless forms becomes a torment. And then one is saved by the realization that even in these things one may discover "the eternal footprint." I know full well what dangers beset me at this time. I might have strayed into metaphysical bypaths and lost sight of my right road forever. And the long circling about might have led to phantasms of the Huschke variety. I thank the Lord that my soul is too sound for that sort of thing. I found a different solution. Ever since then my guiding thought has been the religious foundation of all ancient thinking and life. Here, I am confident, is a key that opens many locks.

Sometimes it even seems to me that something of the divine, eternal meaning of human ideas will be revealed to me at the end of this road. If it is true, as Aristotle says, that like can be grasped only by like, then the divine can only be apprehended by a divine mind, and not by the rationalistic self-conceit that sets itself above history. Abundance of information is not everything, it is not even the essential. It is one of my profoundest convictions that without a thorough transformation of our whole being, without a return to ancient simplicity and health of soul, one cannot gain the merest intimation of the greatness of those ancient times and their thinking, of those days when the human race had not yet, as it has today, departed from its harmony with creation and the transcendent creator. And the same idea, in which the political law of the ancients is grounded, dominates all other aspects of their thought and action. I see more and more that *one* law governs all things, and that primordial man planned and regulated his earthly life with the regularity, as it were, of animal instinct.

To explore this characteristic of the oldest thinking, particularly in matters of law and politics, is the aim of all my study and literary activity. What I am engaged upon now is true study of nature. The material alone is my preceptor. It must first be assembled, then observed and analyzed. Only in this way can one hope to disclose a law that is inherent in the matter itself and not in our subjective spirit. For how few scholars has the material been the supreme judge! My collection of excerpts has so increased in the course of my labors, so much material has accumulated, that, in order not to be overwhelmed by it, I must now think in all seriousness of setting chisel to the stone and advance in my work to the point where the image that still lies dormant within me will at length emerge, in crude form perhaps, but recognizable. In the course of these studies I have encountered so many books that brilliantly elucidate everything and yet fail to disclose any understanding for the merest fragment of the ancient material that I doff my hat with true respect to anyone who can do so even in regard to the most trifling point. To perform my task quickly is not possible, nor is it my desire. I should like to give many years to the enjoyment of this occupation and for a long while experience the satisfaction of studying more for myself than for the public. But insofar as I, like every scholar, am concerned with my name, I hope to acquire glory rather than celebrity. At my present age it becomes necessary, of course, to keep my object well in view, and to limit my intellectual activity more than I should like to—all the more so as my judicial tasks and the legal studies connected with them demand a considerable share of my time.

A distraction of still another kind remains to be mentioned before I conclude this communication. Sometimes I am kept from home for months at a time by my travels. Since my first visit to England I have spent two periods of study at the British Museum, partly to consult literature that is elsewhere inaccessible, and partly for the sake of the Lycian and Assyrian sculpture. But still more important was a journey to Greece undertaken in the spring of 1851, which included all parts of the present kingdom and went off most successfully. Just as I had set out to cover the entire scope of ancient literature by continued reading, I planned in this journey to gain a personal knowledge of the most important scenes of classical antiquity and through this direct contact enhance my understanding of the literature. Now I have gained a living and colorful background for my study of the Greek authors. Whatever I read, a rich setting is present in my mind.

I have come to the end of my confessions. There is no doubt that I have spoken too much of myself and too little of my subject matter. I expect this criticism and find it justified. And I must also own that this communication has been too detailed and long-winded. But I beg your Excellency to pardon this latter fault as proof of a trusting devotion encouraged by your affable reception at Ragaz.

Translated by Ralph Manheim

Leopold von Ranke

History and Philosophy

It has often been noted that there is a certain contradiction between immature philosophy and history. Some thinkers have decided on a priori grounds what must be. Without observing that others, more doubting, will disagree with their ideas, they set forth to rediscover them in the history of the world. Out of the infinite array of facts, they select those which they wish to believe. This has been called the philosophy of history! One of the ideas which is continually repeated in the philosophies of history is the irrefutable proposition that mankind is involved in an uninterrupted progress, a steady development of its own perfection. Fichte, one of the first philosophers of this type, assumed that there are five epochs of what he called a world plan: the rule of reason through instinct, the rule of reason through law, the liberation from the authority of reason, the science of reason, and the art of reason. Or, put otherwise: innocence, original sinfulness, complete sinfulness, initial justification, and completed justification. These stages can also appear in the life of an individual. If this or similar schemes were somehow true, then universal history would have to follow a progression, and the human race would travel in its appointed course from one age to another. History would be completely concerned with the development of such concepts, with their manifestations and representations in the world. But this is largely not so. For one thing, philosophers themselves are extraordinarily at odds about the type and selection of these dominating ideas. Moreover, they consider only a few of the peoples in the world's history, regarding the activity of the rest as nothing, merely superfluous. Nor can they disguise the fact that from the beginning of the world to the present day the peoples of the world have experienced the most varied circumstances.

There are two ways to become acquainted with human affairs: through the knowledge of the particular, and through the knowledge of the abstract. There is no other method. Even revelation consists of the two: abstract principles and history. But these two sources of knowledge must be distinguished. Those historians who disregard this err, as do those who see history as only a vast aggregation of facts which must be arranged according to a utilitarian principle to make them comprehensible. Thus they append one particular fact to another, connected only by a general moral. I believe, instead, that the science of history is called upon to find its perfection within itself, and that it is capable of doing so. By proceeding from the research and consideration of the individual facts in themselves to a general view of events, history is able to raise itself to a knowledge of the objectively present relationships.

To make a true historian, I think that two qualities are needed, the first of which is a participation and joy in the particular in and for itself. If a person has a real fondness for this race of so many, so varied, creatures to which we ourselves belong, and for its essential nature, always ancient and somehow always new, so good and so evil, so noble and so brutish, so refined and so crude, directed toward eternity and living for the moment, satisfied with little yet desirous of everything; if he has a love of the vital manifestation of humanity at all, then he must rejoice in it without any reference to the progress of things. To his observation of humanity's virtues he will add an attention to its accompanying vices, to its happiness and misfortunes, to the development of human nature under so many varied conditions, to its institutions and customs. In summary, he must seek to follow the kings who have ruled over the races, the succession of events, and the development of the chief undertakings. All this he should do for no purpose other than his joy in the life of the particular individual, just as we enjoy flowers without considering to which genus of Linnaeus and Oken they belong. Enough: he must do this without thinking how the whole appears in the individuals.

But this is not enough. It is essential that the historian also have an eye for the universal. He ought not to conceive of it a priori as the philosopher does. Rather, his consideration of particular individuals will show him the course which the development of the world as a whole has taken. This development is related, not to the universal ideas which have ruled in one or another period, but to something completely different. No people in the world has remained out of contact with the others. This relationship, inherent in a people's own nature, is the one by which it enters into universal history, and must be emphasized in universal history.

There are some peoples who have armed themselves more powerfully than their neighbors on the planet, and these above all have exercised an influence upon the rest. They were the chief cause of the changes, for good or ill, which the world has experienced. Our attention ought to be directed, not to the ideas which some see as the directing force, but to the peoples themselves who appear as actors in history, to their struggles with one another, to their own development which took place in the midst of these peaceful or warlike relationships. It would be infinitely wrong to see only the effects of brute force in the struggles of historical powers or to conceive of the past in that way. There appears a spiritual essence in power itself, an original genius which has its own proper life, fulfills more or less its own requirements, and forms its own sphere of action. The business of history is to perceive the existence of this life, which cannot be described by a thought or a word. The spirit which appears in the world is not of such a conceivable nature. It fills all the boundaries of its being with its presence; nothing about it is accidental; its manifestation is founded in everything.

Translated by Roger Wines

Jacob Burckhardt

On Fortune and Misfortune in History

In our private lives, we are wont to regard our personal fate under the two categories "fortunate" and "unfortunate," and we transfer these categories without hesitation to history.

Yet from the outset we should feel misgivings, since, in our own affairs, our judgment may change radically with age and experience. Not until the last hour of our lives can we pronounce a final judgment on the men and things we have known, and that judgment may be totally different according to whether we die in our fortieth or our eightieth year. It has, moreover, no objective validity but only a subjective validity for ourselves. This is the common experience of any man whose youthful desires appear to him folly in later life.

Nevertheless, historical judgments of good and evil fortune in the past have been pronounced both on isolated events and on whole epochs and conditions of life, and it is mainly modern times that are prone to pronounce them.

There are, of course, older expressions of opinion. The well-being of a class with slaves at its command is apparent here and there, for instance in the *Skolion* of Hybreas. Machiavelli praises the year 1298, though only as a contrast to the revolution which immediately followed, and Justinger gives a similar picture of old Berne about 1350. All these judgments are, of course, much too local, and the happiness they praise was in part based on the sufferings of others; nevertheless, they are at least ingenuous, and were not devised to throw light on world history.

We, however, judge as follows:

It was fortunate that the Greeks conquered Persia, and Rome Carthage;

unfortunate that Athens was defeated by Sparta in the Peloponnesian War;

unfortunate that Caesar was murdered before he had time to consolidate the Roman Empire in an adequate political form;

unfortunate that in the migrations of the Germanic tribes so many of the highest creations of the human spirit perished, but fortunate that they refreshed the world with new and healthy stock;

fortunate that Europe, in the eighth century, on the whole held Islam at bay;

unfortunate that the German Emperors were defeated in their struggle with the Papacy and that the Church was able to develop its terrible tyranny;

unfortunate that the Reformation triumphed in only half of Europe and that Protestantism was divided into two sects;

fortunate that first Spain, then Louis XIV were eventually defeated in their plans for world domination, etc.

The nearer we come to the present, of course, the more opinions diverge. We might, however, reply that this does not invalidate our right to form an opinion which, as soon as a wider survey in time enables us to assess at their true value causes and effects, events and their consequences, finds its justification.

By an optical illusion, we see happiness at certain times, in certain countries, and we deck it out with analogies from the youth of man, spring, sunrise and other metaphors. Indeed, we imagine it dwelling in a beautiful part of the country, a certain house, just as the smoke rising from a distant cottage in the evening gives us the impression of intimacy among those living there.

Whole epochs, too, are regarded as happy or unhappy. The happy ones are the so-called high epochs of man. For instance, the claim to such happiness is seriously put forward for the Periclean Age, in which it is recognized that the life of the ancient world reached its zenith in the State, society, art and poetry. Other epochs of the same kind, e.g., the age of the good Emperors, have been abandoned as having been selected from too one-sided a standpoint. Yet even Renan says of the thirty years from 1815 to 1848 that they were the best that France, and perhaps humanity, had ever experienced.

All times of great destruction naturally count as eminently unhappy, since the happiness of the victor is (quite rightly) left out of account.

Judgments of this kind are characteristic of modern times and only imaginable with modern historical methods. The ancient world believed in an original golden age, with respect to which the world had steadily deteriorated. Hesiod paints the "present" age of iron in sinister tints of night. In our day, we may note a theory of perfection (so-called progress) in favor of the present and the future. Discoveries in pre-history reveal at least this much—the pre-historical epochs of the human race were probably spent in profound torpor, half-animal fear, cannibalism, etc. In any case, those epochs which have hitherto been regarded as the youth of the individual peoples, namely those in which they can first be recognized, were actually very derivative and late epochs.

But who is, as a rule, responsible for such judgments?

They arise from a kind of literary consensus which has gradually taken shape out of the desires and arguments of the Age of Reason and the real or imagined conclusions of a number of widely read historians.

Nor do they spread haphazard. They are turned to journalistic uses as arguments for or against certain trends of the time. They form part of the fussy baggage of public opinion and, in part, bear very clearly in the very violence, not to say crudity, of their appearance, the impress of the time from which they issue. They are the deadly enemies of true historical insight.

And now we may enquire into some of their separate sources.

The most important of these is *impatience,* and it is the writer and the reader of history who are most subject to it. It supervenes when we have had to spend too long a time on a period, and the evidence—or perhaps our own effort—is inadequate to enable us to form an opinion. We wish things had moved more quickly, and would, for instance, willingly sacrifice one or two of the twenty-six dynasties of Egypt if only King Amasis and his liberal reform would at last carry the day. The Kings of Media, though only four in number, make us impatient because we know so little about them, while that great mover of the imagination, Cyrus, seems to be already waiting at the door.

In short, we take sides for what our ignorance finds interesting against the tedious, as if for happiness against unhappiness. We confuse what was desirable to remote epochs (if anything was) with the pleasures of our imagination.

From time to time we try to delude ourselves with an apparently nobler explanation, but our only motive is one of retrospective impatience.

We pity for their unhappiness past ages, peoples, parties, creeds and so on which passed through long struggles for a higher good. Today we should like to see the aims with which we sympathize triumph without a struggle, and pluck victory without effort; and we transfer the same wish to the past. We pity, for instance, the Roman plebeians and the pre-Solonian Athenians in their century-long struggle with the hard-hearted patricians and Eupatridae and the pitiless debtors' law.

Yet it was only the long struggle which made victory possible and proved the vitality and great worth of the cause.

But how short-lived was the triumph, and how ready we are to side with one decadence against another! Through the victory of democracy, Athens declined into political impotence; Rome conquered Italy, and ultimately the world, at the cost of infinite suffering to the nations and great degeneration at home.

The state of mind which would like to spare the past its troubles, however, comes out most strongly in connection with the wars of religion. We are indignant that any truth (or what we regard as such) should have only been able to make headway by material force, and that it should be suppressed if that force proved inadequate. And it is true that truth infallibly sacrifices something of its purity and sanctity during prolonged struggles, owing to the worldly intentions of its representatives and devotees. Thus it seems to us a misfortune that the Reformation had to contend with a terrible material opposition and hence had to be represented by governments whose heart was in the property of the Church rather than in religion.

Yet in struggle, and in struggle alone, and not in printed polemics, does the full, complete life develop that must come of religious warfare. Only struggle makes both sides fully conscious. Only through struggle, at all times and in all questions of world history, does mankind realize what it really wants and what it can really achieve.

Firstly, Catholicism again became a religion, which it had almost ceased to be. Then men's minds were opened in a thousand directions, political life and culture were brought into all kinds of contact and contrast with the religious conflict, and ultimately the world was transformed and spiritually vastly enriched. None of these things could have come about in mere smooth obedience to the new creed.

Then comes the judgment according to *Culture*. It consists in appraising the felicity and morality of a people or a state of life in the past by the diffusion of education, of general culture and comfort in the modern sense. Here nothing stands the test and all past ages are disposed of with more or less commiseration. For a time, the "present" was literally synonymous with progress, and the result was the most ridiculous vanity, as if the world were marching towards a perfection of mind or even morality. Imperceptibly, the criterion of security, which will be discussed later, creeps in, and without security, and without the culture just described, *we*, at any rate, could not live. But a simple, strong mode of life, with the physical nobility of the race still intact, and the people perpetually on its guard against enemies and oppressors, is also culture, and possibly productive of a superior quality of feeling. Man's mind was complete early in time. And the enquiry as to "moral progress" we may justifiably leave to Buckle, who was so naïvely astonished that there is none to be found, forgetting that it is relevant to the life of the individual and not to whole epochs. If, even in bygone times, men gave their lives for each other, we have not progressed since.

Now follows the judgment by *personal taste,* under which we may group a number of factors. It regards such times and peoples as happy in and among whom precisely that element was predominant which lies nearest the heart of whoever is passing judgment. According as feeling, imagination or reason is the central value of life, the palm will go to those times and peoples in which the largest possible number of men were seriously occupied with spiritual things, or in which art and poetry were the reigning powers, and the greatest possible amount of time was free for intellectual work and contemplation, or in which the greatest number of people could earn a good livelihood and there was unimpeded activity in trade and traffic.

It would be easy to make the representatives of all these three categories realize how one-sided is their judgment, how inadequately it comprehends the whole life of the age concerned, and how intolerable, for many reasons, they themselves would have found life in that age.

Judgment by *political sympathy* is also common. To one, only republics were happy; to another, only monarchies. To one, only times of great and incessant unrest; to another, only times of calm. We might here quote Gibbon's view of the age of the good Emperors as the happiest the human race had ever lived through.

Even in the cases already mentioned, and more especially in the case of judgment by *culture,* the criterion of *security* creeps in. According to this judgment, the prime condition of any happiness is the subordination of private purposes to a police-protected law, the treatment of all questions of property by an impartial legal code and the most far-reaching safeguarding of profits and commerce. The whole morality of our day is to a large extent oriented towards this security, that is, the individual is relieved of the most vital decisions in the defense of house and home, in the majority of cases at any rate. And what goes beyond the power of the State is taken over by insurance, i.e., the forestalling of definite kinds of misfortune by a corresponding annual sacrifice. As soon as a livelihood or its revenues has become sufficiently valuable, the neglect to insure it is considered culpable.

Now this security was grievously lacking at many times which otherwise shine with an immortal radiance and till the end of time will hold a high place in the history of man.

Piracy was of everyday occurrence, not only in the age which Homer describes, but obviously in that in which he lived, and strangers were quite courteously and ingenuously questioned on the subject. The world was swarming with murderers, voluntary and involuntary, who sat at kings' tables, and even Odysseus, in one of his fictitious stories of his life, lays claim to a murder. And yet what simplicity and nobility of manners those people knew! And an age in which the epic lay was the common property of many singers, and moved from place to place, the common delight of nations, is for ever enviable for its achievements, its emotions, its strength and its simplicity. We have only to think of the figure of Nausicaa.

The Periclean Age in Athens was in every sense of the word an age in which any peaceful and prudent citizen of our time would refuse to live, in which he could not but be mortally unhappy, even if he was neither a member of the slave-majority nor a citizen of a city under the Attic hegemony, but a free man and a full citizen of Athens itself. Huge contributions levied by the State, and perpetual inquisitions into the fulfillment of duties towards the State by demagogues and sycophants, were the order of the day. Yet the Athenians of that age must have felt a plentitude of life which far outweighed any security in the world.

A very popular judgment in our day is the judgment by *greatness*. Those who pass such judgment cannot, of course, deny that great political power rapidly acquired, whether by the State or by the individual, can only be bought at the cost of untold sufferings to others. But they ennoble the character of the ruler and those about him to the utmost limit, and attribute to him the prophetic vision of all the great and good results which later came of his work. Finally, they assume that the spectacle of genius must have transfigured and made happy the people he had to deal with.

They dismiss the sufferings of the multitude with the utmost coolness as a "temporary misfortune"; they point to the undeniable fact that settled conditions, i.e., subsequent "happiness," have only been established when terrible struggles have bestowed power on one side or the other. As a rule, the origin and life of the man who applies this standard is based on conditions established in that fashion, hence his indulgence.

And now at last the common source trickling through all these judgments, and long since perceptible in them, the judgment by *egoism*. "We" judge thus and thus. It is true that somebody else, who is of the contrary opinion—perhaps out of egoism too—also says "we," while in the absolute sense as much is achieved by both as by the prayers of the individual farmer for sun or rain.

Our profound and utterly ridiculous self-seeking first regards those times as happy which are in some way akin to our nature. Further, it considers such past forces and individuals as praiseworthy on whose work our present existence and relative welfare are based.

Just as if the world and its history had existed merely for our sakes! For everyone regards all times as fulfilled in his own, and cannot see his own as one of many passing waves. If he has reason to believe that he has achieved pretty nearly everything that lay in his power, we can understand his standpoint. If he looks for a change, he hopes that he will soon see it come, and may help to bring it about.

But every individual—we too—exists not for his own sake, but for the sake of all the past and all the future.

In face of this great, grave whole, the claims of peoples, times and individuals to happiness and well-being, lasting or fleeting, is of very subordinate importance, for since the life of humanity is one whole, it is only to our frail powers of perception that its fluctuations in time or place are a rise and fall, fortune and misfortune. The truth is that they are governed by a higher necessity.

We should try to rid the life of nations entirely of the word "happiness" and replace it by some other, while, as we shall see later, we cannot do without the word "unhappiness." Natural history shows us a fearful struggle for life, and that same struggle encroaches far upon the historical life of nations.

"Happiness" is a desecrated word, exhausted by common use. Supposing that there was a world plebiscite to decide on the definition of the word. How far should we get?

And above all, only the fairy tale equates changelessness with happiness. From its childish standpoint it may strive to hold fast to the image of a permanent, joyous well-being (about half-way between Olympus and the Land of Cockayne). But even the fairy tale does not take it really seriously. When the wicked magician at last lies dead and the wicked fairies are punished, Abdullah and

Fatima live happily ever after into a ripe old age, but imagination, their trials over, forthwith dismisses them, to claim our interest for Hassan and Zuleika or Leila, or some other couple. The end of the *Odyssey* is so much nearer the truth. The trials of him who has suffered so much are to continue, and he must at once set out on a grievous pilgrimage.

The conception of a happiness which consists in the permanence of certain conditions is of its very nature false. The moment we set aside a primitive state, or state of nature, in which every day is like every other day, and every century like every other century, until, by some rupture, historical life begins, we must admit that permanence means paralysis and death. Only in movement, with all its pain, is life. And above all, the idea of happiness as a positive feeling is false in itself. Happiness is mere absence of pain, at best associated with a faint sense of growth.

There have been, of course, arrested peoples who present the same general picture for centuries and hence give the impression of tolerable contentment with their fate. As a rule, however, that is the product of despotism, which inevitably appears when a form of State and society has been achieved (presumably at great cost) and has to be defended against the rise of opposing forces, and with all available measures, even the most extreme. The first generation must, as a rule, have been very unhappy, but succeeding ones grow up in that order of ideas, and ultimately they pronounce sacred everything that they cannot and do not wish to change, praising it perhaps as supreme happiness. When Spain was on the point of material extinction, she was still capable of deep feeling as soon as the splendor of the Castilian name came into question. The oppression of the government and the Inquisition seems to have been powerless to humiliate her soul. Her greatest artists and poets belong to that age.

These stationary peoples and national epochs may exist in order to preserve definite spiritual, intellectual and material values from earlier times and to pass them on uncontaminated as a leaven to the future. And their calm is not absolute and deathly; it is rather of the nature of a refreshing sleep.

There are other ages, peoples, men, on the other hand, which at times spend their strength, indeed their whole strength, in rapid movement. Their importance resides in the destruction of the old and the clearing of the way for the new. But they were not made for any lasting happiness, or indeed for any passing joy, save for the short-lived rejoicing of victory. For their power of regeneration is born of perpetual discontent, which finds any halt tedious and demands to advance.

Now this striving, however important its consequences, however great its political consequences may be, actually appears in time in the garb of the most unfathomable human egoism, which must of necessity subdue others to its will and find its satisfaction in their obedience, yet which is insatiable in its thirst for obedience and admiration and claims the right to use force in all great issues.

Now evil on earth is assuredly a part of the great economy of world history. It is force, the right of the stronger over the weaker, prefigured in that struggle for life which fills all nature, the animal and the vegetable worlds, and is carried on in the early stages of humanity by murder and robbery, by the eviction, extermination or enslavement of weaker races, or of weaker peoples within the same race, of weaker States, of weaker social classes within the same State and people.

Yet the stronger, as such, is far from being the better. Even in the vegetable kingdom, we can see baser and bolder species making headway here and there. In history, however, the defeat of the noble simply because it is in the minority is a grave danger, especially in times ruled by a very general culture which arrogates to itself the rights of the majority. The forces which have succumbed were perhaps nobler and better, but the victorious, though their only motive was ambition, inaugurate a future of which they themselves have no inkling. Only in the exemption of States from the general moral law, which continues to be binding on the individual, can something like a premonition of it be divined.

The greatest example is offered by the Roman Empire, inaugurated by the most frightful methods soon after the end of the struggle between the patricians and plebeians in the guise of the Samnite War, and completed by the subjection of East and West in rivers of blood.

Here, on the grand scale, we can discern a historical purpose which is, to us at any rate, plainly apparent, namely the creation of a common world culture, which also made possible the spread of a world religion, both capable of being transmitted to the Teutonic barbarians of the Völkerwanderung as the future bond of a new Europe. Yet from the fact that good came of evil, and relative happiness of misery, we cannot in any way deduce that evil and misery were not, at the outset, what they were. Every successful act of violence is evil, and at the very least a dangerous example. But when that act was the foundation of power, it was followed by the indefatigable efforts of men to turn mere power into law and order. With their healthy strength, they set to work to cure the State of violence.

And, at times, evil reigns long as evil on earth, and not only among Fatimids and Assassins. According to Christian doctrine, the prince of this world is Satan. There is nothing more un-christian than to promise virtue a lasting reign, a material divine reward here below, as the early Church writers did to the Christian Emperors. Yet evil, as ruler, is of supreme importance; it is the one condition of selfless good. It would be a horrible sight if, as a result of the consistent reward of good and punishment of evil on this earth, all men were to behave well with an ulterior motive, for they would continue to be evil men and to nourish evil in their hearts. The time might come when men would pray Heaven for a little impunity for evildoers, simply in order that they might show their real nature once more. There is enough hypocrisy in the world as it is.

Let us now try to see whether the consolation we have divined will stand the test of a few of the most justified indictments of history.

Firstly, by no means every destruction entails regeneration. Just as the destruction of a finer vegetation may turn a land into an arid waste for ever, a people which has been too brutally handled will never recover. There are (or at any rate there seem to be) absolutely destructive forces under whose hoofs no grass grows. The essential strength of Asia seems to have been permanently and for ever broken by the two periods of Mongol rule. Timur in particular was horribly devastating with his pyramids of skulls and walls of lime, stone and living men. Confronted with the picture of the destroyer, as he parades his own and his people's self-seeking through the world, it is good to realize the irresistible might with which evil may at times spread over the world. In such countries, men will never again believe in right and human kindness. Yet he may have saved Europe from the Osmanlis. Imagine history without him, and Bajazet and the Hussites hurling themselves simultaneously on Germany and Italy. The later Osmanlis, people and sultans, whatever terror they may have meant for Europe, never again approached the climax of power represented by Bajazet I before the battle of Angora.

Even ancient times present a picture of horror when we imagine the sum of despair and misery which went to establish the old world Empires, for instance. Our deepest compassion, perhaps, would go out to those individual peoples who must have succumbed to the Kings of Persia, or even to the Kings of Assyria and Media, in their desperate struggle for independence. All the lonely royal fortresses of individual peoples (Hyrcanians, Bactrians, Sogdanians, Gedrosians) which Alexander encountered marked the scenes of ghastly last struggles, of which all knowledge has been lost. Did they fight in vain?

We feel quite differently about the peoples whose last struggle and end are known to us; that of the Lydian cities against Harpagus, Carthage, Numantia, Jerusalem against Titus. They seem to us to have taken their place in the ranks of those who have been the teachers and examples of mankind in the one great cause—that all must be staked on the cause of the whole and that individual life is not the supreme value. And thus, of their despair, a happiness, harsh but sublime, is born for all the world.

And if Persian tablets should be discovered bringing us greater knowledge of the end of those peoples in the Eastern provinces, were they only conceived in the bombastic Ormuzd style of the mindless victor, they would go to swell the number of those great memories.

We may here leave out of account the consolation we derive from the thought that without such temporary destroyers as Assyria and Persia, Alexander could not have borne the elements of Greek culture so far into Asia. Beyond Mesopotamia it had little influence. We must always be on our guard against taking our historical perspectives for the decrees of history.

One thing, however, must be said of all great destructions: since we cannot fathom the economy of world history, we never know what would have happened if some event, however terrible, had not occurred. Instead of one wave of history which we know, another, which we do not know, would have risen; instead of one evil oppressor, perhaps one still more evil.

Yet no man of power should imagine that he can put forward for his exculpation the plea: "If we do not do it, others will." For then every crime would be justified. (Such men in any case feel no need of exculpation, but say: "What *we* do turns out well because *we* do it.")

It may be, too, that if those who succumbed had lived longer, they would no longer have seemed worthy of our compassion. A people, for instance, that succumbed early in the glorious struggle might later not have been very happy, not very civilized, early corrupted by its own iniquity and deadly to its neighbors. But, having perished in the flower of its strength, we feel toward it as we feel towards exceptional men who have died young; we imagine that, had they lived, they could not but have progressed in good fortune and greatness, while perhaps their meridian already lay behind them.

Consolation comes from another direction in the mysterious law of compensation, which becomes apparent in one point at least, namely in the increase of populations after great plagues and wars. There seems to be a total life of humanity which makes losses good.

Thus it is not certain, yet it appears to us probable, that the retreat of culture from the eastern half of the Mediterranean in the fifteenth century was made good, spiritually and materially, by the expansion overseas of the people of Western Europe. The accent of the world shifted.

Thus as, in the one case, another manner of death would have come instead of the one we know, in this case the vital power of the world replaces a vanished life by a new one.

The compensation, however, must not be taken as a substitute for suffering, to which its originator might point, but only as a continuance of the life of wounded humanity with its centre of gravity shifted. Nor must we hold it out to the sufferers and their dependents. The Völkerwanderung was a great rejuvenation for the moribund Roman Empire, but if we had asked the Byzantine, living under the Comneni in the twelfth century in the Eastern remnant of it, he would have spoken with all the pride in the world of the continued life of Rome on the Bosphorus, and with an equal contempt of the "renewed and refreshed" Occident. Even the Greco-Slav of our day under the Turks does not consider himself inferior to, and probably not more unhappy than, the man of the West. Indeed, if people were consulted, they could not pay for the greatest regeneration in the world, if the price were their own end and the influx of savage hordes.

The theory of compensation is, after all, generally the theory of desirability in disguise, and it is and remains advisable to be exceedingly chary in the use of such consolation as is to be gained from it, since we cannot finally assess these losses and gains. Bloom and decay are certainly the common lot, but every really personal life that is cut off by violence, and (in our opinion) prematurely, must be regarded as absolutely irreplaceable, indeed as irreplaceable even by one of equal excellence.

Another variant of compensation is the postponement of an event which seemed imminent. From time to time a great event, ardently desired, does not take place because some future time will fulfill it in greater perfection. In the Thirty Years' War, Germany was twice on the point of union, in 1629 by Wallenstein, in 1631 by Gustavus Adolphus. In both cases a terrible, unbridgeable breach would have remained in the nation. The birth of the nation was postponed for 240 years, and came at a moment when that breach had ceased to be a menace. In the realm of art we may say that Pope Nicholas V's new St. Peter's would have been immeasurably inferior to the St. Peter's of Bramante and Michaelangelo.

Another variant is the substitution of one branch of culture for another. In the first half of the eighteenth century, when poetry was almost completely negligible and painting half dead, music reached its sublimest heights. Yet here too there are imponderabilia which we must not play off against each other too glibly. The one thing certain is that *one* time, *one* people cannot possess everything at the same time, and that a great many talents, of themselves indeterminate, are attracted by the art that has already reached its zenith.

The most justified indictments which we seem to have the right to bring against fate are those which concern the destruction of great works of art and literature. We might possibly be ready to forgo the learning of the ancient world, the libraries of Alexandria and Pergamum; we have enough to do to cope with the learning of modern times, but we mourn for the supreme poets whose works have been lost, and the historians too represent an irreparable loss because the continuity of intellectual tradition has become fragmentary over long and important periods. But that continuity is a prime concern of man's earthly life, and a metaphysical proof of the significance of its duration, for whether a spiritual continuity existed without our knowledge, an organ unknown to us, we cannot tell, and in any case cannot imagine it, hence we most urgently desire that the awareness of that continuity should remain living in our minds.

Yet our unfulfilled longing for the lost is worth something too. We owe to it, and to it alone, the fact that so many fragments have been rescued and pieced together by incessant study. Indeed, the worship of relics of art and the indefatigable combination of the relics of history form part of the religion of our day.

Our capacity for worship is as important as the object we worship.

It may be, too, that those great works of art had to perish in order that later art might create in freedom. For instance, if, in the fifteenth century, vast numbers of well-preserved Greek sculptures and paintings had been discovered, Leonardo, Raphael, Titian, and Correggio would not have done their work, while they could, in their own way, sustain the comparison with what had been inherited from Rome. And if, after the middle of the eighteenth century, in the enthusiastic revival of philological and antiquarian studies, the lost Greek lyric poets had suddenly been rediscovered, they might well have blighted the full flowering of German poetry. It is true that, after some decades, the mass of rediscovered ancient poetry would have become assimilated with it, but the decisive moment of bloom, which never returns in its full prime, would have been irretrievably past. But enough had survived in the fifteenth century for art, and in the eighteenth for poetry, to be stimulated and not stifled.

Having reached this point, we must stop. Imperceptibly we have passed from the question of good and evil fortune to that of the survival of the human spirit, which in the end presents itself to us as the life of *one* human being. That life, as it becomes self-conscious *in* and *through* history, cannot fail in time so to fascinate the gaze of the thinking man, and the study of it so to engage his power, that the ideas of fortune and misfortune inevitably fade.

"Ripeness is all." Instead of happiness, the able mind will, *nolens volens,* take knowledge as its goal. Nor does that happen from indifference to a wretchedness that may befall us too—whereby we are guarded against all pretence of cool detachment—but because we realize the blindness of our desires, since the desires of peoples and of individuals neutralize each other.

If we could shake off our individuality and contemplate the history of the immediate future with exactly the same detachment and agitation as we bring to a spectacle of nature—for instance, a storm at sea seen from land—we should perhaps experience in full consciousness one of the greatest chapters in the history of the human mind.

At a time when the illusory peace of thirty years in which we grew up has long since utterly vanished, and a series of fresh wars seems to be imminent;

when the established political forms of the greatest civilized peoples are tottering or changing;

when, with the spread of education and communications, the realization and impatience of suffering is visibly and rapidly growing;

when social institutions are being shaken to their foundations by world movements, not to speak of all the accumulated crises which have not yet found their issues;

it would be a marvelous spectacle—though not for contemporary earthly beings—to follow with enlightened perception the spirit of man as it builds its new dwelling, soaring above, yet closely bound up with all these manifestations. Any man with such a vision in mind would completely forget about fortune and misfortune, and would spend his life in the quest of that knowledge.

Translated by James Nichols

Rudolf von Ihering

The Struggle for Law

1

The end of the law is peace. The means to that end is war. So long as the law is compelled to hold itself in readiness to resist the attacks of wrong—and this it will be compelled to do until the end of time—it cannot dispense with war. The life of the law is a struggle, a struggle of nations, of the state power, of classes, of individuals.

All the law in the world has been obtained by strife. Every principle of law which obtains had first to be wrung by force from those who denied it; and every legal right—the legal rights of a whole nation as well as those of individuals—supposes a continual readiness to assert it and defend it. The law is not mere theory, but living force. And hence it is that Justice which, in one hand, holds the scales, in which she weighs the right, carries in the other the sword with which she executes it. The sword without the scales is brute force, the scales without the sword is the impotence of law. The scales and the sword belong together, and the state of the law is perfect, only where the power with which Justice carries the sword is equaled by the skill with which she holds the scales.

Law is an uninterrupted labor, and not of the state power only, but of the entire people. The entire life of the law, embraced in one glance, presents us with the same spectacle of restless striving and working of a whole nation, afforded by its activity in the domain of economic and intellectual production. Every individual placed in a position in which he is compelled to defend his legal rights, takes part in this work of the nation, and contributes his might toward the realization of the idea of law on earth.

Doubtless, this duty is not incumbent on all to the same extent. Undisturbed by strife and without offense, the life of thousands of individuals passes away, within the limits imposed by the law to human action; and if we were to tell them: The law is a warfare, they would not understand us, for they know it only as a condition of peace and of order. And from the point of view of their own experience, they are entirely right, just as is the rich heir, into whose lap the fruit of the labor of others has fallen, without any toil to him, when he questions the principle: property is labor. The cause of the illusion of both is that the two sides of the ideas of property and of law may be subjectively separated from each other, in such a manner that enjoyment and peace become the part of one and labor and strife of the other. If we were to address ourselves to the latter, he would give us an entirely opposite answer. And, indeed, property, like the law, is a Janus-head with a double face. To some it turns only one side, to others only the other; and hence the difference of the picture of it obtained by the two. This, in relation to the law, applies to whole generations as well as to single individuals. The life of one generation is war, of another peace; and nations, in consequence of this difference of subjective division, are subject to the same illusion precisely as individuals. A long period of peace, and, as a consequence thereof, faith in eternal peace, is richly enjoyed, until the first gun dispels the pleasant dream, and another generation takes the place of the one which had enjoyed peace without having had to toil for it, another generation which is forced to earn it again by the hard work of war. Thus in property and law do we find labor and enjoyment distributed. But the fact that they belong together does not suffer any prejudice, in consequence. One person has been obliged to battle and to labor for another who enjoys, and lives in peace. Peace without strife, and enjoyment without work, belong to the days of Paradise. History knows both only as the result of painful, uninterrupted effort.

That, to struggle, is, in the domain of law, what to labor, is, in that of economy, and, that, in what concerns its practical necessity as well as its moral value, that struggle is to be placed on an equal footing with labor in the case of property, is the idea which I propose to develop further below. I think that in so doing I shall be performing no work of supererogation, but, on the contrary, that I shall be making amends for a sin of omission which may rightly be laid at the door of our theory of law; and not simply at the door of our philosophy of law, but of our positive jurisprudence also. Our theory of law, it is only too easy to perceive, is busied much more with the scales than with the sword of Justice. The one-sidedness of the purely scientific standpoint from which it considers the law, looking at it not so much as it really is, as an idea of force, but as it is logically, a system of abstract legal principles, has, in my opinion, impressed on its whole way of viewing the law, a character not in harmony with the bitter reality. This I intend to prove.

The expression law *(Recht)* is, it is well known, used in a twofold sense, in an objective sense and in a subjective sense. Law *(Recht),* in the objective sense of the word embraces all the principles of law enforced by the state; it is the legal ordering of life. Law *(Recht),* in the subjective sense of the word, is, so to speak, the precipitate of the abstract rule into the concrete legal right of the person. In both directions the law meets with opposition. In both directions, it has to overcome that opposition; that is, it has to fight out or assert its existence through a struggle. As the real object of my considerations, I have selected the struggle in the second direction, but I must not omit to demonstrate that my assertion that to struggle is of the very essence of the law, in the former direction also, is correct.

In regard to the realization of the law, on the part of the state, this is not contested, and it, therefore, does not call for any further exposition. The maintenance of law and order by the state is nothing but a continual struggle against the lawlessness which violates them. But it is otherwise in regard to the origin of the law, not only to the origin of the most primitive of all law, at the beginning of history, but to the rejuvenescance of law which is taking place daily under our eyes, the doing away with existing institutions, the putting to one side of existing principles of law by new ones; in short, in regard to progress in the domain of the law. For here, to the view which I maintain, that the principles of jurisprudence are subject to the same law in their origin as in the rest of their history, there is, nevertheless, another theory opposed, one which is still, at least in our science of Roman law, universally admitted, and which I may briefly characterize after its two chief representatives as the Savigny-Puchta theory of the origin of the law. According to this theory, the formation of the body of principles of jurisprudence is effected by a process as unnoticed and as painless as is the formation or growth of language. The building up of the body of principles of jurisprudence calls for no strife, no struggle. It is not even necessary, according to this theory, to go in search of them, for the principles of jurisprudence are nothing but the quiet working power of truth which, without any violent effort, slowly but surely makes its way; the power of conviction to which minds gradually open and to which they give expression by their acts: a new principle of jurisprudence comes into being with as little trouble as any rule of grammar. The principle of the old Roman law, that the creditor might sell his insolvent debtor as a slave in foreign parts, or that the owner of a thing might claim it from any one in whose possession he found it, would have been formed in ancient Rome, according to this view, scarcely in any other manner than that in which the grammatical rule that *cum* governs the ablative was formed.

This is the idea of the origin of the law which I myself had when I left the university, and under the influence of which I lived for a good many years. Has this idea any claim to truth? It must be admitted that the law, like language, has an unintended, unconscious development, or, to call it by the traditional expression, an organic development from within outward. To this development, we owe all those principles of law which are gradually accumulated from the autonomous balancing of the accounts of the legal rights of men in their dealings with one another, as well as all those abstractions, consequences and rules deduced by science from existing laws, and presented by it to the consciousness. But the power of these two factors, the intercourse of man with man, and science, is a limited one. It can regulate the motion of the stream, within existing limits, and even hasten it; but it is not great enough to throw down the dikes which keep the current from taking a new direction. Legislation alone can do this; that is, the action of the state power intentionally directed to that end; and hence it is not mere chance, but a necessity, deeply rooted in the nature of the law, that all thorough reforms of the mode of procedure and of positive law may be traced back to legislation. True it is, that the influence of a change made by the legislative power in the existing law, may possibly be limited entirely to the sphere of the abstract, without extending its effects down into the region of the concrete

relations which have been formed on the basis of the law hitherto—to a new change in the machinery of law, a replacing of a
worn out screw or roller by a more perfect one. But it very frequently happens that things are in such a condition that the change
can be effected only at the expense of an exceedingly severe en-
croachment on existing rights and private interests. In the course
of time, the interests of thousands of individuals, and of whole
classes, have become bound up with the existing principles of law
in such a manner that these cannot be done away with, without
doing the greatest injury to the former. To question the principle
of law or the institution, means a declaration of war against all
these interests, the tearing away of a polyp which resists the effort
with a thousand arms. Hence every such attempt, in natural obedience to the law of self-preservation, calls forth the most violent
opposition of the imperiled interests, and with it a struggle in
which, as in every struggle, the issue is decided not by the weight
of reason, but by the relative strength of opposing forces; the result
being not unfrequently the same as in the parallelogram of forces—
a deviation from the original line towards the diagonal. Only thus
does it become intelligible, that institutions on which public opinion has long since passed sentence of death continue to enjoy life
for a great length of time. It is not the *vis inertiae* that preserves
their life, but the power of resistance of the interests centering
about their existence.

But in all such cases, wherever the existing law is backed by
interests, the new has to undergo a struggle to force its way into
the world—a struggle which not unfrequently lasts over a whole
century. This struggle reaches its highest degree of intensity when
the interests in question have assumed the form of vested rights.
Here we find two parties opposed each to the other, each of which
takes as its device the sacredness of the law; the one that of the
historical law, the law of the past; the other that of the law which
is ever coming into existence, ever renewing its youth, the eternal,
primordial law of mankind. A case of conflict of the idea of law
with itself which, for the individuals who have staked all their
strength and their very being for their convictions and finally succumb to the supreme decree of history, has in it something that is
really tragic. All the great achievements that the history of the law
has to record—the abolition of slavery, of serfdom, the freedom of
landed property, of industry, of conscience, etc.—all have had to

be won, in the first instance, in this manner, by the most violent struggles, which often lasted for centuries. Not unfrequently streams of blood, and everywhere rights trampled under foot, mark the way which the law has traveled during such conflict. For the law is Saturn devouring his own children. The law can renew its youth only by breaking with its own past. A concrete legal right or principle of law, which, simply because it has come into existence, claims an unlimited and therefore eternal existence, is a child lifting its arm against its own mother; it despises the idea of the law when it appeals to that idea; for the idea of the law is an eternal Becoming; but That Which Has Become must yield to the new Becoming, since

> —*Alles was entsteht,*
> *Ist werth dass es zu Grunde geht.*

And thus the historical development of law presents us with a picture of research, struggle, fight, in short of toilsome, wearying endeavor. The human mind working unconsciously towards the formation of language is met by no forcible resistance, and art has no opponent to overcome but its own past—the prevailing taste. It is not so with law considered as an end. Cast into the chaotic whirl of human aims, endeavors, interests, it has forever to feel and seek in order to find the right way, and when it has found it, to overthrow the obstacles which would impede its course. If it be an undoubted fact, that this development, like that of art or language, is governed by law and is uniform, it cannot be denied that it departs largely from the latter in the manner in which it takes place; and in this sense, therefore, we are compelled decidedly to reject the parallel instituted by Savigny—a parallel which found universal favor so rapidly—between law on the one hand and language and art on the other. This doctrine is false, but not dangerous as a philosophical opinion. As a political maxim, however, it contains an error pregnant with the most ominous consequences imaginable, because it feeds man with hope where he should act, and act with a full and clear consciousness of the object aimed at, and with all his strength. It feeds him with the hope, that things will take care of themselves and that the best he can do, is to fold his arms and confidently wait for what may gradually spring to light from that primitive source of all law called: the natural conviction of legal right. Hence the aversion of Savigny and of all his disciples for the interference of legislation, and hence the complete ignoring of the real meaning of custom, in the Puchta theory of the law of custom. Custom to Puchta is nothing but a mere mode of discovering what conviction as to the legally right is: but that this very conviction is first formed through the agency of its own action, that through this action it first demonstrates its power and its calling to govern life; in short that the principle: the law is an idea which involves force—to this the eyes of this great mind were entirely closed. But, in this, Puchta was only paying tribute to the time in which he lived. For his time was the romantic in our poetry, and the person who does not recoil from transferring the idea of the romantic to jurisprudence, and who will take the trouble to compare the corresponding directions followed in the two spheres with one another, will perhaps not find fault with me, when I allege that the historical school in law might just as well have been called the romantic. That law or the principles of legal right comes into existence or is formed painlessly, without trouble, without action, like the vegetable creation, is a really romantic notion, that is, a notion based on a false idealization of past conditions. Stern reality teaches us the contrary, and not alone that small part of that reality which we have before our eyes ourselves, and which presents us, almost everywhere, with the most strenuous endeavors of nations in respect to the formation of their legal relations—questions of the gravest nature which crowd one upon another; but the impression remains the same, no matter what part of the past we contemplate. Savigny's theory can, therefore, appeal to nothing but pre-historic times of which we have no information. But if we may be permitted to indulge in hypothesis in relation to them, I am willing to oppose to Savigny's, which represents them as the time of the peaceable, gentle evolution of the principles of law from the inner consciousness of popular conviction, my own hypothesis, which is diametrically opposed to his; and it will have to be granted to me that, to say the least, it has in its favor, the analogy of what we can see of the historical development of law, and as I believe, the advantage, likewise, of greater psychological probability. Primitive times! It was once the fashion to deck them out in every beautiful quality: truth, frankness, fidelity, simplicity, religious faith; and in such soil, principles of law would, certainly have been able to thrive without any other force to assist their growth than the power of the conviction of right: they would not have needed the sword, nor even the unassisted arm. But to-day we all know that the pious and hoary past was noted for qualities the very opposite of these, and the supposition that they were able to get their principles of law in an easier manner than all later generations can scarcely expect to be credited now. For my part, I am convinced that the labor which they must have expended on their task, was one still more difficult, and that even the simplest principles of law, such for instance as those named above, from the most ancient Roman law, of the authority of the owner to claim back his chattel from any one in whose possession it was found, and of the creditor to sell his insolvent debtor into foreign servitude, had to be first fought out by the hardest battles, before they obtained unquestioned recognition. But be this as it may, we may leave the most primitive times out of consideration. The information afforded us by the remotest history on the origin of law is sufficient. But this information is to the effect: the birth of law like that of men has been uniformly attended by the violent throes of childbirth.

And why should we complain that it is thus attended? The very fact that their law does not fall to the lot of nations without trouble, that they have had to struggle, to battle and to bleed for it, creates between nations and their laws the same intimate bond as is created between the mother and her child when, at its birth, she stakes her own life. A principle of law won without toil is on a level with the children brought by the stork: what the stork has brought, the fox or the vulture can take away again. But from the mother who gave it birth, neither the fox nor the vulture can take the child away; and just as little can a people be deprived of the laws or institutions which they have had to labor and to bleed for; in order to obtain. We may even claim that the energy and love with which a people hold to and assert their laws, are determined by the amount of toil and effort which it cost them to obtain them. Not mere custom, but sacrifice, forges the strongest bond between a people and their principles of legal right; and God does not make a gift of what it needs to the nation He wishes well, nor does He make the labor necessary to its acquisition easy, but difficult. In this sense, I do not hesitate to say: The struggle needed by laws to fight their way into existence is not a curse, but a blessing.

Translated by John J. Taylor

Friedrich Carl von Savigny

Origin of Positive Law

We first inquire of history, how law has actually developed itself among nations of the nobler races; the question—What may be good, or necessary, or, on the contrary, censurable herein?—will be not at all prejudiced by this method of proceeding.

In the earliest times to which authentic history extends, the law will be found to have already attained a fixed character, peculiar to the people, like their language, manners, and constitution. Nay, these phenomena have no separate existence, they are but the particular faculties and tendencies of an individual people, inseparably united in nature, and only wearing the semblance of distinct attributes to our view. That which binds them into one whole is the common conviction of the people, the kindred consciousness of an inward necessity, excluding all notion of an accidental and arbitrary origin.

How these peculiar attributes of nations, by which they are first individualized, originated—this is a question which cannot be answered historically. Of late, the prevalent opinion has been that all lived at first a sort of animal life, advancing gradually to a more passable state, until at length the height on which they now stand, was attained. We may leave this theory alone, and confine ourselves to the mere matter of fact of that first authentic condition of the law. We shall endeavor to exhibit certain general traits of this period, in which the law, as well as the language, exists in the consciousness of the people.

This youth of nations is poor in ideas, but enjoys a clear perception of its relations and circumstances, and feels and brings the whole of them into play; whilst we, in our artificial complicated existence, are overwhelmed by our own riches, instead of enjoying and controlling them. This plain natural state is particularly observable in the law; and as, in the case of an individual, his family relations and patrimonial property may possess an additional value in his eyes from the effect of association—so on the same principle, it is possible for the rules of the law itself to be among the objects of popular faith. But these moral faculties require some bodily existence to fix them. Such, for language, is its constant uninterrupted use; such, for the constitution, are palpable and public powers—but what supplies its place with regard to the law? In our times it is supplied by rules, communicated by writing and word of mouth. This mode of fixation, however, presupposes a high degree of abstraction, and is, therefore, not practicable in the early time alluded to. On the contrary, we then find symbolical acts universally employed where rights and duties were to be created or extinguished: it is their palpableness which externally retains law in a fixed form; and their solemnity and weight correspond with the importance of the legal relations themselves, which have been already mentioned as peculiar to this period. In the general use of such formal acts, the Germanic races agree with the ancient Italic, except that, amongst these last, the forms themselves appear more fixed and regular, which perhaps arose from their city constitutions. These formal acts may be considered as the true grammar of law in this period; and it is important to observe that the principal business of the early Roman jurists consisted in the preservation and accurate application of them. We, in latter times, have often made light of them as the creation of barbarism and superstition, and have prided ourselves on not having them, without considering that we, too, are at every step beset with legal forms, to which, in fact, only the principal advantages of the old forms are wanting, namely, their palpableness, and the popular prejudice in their favor, whilst ours are felt by all as something arbitrary, and therefore burdensome. In such partial views of early times we resemble the travelers, who remark, with great astonishment, that in France the little children, nay, even the common people, speak French with perfect fluency.

But this organic connection of law with the being and character of the people, is also manifested in the progress of the times; and here, again, it may be compared with language. For law, as for language, there is no moment of absolute cessation; it is subject to the same movement and development as every other popular tendency; and this very development remains under the same law of inward necessity, as in its earliest stages. Law grows with the growth, and strengthens with the strength of the people, and finally dies away as the nation loses its nationality. But this inward progressive tendency, even in highly cultivated times, throws a great difficulty in the way of discussion. It has been maintained above, that the common consciousness of the people is the peculiar seat of law. This, for example, in the Roman law, is easily conceivable of its essential parts, such as the general definition of marriage, of property, and so forth, but with regard to the endless detail, of which we have only a remnant in the Pandects, every one must regard it as impossible.

This difficulty leads us to a new view of the development of law. With the progress of civilization, national tendencies become more and more distinct, and what otherwise would have remained common, becomes appropriated to particular classes; the jurists now become more and more a distinct class of the kind; law perfects its language, takes a scientific direction, and, as formerly it existed in the consciousness of the community, it now devolves upon the jurists, who thus, in this department, represent the community. Law is henceforth more artificial and complex, since it has a twofold life; first, as part of the aggregate existence of the community, which it does not cease to be; and, secondly, as a distinct branch of knowledge in the hands of the jurists. All the latter phenomena are explicable by the cooperation of those two principles of existence; and it may now be understood, how even the whole of that immense detail might arise from organic causes, without any exertion of arbitrary will or intention. For the sake of brevity, we call, technically speaking, the connection of law with the general existence of the people—the political element; and the distinct scientific existence of law—the technical element.

At different times, therefore, amongst the same people, law will be natural law (in a different sense from our law of nature), or learned law, as the one or the other principle prevails, between which a precise line of demarcation is obviously impossible. Under a republican constitution, the political principle will be able to preserve an immediate influence longer than in monarchical states; and under the Roman republic in particular, many causes cooperated to keep this influence alive, even during the progress of civilization. But in all times, and under all constitutions, this influence continues to show itself in particular applications, as where the same constantly-recurring necessity makes a general consciousness of the people at large possible. Thus, in most cities, a separate law for menial servants and house renting will grow up and continue to exist, equally independent of positive rules and scientific jurisprudence: such laws are the individual remains of the primitive legal formations. Before the great overthrow of almost all institutions, which we have witnessed, cases of this sort were of much more frequent occurrence in the small German states than now, parts of the old Germanic institutions having frequently survived all revolutions whatever. The sum, therefore, of this theory is, that all law is originally formed in the manner, in which, in ordinary but not quite correct language, customary law is said to have been formed: i.e., that it is first developed by custom and popular faith, next by jurisprudence,—everywhere, therefore, by internal silently-operating powers, not by the arbitrary will of a law-giver.

This state of things has hitherto been only historically set forth; whether it be praiseworthy and desirable, the following enquiry will show. But even in an historical point of view, this state of law requires to be more accurately defined. In the first place, in treating of it, a complete undisturbed national development is assumed; the influence of an early connection with foreign jurisprudence will, farther on, be illustrated by the example of Germany. It will likewise appear, that a partial influence of legislation on jurisprudence may sometimes produce a beneficial, and sometimes an injurious, effect. Lastly, there are great variations within the limits of the validity and application of the law. For, as the same nation branches off into many stocks, and states are united or disunited, the same law may sometimes be common to several independent states; and sometimes, in different parts of the same state, together with the same fundamental principles, a great diversity of particular provisions may prevail.

Amongst the German jurists, Hugo has the great merit of having, in most of his works, systematically striven against the prevailing theories. In this respect, also, high honor is due to the memory of Möser, who generally aimed at interpreting history in the most comprehensive sense, and often with peculiar reference to law. That his example has been in a great degree neglected by jurists, was to be expected, since he was not of their craft, and has neither delivered lectures nor composed class books.

Translated by Abraham Hayward

Carl von Clausewitz

On Military Genius

Any complex activity, if it is to be carried on with any degree of virtuosity, calls for appropriate gifts of intellect and temperament. If they are outstanding and reveal themselves in exceptional achievements, their possessor is called a "genius."

We are aware that this word is used in many senses, differing both in degree and in kind. We also know that some of these meanings make it difficult to establish the essence of genius. But since we claim no special expertise in philosophy or grammar, we may be allowed to use the word in its ordinary meaning, in which "genius" refers to a very highly developed mental aptitude for a particular occupation.

Let us discuss this faculty, this distinction of mind for a moment, setting out its claims in greater detail, so as to gain a better understanding of the concept. But we cannot restrict our discussion to *genius* proper, as a superlative degree of talent, for this concept lacks measurable limits. What we must do is to survey all those gifts of mind and temperament that in combination bear on military activity. These, taken together, constitute *the essence of military genius*. We have said *in combination*, since it is precisely the essence of military genius that it does not consist in a single appropriate gift—courage, for example—while other qualities of mind or temperament are wanting or are not suited to war. Genius consists *in a harmonious combination of elements*, in which one or the other ability may predominate, but none may be in conflict with the rest.

If every soldier needed some degree of military genius our armies would be very weak, for the term refers to a special cast of mental or moral powers which can rarely occur in an army when a society has to employ its abilities in many different areas. The smaller the range of activities of a nation and the more the military factor dominates, the greater will be the incidence of military genius. This, however, is true only of its distribution, not of its quality. The latter depends on the *general intellectual development* of a given society. In any primitive, warlike race, the warrior spirit is far more common than among civilized peoples. It is possessed by almost every warrior: but in civilized societies only necessity will stimulate it in the people as a whole, since they lack the natural disposition for it. On the other hand, we will never find a savage who is a truly great commander, and very rarely one who would be considered a military genius, since this requires a degree of intellectual powers beyond anything that a primitive people can develop. Civilized societies, too, can obviously possess a warlike character to greater or lesser degree, and the more they develop it, the greater will be the number of men with military spirit in their armies. Possession of military genius coincides with the higher degrees of civilization: the most highly developed societies produce the most brilliant soldiers, as the Romans and the French have shown us. With them, as with every people renowned in war, the greatest names do not appear before a high level of civilization has been reached.

We can already guess how great a role intellectual powers play in the higher forms of military genius. Let us now examine the matter more closely.

War is the realm of danger; therefore *courage* is the soldier's first requirement.

Courage is of two kinds: courage in the face of personal danger, and courage to accept responsibility, either before the tribunal of some outside power or before the court of one's own conscience. Only the first kind will be discussed here.

Courage in face of personal danger is also of two kinds. It may be indifference to danger, which could be due to the individual's constitution, or to his holding life cheap, or to habit. In any case, it must be regarded as a permanent *condition*. Alternatively, courage may result from such positive motives as ambition, patriotism, or enthusiasm of any kind. In that case courage is a feeling, an emotion, not a permanent state.

These two kinds of courage act in different ways. The first is the more dependable; having become second nature, it will never fail. The other will often achieve more. There is more reliability in the first kind, more boldness in the second. The first leaves the mind calmer; the second tends to stimulate, but it can also blind. *The highest kind of courage is a compound of both.*

War is the realm of physical exertion and suffering. These will destroy us unless we can make ourselves indifferent to them, and for this birth or training must provide us with a certain strength of body and soul. If we do possess those qualities, then even if we have nothing but common sense to guide them we shall be well equipped for war: it is exactly these qualities that primitive and semicivilized peoples usually possess.

If we pursue the demands that war makes on those who practice it, we come to the region dominated by the *powers of intellect.* War is the realm of uncertainty; three quarters of the factors on which action in war is based are wrapped in a fog of greater or lesser uncertainty. A sensitive and discriminating judgment is called for; a skilled intelligence to scent out the truth.

Average intelligence may recognize the truth occasionally, and exceptional courage may now and then retrieve a blunder; but usually intellectual inadequacy will be shown up by indifferent achievement.

War is the realm of chance. No other human activity gives it greater scope: no other has such incessant and varied dealings with this intruder. Chance makes everything more uncertain and interferes with the whole course of events.

Since all information and assumptions are open to doubt, and with chance at work everywhere, the commander continually finds that things are not as he expected. This is bound to influence his plans, or at least the assumptions underlying them. If this influence is sufficiently powerful to cause a change in his plans, he must usually work out new ones; but for these the necessary information may not be immediately available. During an operation decisions have usually to be made at once: there may be no time to review the situation or even to think it through. Usually, of course, new information and reevaluation are not enough to make us give up our intentions: they only call them in question. We now know more, but this makes us more, not less uncertain. The latest reports do not arrive all at once: they merely trickle in. They continually impinge on our decisions, and our mind must be permanently armed, so to speak, to deal with them.

If the mind is to emerge unscathed from this relentless struggle with the unforeseen, two qualities are indispensable: *first, an intellect that, even in the darkest hour, retains some glimmerings of the inner light which leads to truth; and second, the courage to follow this faint light wherever it may lead.* The first of these qualities is described by the French term, *coup d'oeil;* the second is *determination.*

The aspect of war that has always attracted the greatest attention is the engagement. Because time and space are important elements of the engagement, and were particularly significant in the days when the cavalry attack was the decisive factor, the *idea of a rapid and accurate decision* was first based on an evaluation of time and space, and consequently received a name which refers to visual estimates only. Many theorists of war have employed the term in that limited sense. But soon it was also used of any sound decision taken in the midst of action—such as recognizing the right point to attack, etc. *Coup d'oeil* therefore refers not alone to the physical but, more commonly, to the inward eye. The expression, like the quality itself, has certainly always been more applicable to tactics, but it must also have its place in strategy, since here as well quick decisions are often needed. Stripped of metaphor and of the restrictions imposed on it by the phrase, the concept merely refers to the quick recognition of a truth that the mind would ordinarily miss or would perceive only after long study and reflection.

Determination in a single instance is an expression of courage; if it becomes characteristic, a mental habit. But here we are referring not to physical courage but to the courage to accept responsibility, courage in the face of a moral danger. This has often been called *courage d'esprit,* because it is created by the intellect. That, however, does not make it an act of the intellect: it is an act of temperament. Intelligence alone is not courage; we often see that the most intelligent people are irresolute. Since in the rush of events a man is governed by feelings rather than by thought, the intellect needs to arouse the quality of courage, which then supports and sustains it in action.

Looked at in this way, the role of determination is to limit the agonies of doubt and the perils of hesitation when the motives for action are inadequate. Colloquially, to be sure, the term "determination" also applies to a propensity for daring, pugnacity, boldness, or temerity. But when a man has adequate grounds for action—whether subjective or objective, valid or false—he cannot properly be called "determined." This would amount to putting oneself in his position and weighting the scale with a doubt that he never felt. In such a case it is only a question of strength or weakness. I am not such a pedant as to quarrel with common usage over a slight misuse of a word; the only purpose of these remarks is to preclude misunderstandings.

Determination, which dispells doubt, is a quality that can be aroused only by the intellect, and by a specific cast of mind at that. More is required to create determination than a mere conjunction of superior insight with the appropriate emotions. Some may bring the keenest brains to the most formidable problems, and may possess the courage to accept serious responsibilities; but when faced with a difficult situation they still find themselves unable to reach a decision. Their courage and their intellect work in separate compartments, not together; determination, therefore, does not result. It is engendered only by a *mental act;* the mind tells man that boldness is required, and thus gives direction to his will. This particular cast of mind, which employs the fear of *wavering* and *hesitating* to suppress all other fears, is the force that makes strong men determined. Men of low intelligence, therefore, cannot possess determination in the sense in which we use the word. They may act without hesitation in a crisis, but if they do, they act *without reflection;* and a man who acts without reflection cannot, of course, be torn by doubt. From time to time action of this type may even be appropriate; but, as I have said before, it is the *average result* that indicates the existence of military genius. The statement may surprise the reader who knows some determined cavalry officers who are little given to deep thought; but he must remember that we are talking about a special kind of intelligence, not about great powers of meditation.

In short, we believe that determination proceeds from a special type of mind, from a strong rather than a brilliant one. We can give further proof of this interpretation by pointing to the many examples of men who show great determination as junior officers, but lose it as they rise in rank. Conscious of the need to be decisive, they also recognize the risks entailed by a *wrong* decision; since they are unfamiliar with the problems now facing them, their mind loses its former incisiveness. The more used they had been to instant action, the more their timidity increases as they realize the dangers of the vacillation that ensnares them.

Having discussed *coup d'oeil* and determination it is natural to pass to a related subject: *presence of mind*. This must play a great role in war, the domain of the unexpected, since it is nothing but an increased capacity of dealing with the unexpected. We admire presence of mind in an apt repartee, as we admire quick thinking in the face of danger. Neither needs to be exceptional, so long as it meets the situation. A reaction following long and deep reflection may seem quite commonplace; as an immediate response, it may give keen pleasure. The expression "presence of mind" precisely conveys the speed and immediacy of the help provided by the intellect.

Whether this splendid quality is due to a special cast of mind or to steady nerves depends on the nature of the incident, but neither can ever be entirely lacking. A quick retort shows wit; resourcefulness in sudden danger calls, above all, for steady nerve.

Four elements make up the climate of war: danger, exertion, uncertainty, and chance. If we consider them together, it becomes evident how much fortitude of mind and character are needed to make progress in these impeding elements with safety and success. According to circumstance, reporters and historians of war use such terms as *energy, firmness, staunchness, emotional balance,* and *strength of character.* These products of a heroic nature could almost be treated as one and the same force—strength of will—which adjusts itself to circumstances: but though closely linked, they are not identical. A closer study of the interplay of psychological forces at work here may be worth while.

To begin with, clear thought demands that we keep one point in mind: of the weight, the burden, the resistance—call it what you like—that challenges the psychological strength of the soldier, only a small part is the *direct result of the enemy's activity, his resistance, or his operations.* The direct and primary impact of enemy activity falls, initially, on the soldier's person without affecting him in his capacity as commander. If, for example, the enemy resists four hours instead of two, the commander is in danger twice as long; but the higher an officer's rank, the less significant this factor becomes, and to the commander-in-chief it means nothing at all.

A second way in which the enemy's resistance *directly* affects the commander is the loss that is caused by prolonged resistance and the influence this exerts on his sense of responsibility. The deep anxiety which he must experience works on his strength of will and puts it to the test. Yet we believe that this is not by any means the heaviest burden he must bear, for he is answerable to himself alone. All other effects of enemy action, however, are felt by the men under his command, and *through them react on him.*

So long as a unit fights cheerfully, with spirit and elan, great strength of will is rarely needed; but once conditions become difficult, as they must when much is at stake, things no longer run like a well-oiled machine. The machine itself begins to resist, and the commander needs tremendous willpower to overcome this resistance. The machine's *resistance* need not consist of disobedience and argument, though this occurs often enough in individual soldiers. It is the impact of the ebbing of moral and physical strength, of the heart-rending spectacle of the dead and wounded, that the commander has to withstand—first in himself, and then in all those who, directly or indirectly, have entrusted him with their thoughts and feelings, hopes and fears. As each man's strength gives out, as it no longer responds to his will, the inertia of the whole gradually comes to rest on the commander's will alone. The ardor of his spirit must rekindle the flame of purpose in all others; his inward fire must revive their hope. Only to the extent that he can do this will he retain his hold on his men and keep control. Once that hold is lost, once his own courage can no longer revive the courage of his men, the mass will drag him down to the brutish world where danger is shirked and shame is unknown. Such are the burdens in battle that the commander's courage and strength of will must overcome if he hopes to achieve outstanding success. The burdens increase with the number of men in his command, and therefore the higher his position, the greater the strength of character he needs to bear the mounting load.

Energy in action varies in proportion to the strength of its motive, whether the motive be the result of intellectual conviction or of emotion. Great strength, however, is not easily produced where there is no emotion.

Of all the passions that inspire man in battle, none, we have to admit, is so powerful and so constant as the longing for honor and renown. The German language unjustly tarnishes this by associating it with two ignoble meanings in the terms "greed for honor" *(Ehrgeiz)* and "hankering after glory" *(Ruhmsucht)*. The abuse of these noble ambitions has certainly inflicted the most disgusting outrages on the human race; nevertheless their origins entitle them to be ranked among the most elevated in human nature. In war they act as the essential breath of life that animates the inert mass. Other emotions may be more common and more venerated—patriotism, idealism, vengeance, enthusiasm of every kind—but they are no substitute for a thirst for fame and honor. They may, indeed, rouse the mass to action and inspire it, but they cannot give the commander the ambition to strive higher than the rest, as he must if he is to distinguish himself. They cannot give him, as can ambition, a personal, almost proprietary interest in every aspect of fighting, so that he turns each opportunity to best advantage—plowing with vigor, sowing with care, in the hope of reaping with abundance. It is primarily this spirit of endeavor on the part of commanders at all levels, this inventiveness, energy, and competitive enthusiasm, which vitalizes an army and makes it victorious. And so far as the commander-in-chief is concerned, we may well ask whether history has ever known a great general who was not ambitious; whether, indeed, such a figure is conceivable.

Staunchness indicates the will's resistance to a single blow; *endurance* refers to prolonged resistance.

Though the two terms are similar and are often used interchangeably, the difference between them is significant and unmistakable. Staunchness in face of a single blow may result from strong emotion, whereas intelligence helps sustain endurance. The longer an action lasts, the more deliberate endurance becomes, and this is one of its sources of strength.

We now turn to *strength of mind,* or of *character,* and must first ask what we mean by these terms.

Not, obviously, vehement display of feeling, or passionate temperament: that would strain the meaning of the phrase. We mean the ability to keep one's head at times of exceptional stress and violent emotion. Could strength of intellect alone account for such a faculty? We doubt it. Of course the opposite does not flow from the fact that some men of outstanding intellect do lose their self-control; it could be argued that a powerful rather than a capacious mind is what is needed. But it might be closer to the truth to assume that the faculty known as *self-control*—the gift of keeping calm even under the greatest stress—is rooted in temperament. It is itself an emotion which serves to balance the passionate feelings in strong characters without destroying them, and it is this balance alone that assures the dominance of the intellect. The counterweight we mean is simply the sense of human dignity, the noblest pride and deepest need of all: the urge *to act rationally at all times.* Therefore we would argue that a strong character is one *that will not be unbalanced by the most powerful emotions.*

If we consider how men differ in their emotional reactions, we first find a group with small capacity for being roused, usually known as "stolid" or "phlegmatic."

Second, there are men who are extremely active, but whose feelings never rise above a certain level, men whom we know to be sensitive but calm.

Third, there are men whose passions are easily inflamed, in whom excitement flares up suddenly but soon burns out, like gunpowder. And finally we come to those who do not react to minor matters, who will be moved only very gradually, not suddenly, but whose emotions attain great strength and durability. These are the men whose passions are strong, deep, and concealed.

These variants are probably related to the *physical forces* operating in the human being—they are part of that dual organism we call the nervous system, one side of which is physical, the other psychological. With our slight scientific knowledge we have no business to go farther into that obscure field; it is important nonetheless to note the ways in which these various psychological combinations can affect military activity, and to find out how far one can look for great strength of character among them.

Stolid men are hard to throw off balance, but total lack of vigor cannot really be interpreted as strength of character. It cannot be denied, however, that the imperturbability of such men gives them a certain narrow usefulness in war. They are seldom strongly motivated, lack initiative and consequently are not particularly active; on the other hand they seldom make a serious mistake.

The salient point about the second group is that trifles can suddenly stir them to act, whereas great issues are likely to overwhelm them. This kind of man will gladly help an individual in need, but the misfortune of an entire people will only sadden him; they will not stimulate him to action.

In war such men show no lack of energy or balance, but they are unlikely to achieve anything significant unless they possess a *very powerful intellect* to provide the needed stimulus. But it is rare to find this type of temperament combined with a strong and independent mind.

Inflammable emotions, feelings that are easily roused, are in general of little value in practical life, and therefore of little value in war. Their impulses are strong but brief. If the energy of such men is joined to courage and ambition they will often prove most useful at a modest level of command, simply because the action controlled by junior officers is of short duration. Often a single brave decision, a burst of emotional force, will be enough. A daring assault is the work of a few minutes, while a hard-fought battle may last a day, and a campaign an entire year.

Their volatile emotions make it doubly hard for such men to preserve their balance; they often lose their heads, and nothing is worse on active service. All the same, it would be untrue to say that highly excitable minds could never be strong—that is, could never keep their balance even under the greatest strain. Why should they not have a sense of their own dignity, since as a rule they are among the finer natures? In fact, they usually have such a sense, but there is not time for it to take effect. Once the crisis is past, they tend to be ashamed of their behavior. If training, self-awareness, and experience sooner or later teaches them how to be on guard against themselves, then in times of great excitement an internal counterweight will assert itself so that they too can draw on great strength of character.

Lastly, we come to men who are difficult to move but have strong feelings—men who are to the previous type like heat to a shower of sparks. These are the men who are best able to summon the titanic strength it takes to clear away the enormous burdens that obstruct activity in war. Their emotions move as great masses do— slowly but irresistibly.

These men are not swept away by their emotions so often as is the third group, but experience shows that they too can lose their balance and be overcome by blind passion. This can happen whenever they lack the noble pride of self-control, or whenever it is inadequate. We find this condition mostly among great men in primitive societies, where passion tends to rule for lack of intellectual discipline. Yet even among educated peoples and civilized societies men are often swept away by passion, just as in the Middle Ages poachers chained to stags were carried off into the forest. We repeat again: strength of character does not consist solely in having powerful feelings, but in maintaining one's balance in spite of them. Even with the violence of emotion, judgment and principle must still function like a ship's compass, which records the slightest variations however rough the sea.

We say a man has strength of character, or simply has character, if he sticks to his convictions, whether these derive from his own opinions or someone else's, whether they represent principles, attitudes, sudden insights, or any other mental force. Such *firmness* cannot show itself, of course, if a man keeps changing his mind. This need not be the consequence of external influence; the cause may be the workings of his own intelligence, but this would suggest a peculiarly insecure mind. Obviously a man whose opinions are constantly changing, even though this is in response to his own reflections, would not be called a *man of character*. The term is applied only to men whose views are *stable and constant*. This may be because they are well thought-out, clear, and scarcely open to revision; or, in the case of indolent men, because such people are not in the habit of mental effort and therefore have no reason for altering their views; and finally, because a firm decision, based on fundamental principle derived from reflection, is relatively immune to changes of opinion.

With its mass of vivid impressions and the doubts which characterize all information and opinion, there is no activity like war to rob men of confidence in themselves and in others, and to divert them from their original course of action.

In the dreadful presence of suffering and danger, emotion can easily overwhelm intellectual conviction, and in this psychological fog it is so hard to form clear and complete insights that changes of view become more understandable and excusable. Action can never be based on anything firmer than instinct, a sensing of the truth. Nowhere, in consequence, are differences of opinion so acute as in war, and fresh opinions never cease to batter at one's convictions. No degree of calm can provide enough protection: new impressions are too powerful, too vivid, and always assault the emotions as well as the intellect.

Only those general principles and attitudes that result from clear and deep understanding can provide a *comprehensive* guide to action. It is to these that opinions on specific problems should be anchored. The difficulty is to hold fast to these results of contemplation in the torrent of events and new opinions. Often there is a gap between principles and actual events that cannot always be bridged by a succession of logical deductions. Then a measure of self-confidence is needed, and a degree of skepticism is also salutary. Frequently nothing short of an imperative principle will suffice, which is not part of the immediate thought-process, but dominates it: that principle is in all doubtful cases to *stick to one's first opinion and to refuse to change unless forced to do so by a clear conviction.* A strong faith in the overriding truth of tested principles is needed; the *vividness* of transient impressions must not make us forget that such truth as they contain is of a lesser stamp. By giving precedence, in case of doubt, to our earlier convictions, by holding to them stubbornly, our actions acquire that quality of steadiness and consistency which is termed strength of character.

It is evident how greatly strength of character depends on balanced temperament; most men of emotional strength and stability are therefore men of powerful character as well.

Strength of character can degenerate into *obstinacy.* The line between them is often hard to draw in a specific case; but surely it is easy to distinguish them in theory.

Obstinacy *is not an intellectual defect;* it comes from reluctance to admit that one is wrong. To impute this to the mind would be illogical, for the mind is the seat of judgment. Obstinacy *is a fault of temperament.* Stubbornness and intolerance of contradiction result from a special kind of *egotism,* which elevates above everything else *the pleasure of its autonomous intellect, to which others must bow.* It might also be called vanity, if it were not something superior: vanity is content with the appearance alone; obstinacy demands the material reality.

We would therefore argue that strength of character turns to obstinacy as soon as a man resists another point of view not from superior insight or attachment to some higher principle, but because he *objects instinctively.* Admittedly, this definition may not be of much practical use; but it will nevertheless help us avoid the interpretation that obstinacy is simply a more intense form of strong character. There is a basic difference between the two. They are closely related, but one is so far from being *a higher degree* of the other that we can even find extremely obstinate men who are too dense to have much strength of character.

So far our survey of the attributes that a great commander needs in war has been concerned with qualities in which mind and temperament work together. Now we must address ourselves to a special feature of military activity—possibly the most striking even though it is not the most important—which is not related to temperament, and involves merely the intellect. I mean the relationship between warfare and terrain.

This relationship, to begin with, is *a permanent factor*—so much so that one cannot conceive of a regular army operating except in a definite space. Second, its importance is *decisive in the highest degree,* for it affects the operations of all forces, and at times entirely alters them. Third, its influence may be felt in the *very smallest feature of the ground,* but it can also dominate *enormous areas.*

In these ways the relationship between warfare and terrain determines the peculiar character of military action. If we consider other activities connected with the soil—gardening, for example, farming, building, hydraulic engineering, mining, game-keeping, or forestry—none extends to more than a very limited area, and a working knowledge of that area is soon acquired. But a commander must submit his work to a partner, space, which he can never completely reconnoiter, and which because of the constant movement and change to which he is subject he can never really come to know. To be sure, the enemy is generally no better off; but the handicap, though shared, is still a handicap, and the man with enough talent and experience to overcome it will have a real advantage. Moreover it is only in a general sense that the difficulty is the same for both sides; in any particular case the defender usually knows the area far better than his opponent.

This problem is unique. To master it a special gift is needed, which is given the too restricted name of *a sense of locality.* It is the faculty of *quickly and accurately grasping the topography of any area* which enables a man to find his way about at any time. Obviously this is an act of the imagination. Things are perceived, of course, partly by the naked eye and partly by the mind, which fills the gaps with guesswork based on learning and experience, and thus constructs a whole out of the fragments that the eye can see; but if the whole is to be vividly present to the mind, imprinted like a picture, like a map, upon the brain, without fading or blurring in detail, *it can only be achieved by the mental gift that we call imagination.* A poet or painter may be shocked to find that his Muse dominates these activities as well: to him it might seem odd to say that a young gamekeeper needs an unusually powerful imagination in order to be competent. If so, we gladly admit that this is to apply the concept narrowly and to a modest task. But however remote the connection, his skill must still derive from this natural gift, for if imagination is entirely lacking it would be difficult to combine details into a clear, coherent image. We also admit that a good memory can be a great help; but are we then to think of memory as a separate gift of the mind, or does imagination, after all, imprint those pictures in the memory more clearly? The question must be left unanswered, especially since it seems difficult even to conceive of these two forces as operating separately.

That practice and a trained mind have much to do with it is undeniable. Puységur, the celebrated quarter-master-general of Marshal Luxembourg, writes that at the beginning of his career he had little faith in his sense of locality; when he had to ride any distance at all to get the password, he invariably lost his way.

Scope for this talent naturally grows with increased authority. A hussar or scout leading a patrol must find his way easily among the roads and tracks. All he needs are a few landmarks and some modest powers of observation and imagination. A commander-in-chief, on the other hand, must aim at acquiring an overall knowledge of the configuration of a province, of an entire country. His mind must hold a vivid picture of the road-network, the river-lines and the mountain ranges, without ever losing a sense of his immediate surroundings. Of course he can draw general information from reports of all kinds, from maps, books, and memoirs. Details will be furnished by his staff. Nevertheless it is true that with a quick, unerring sense of locality his dispositions will be more rapid and assured; he will run less risk of a certain awkwardness in his concepts, and be less dependent on others.

We attribute this ability to the imagination; but that is about the only service that war can demand from this frivolous goddess, who in most military affairs is liable to do more harm than good.

With this, we believe, we have reached the end of our review of the intellectual and moral powers that human nature needs to draw upon in war. The vital contribution of intelligence is clear throughout. No wonder then, that war, though it may appear to be uncomplicated, cannot be waged with distinction except by men of outstanding intellect.

Once this view is adopted, there is no longer any need to think that it takes a great intellectual effort to outflank an enemy position (an obvious move, performed innumerable times) or to carry out a multitude of similar operations.

It is true that we normally regard the plain, efficient soldier as the very opposite of the contemplative scholar, or of the inventive intellectual with his dazzling range of knowledge. This antithesis is not entirely unrealistic; but it does not prove that courage alone will make an efficient soldier, or that having brains and using them is not a necessary part of being a good fighting man. Once again we must insist: no case is more common than that of the officer whose energy declines as he rises in rank and fills positions that are beyond his abilities. But we must also remind the reader that outstanding effort, the kind that gives men a distinguished name, is what we have in mind. Every level of command has its own intellectual standards, its own prerequisites for fame and honor.

A major gulf exists between a commander-in-chief—a general who leads the army as a whole or commands in a theater of operations—and the senior generals immediately subordinate to him. The reason is simple: the second level is subjected to much closer control and supervision, and thus gives far less scope for independent thought. People therefore often think outstanding intellectual ability is called for only at the top, and that for all other duties common intelligence will suffice. A general of lesser responsibility, an officer grown gray in the service, his mind well-blinkered by long years of routine, may often be considered to have developed a certain stodginess; his gallantry is respected, but his simplemindedness makes us smile. We do not intend to champion and promote these good men; it would contribute nothing to their efficiency, and little to their happiness. We only wish to show things as they are, so that the reader should not think that a brave but brainless fighter can do anything of outstanding significance in war.

Since in our view even junior positions of command require outstanding intellectual qualities for outstanding achievement, and since the standard rises with every step, it follows that we recognize the abilities that are needed if the second positions in an army are to be filled with distinction. Such officers may appear to be rather simple compared to the polymath scholar, the far-ranging business executive, the statesman; but we should not dismiss the value of their practical intelligence. It sometimes happens of course that someone who made his reputation in one rank carries it with him when he is promoted, without really deserving to. If not much is demanded of him, and he can avoid exposing his incompetence, it is difficult to decide what reputation he really deserves. Such cases often cause one to hold in low estimate soldiers who in less responsible positions might do excellent work.

Appropriate talent is needed at all levels if distinguished service is to be performed. But history and posterity reserve the name of "genius" for those who have excelled in the highest positions—as commanders-in-chief—since here the demands for intellectual and moral powers are vastly greater.

To bring a war, or one of its campaigns, to a successful close requires a thorough grasp of national policy. On that level strategy and policy coalesce: the commander-in-chief is simultaneously a statesman.

Charles XII of Sweden is not thought of as a great genius, for he could never subordinate his military gifts to superior insights and wisdom, and could never achieve a great goal with them. Nor do we think of Henry IV of France in this manner: he was killed before his skill in war could affect the relations between states. Death denied him the chance to prove his talents in this higher sphere, where noble feelings and a generous disposition, which effectively appeased internal dissension, would have had to face a more intractable opponent.

The great range of business that a supreme commander must swiftly absorb and accurately evaluate has been indicated in the first chapter. We argue that a commander-in-chief must also be a statesman, but he must not cease to be a general. On the one hand, he is aware of the entire political situation; on the other, he knows exactly how much he can achieve with the means at his disposal.

Circumstances vary so enormously in war, and are so indefinable, that a vast array of factors has to be appreciated—mostly in the light of probabilities alone. The man responsible for evaluating the whole must bring to his task the quality of intuition that perceives the truth at every point. Otherwise a chaos of opinions and considerations would arise, and fatally entangle judgment. Bonaparte rightly said in this connection that many of the decisions faced by the commander-in-chief resemble mathematical problems worthy of the gifts of a *Newton* or an *Euler*.

What this task requires in the way of higher intellectual gifts is a sense of unity and a power of judgment raised to a marvelous pitch of vision, which easily grasps and dismisses a thousand remote possibilities which an ordinary mind would labor to identify and wear itself out in so doing. Yet even that superb display of divination, the sovereign eye of genius itself, would still fall short of historical significance without the qualities of character and temperament we have described.

Truth in itself is rarely sufficient to make men act. Hence the step is always long from cognition to volition, from knowledge to ability. The most powerful springs of action in men lie in his emotions. He derives his most vigorous support, if we may use the term, from that blend of brains and temperament which we have learned to recognize in the qualities of determination, firmness, staunchness, and strength of character.

Naturally enough, if the commander's superior intellect and strength of character did not express themselves in the final success of his work, and were only taken on trust, they would rarely achieve historical importance.

What the layman gets to know of the course of military events is usually nondescript. One action resembles another, and from a mere recital of events it would be impossible to guess what obstacles were faced and overcome. Only now and then, in the memoirs of generals or of their confidants, or as the result of close historical study, are some of the countless threads of the tapestry revealed. Most of the arguments and clashes of opinion that precede a major operation are deliberately concealed because they touch political interests, or they are simply forgotten, being considered as scaffolding to be demolished when the building is complete.

Finally, and without wishing to risk a closer definition of the higher reaches of the spirit, let us assert that the human mind (in the normal meaning of the term) is far from uniform. If we then ask what sort of mind is likeliest to display the qualities of military genius, experience and observation will both tell us that it is the inquiring rather than the creative mind, the comprehensive rather than the specialized approach, the calm rather than the excitable head to which in war we would choose to entrust the fate of our brothers and children, and the safety and honor of our country.

Translated by Michael Howard and Peter Paret

Economy
and
Technology

Friedrich List

Labor and the Division of Labor

Labor is that bodily and more or less intellectual activity of man
directed either at producing a thing useful and valuable to himself
or to others, or at producing a force that would further this end.

After nature, labor is the main source of wealth, insofar as it is
only with its help that man is able to extract from nature the
physical means for his existence and his welfare, as well as reserve
supplies and tools (capital), with the help of which he can in a
more effective and persistent manner achieve this purpose.

Labor in and of itself exerts an almost incalculable influence
upon the well-being of society, insofar as peoples compelled by
circumstances to procure for themselves through exertion the most
basic necessities of life develop their physical and mental powers
to a much higher degree and are much less subject to the influences
of vice than peoples to whom nature voluntarily proffers these
necessities. In this respect, one could regard the winter of the temperate zone as the progenitor of labor and of culture, inasmuch as
it instills in man, through the diverse and dire needs to which it
gives rise, and through the prudence and exertions it demands as
man's duty during the milder seasons, the qualities of industry

and thrift. Once he has developed thereby habits of activity and prudence, man strides henceforth in the temperate zone boldly onwards in the development of his powers, while in those regions where nature has been too good to him, he not seldom remains standing on the first rung of culture. This as well is certainly one of the main reasons why art and science, industry and prosperity, domestic virtues and civic freedom thrive better in the temperate zones than in the warm and the torrid zones.

In the raw state of nature, man everywhere regards labor as an evil. Thence the subservient position of the children and women in the wild and patriarchal state; thence the slavery, the caste system, the assumption of privileges. Slavery and the caste system, as much as they stand in the way of the expansion and progress of civilization given today's level of culture, seem for all that to have been a necessary school that raw humanity had to pass through in order to be able to partake of the blessings of free and voluntary labor. Through these institutions the division of labor was promoted, the first improvements to machines and processes were carried out, people were accustomed to physical exertion and prepared for the periods when they should find in labor the means to buy themselves free from the domination of their oppressors and secure guarantees for the preservation of their rights.

In man's endeavor to shift the burden of labor, that curse that was pronounced upon him when he was cast out of paradise, from his own shoulders to those of another, we recognize even today the ultimate foundation of the aspiration to domination and privilege, the ultimate foundation of the war and hostility that exist among the nations of the earth. And just as we acknowledge labor to be the only rational and legitimate, the surest and the most effective means for individuals and nations to attain wealth and achieve prosperity, so do all societal configurations that do not rest upon this basis appear to us as ones that will have to change with the progress of enlightenment and the improvement of human institutions. Take war, for example: What has it been throughout history, with only a few exceptions, but a means for the generals to enrich themselves, to assert their courage and talents, to expand their power? And who had to bear the costs but those who by the sweat of their brow had planted the grain, had scraped forth the iron from the bowels of the earth, had spun and woven the clothing? But it was not only at the cost of the fruits of labor that this game, rooted in idleness and the inclination to destroy, was played. This game blighted even the roots of labor, by robbing it of the honor it was due, by destroying the custom, without which no diligence is possible, by shaking the foundations of the security of property and travel, without which security diligence is capable of very little. We should remember how in the middle ages the inhabitants of individual valleys, districts, and provinces annihilated each other in this way, and how in our day it has come even to the point that entire leagues of states recognize the rule of law; indeed, that a system of states exists, which, having arisen purely from labor and being organized in a fashion commensurate with its origin, knows outwardly no other war than that of defense against unjust attacks, undergoes inwardly no other struggle than that with nature, and among themselves know no other jealousy than the effort to outdo each other in the institutions of civilization. Thus, the hope that the principle of labor shall one day conquer and dominate the earth is certainly no chimera. The most perfect state of the human race of which reason can in this respect conceive is surely that when it reaches the point where it is able to have all excessively strenuously tasks performed by the forces of nature, when man is left with just enough physical exertion as is necessary to his physical welfare, and when every person is placed in a position to be able to spend his life in a succession of intellectual and physical exertions, of intellectual and physical pleasures. That humanity is striving toward this goal cannot be denied. The machines and inventions of civilized Europe are already replacing the slave labor of antiquity and of the modern-day Orient. Absolute idleness has already reached its lowest level in the civilized states; intellectual labor is already leading here to honor and dignity, physical labor to respect and prestige, and everyone can now enjoy, free and unmolested, its fruits, and shall be able to do so all the more, the more the political institutions perfect themselves, i.e., the less labor is called upon to share its fruits with idleness and with brute force.

The less that remains for their enjoyment to that segment of society that must subject itself to physical labor, the more tension the mainspring of labor will lose, and the more negligible will be its influence upon the general well-being. We can discern this most clearly from the situation in the slave states. There exists, however, a condition almost worse than that of slavery; namely that in which the taxes are so high that the free worker, after excessive exertions, is left with no intellectual pleasures, and physical pleasures sufficient only to keep him from starving. Such privations oppress not only the spirit, but gradually cripple the nation bodily as well. In the conditions of slavery and serfdom, the master has a stake in keeping his slave well nourished, since crippling him would decrease his value and productivity.

But such a degradation of the working classes avenges itself in yet another way than by impoverishing and crippling the nation. Nature has namely sown talent and potential among the people with an even hand, and if we find for example that of a thousand nonlaboring people, ten have had some exceptional talent bestowed upon them, then we may assume that a group of nine thousand laborers will contain ninety equally talented people. If each then receives a healthy, well-nourished body and a grain of intellectual education, then it is all the easier for the favored minds from the group of the laborers to work up to the position allotted to them by creation, while they will never develop under the pressure of excessive exertions and privations and with a lack of intellectual stimulation, and will perhaps out of aversion to an occupation incommensurate with their intellectual capabilities become wastrels and criminals. If one bears in mind that the class of society whose lot is to perform heavy labor is in all countries by far the more numerous, then one will know why despotically ruled countries have such a great lack of talent, and free ones such a great abundance thereof.

Even physical labor is of more or less intellectual origin. The more civilized and prudent a person is, the greater his concern for the well-being of his dependants, the more optimistically he looks to the future, the more free play his energies have in shaping his future, the more firmly the fruits of his labor are secured, and the more value he places on honor and deportment, the greater will be his efforts to attain skills and to bring forth with their help things of value. This is why he works more and better in free, religious countries than in despotic and morally depraved ones; this is why slave labor is the most expensive labor.

But intellectual labor is to the social economy what the soul is to the body. Through new inventions, the power of man is constantly increasing. Let us just think of the accomplishments of those few whose work we can thank for the invention and perfection of the steam engine. Not only have they given to a small number of people the power to perform tasks whose completion would previously have required a thousand hands, they have also enabled man to bring forth the treasures of the earth from the deepest, previously impenetrable abysses, to battle the power of the wind and the waves, to move from one place to the other with the speed of a bird; they have increased the prosperity and the pleasures and the populations of the lands, and the beneficent effects of their labor grow on and on from generation to generation. Furthermore, intellectual labor plants and nurtures the productive forces of the future generation, by instilling in the young the ideals of activity, morality, and intelligence; it preserves law and order, cultivates and promotes public institutions, arts, and sciences, eliminates or alleviates physical and moral evils and infirmities.

Ever since people have been thinking and writing about issues of political economy, a difference has been drawn between productive and nonproductive labor, but a whole succession of errors was necessary before a simple truth could be arrived at. The encyclopedists or economists maintain that only labor expended on agriculture is productive, because it is the only kind that yields an absolute surplus or revenue; labor expended on manufactured articles, on the other hand, while creating value consumes an equal value in products, and is thus unproductive. It is difficult to understand how sophistry has been able to make unclear such a clear matter as this, that agriculture and industrial production mutually support and elevate one another. Thus, the eminent English political economist, Adam Smith, the first person to show that labor is one of the primary causes of wealth, (although the sages of antiquity, among them King Solomon, demonstrated long before him that idleness and indolence are the causes of poverty) had no trouble refuting this weak argument of the economists. By limiting too severely the concept of wealth and taking it to mean only the exchange value that labor is capable of bestowing upon tangible things, Smith committed for his part the error of declaring intellectual labor and mere personal services to be unproductive. The eminent French political economist Jean Baptiste Say laid bare this error and demonstrated the productivity of intellectual labor, but in a way that appears to us insufficient: by deeming the accomplishments of such labor productive (thus transposing them to the realm of values) on the basis of their instrumentality for obtaining material goods.

Count von Soden has the honor of having been the first to demonstrate, in his work on political economy, that a distinction is to be made between productive energies and the production of material value. He neglected, however, to represent each as distinctly different systems; a close interrelationship admittedly obtains between the two, but the failure to uphold a clear boundary between them is most detrimental to the clear insight into the effects of the various types of labor.

Labor is productive, either insofar as it creates exchange value, or insofar as it increases the productive energies. The horse breeder produces exchange value, the teacher produces productive energies. The labor of the latter is in its relation to the general public productive not for the reason that the teacher receives a value, i.e., school fees, in return for his services, but because he enables the future generation, through the service he provides, to take part in the production process. The material goods of society are reduced by the entire sum of the values consumed by the teacher; they are restored to society as energies. But values and energies are as different from one another as mind and body, and if one confuses the system of the one with the system of the other, if one assesses energies on the basis of values, one can come only to the most absurd conclusions. Thus, for example, would a man who expended nothing for the education of his children while saving up the products of his labor appear productive, while another, who expended all the fruits of his labor on the education of his children, would appear unproductive; a slaveholder who cultivates value in his young slaves would be more productive than a man who is rearing his own children provides his country with producers. Just as in this way society attains energies by sacrificing values, so is it conversely not uncommon for society to sacrifice productive energies for the production of values. Thus, only by sacrificing a large portion of the productive energies of human beings can slaveholders reduce these energies to a thing with exchange value. Thus also do many types of labor exist, through which values are produced but energies destroyed; we need only think of distilled spirits, of opium, of weapons and tools that are misused for purposes of spiritual or bodily murder, etc.

All types of labor undertaken to uphold law and order in society, to prevent vice and crime, to promote ethical behavior, to reduce bodily afflictions, etc., as well as that performed by jurists, administrators, clergymen, and physicians, are productive for the particular reason that they maintain, preserve, and increase the productive energies of society, not because they are compensated with exchange values. The types of labor applied to the practice of the polite arts and the sciences provide recreation, elevate the spirit, and lend beauty to life, thus producing pleasures that on the higher pinnacles of civilization are no less desirable than the material ones, and that furthermore spur people on to higher intellectual and material production. The labors of the servants enable the master of the household to attend to more important business and allow the lady of the house to devote her energies to the upbringing of her children, thus increasing the productive energies of society.

This does not mean, by the way, that all intellectual labor and all servants are in all circumstances productive. A country can have too many public servants and soldiers, too many clergymen, scholars, artists, and domestic servants, or these may carry out their respective pursuits in a manner that does not promote the common good. What matters is that the proper proportion among the various classes be brought about, and that each class fulfill its respective duty. The more this proportion is upset, the more unproductive do intellectual labors become. The same, by the way, can occur with labor applied to the production of material things as well. Given the conditions prevalent in a particular country, too much or too little labor can be expended on agriculture, or on trade or individual branches thereof; these can consequently be either more or less productive. Insofar as disproportions of this or of the previously mentioned type are not grounded in existing legal or societal regulations or institutions, they are best given the opportunity to correct themselves; otherwise, this would most likely be impossible without the assistance of the legal apparatus.

The only ones who are actually unproductive are the idle; those who occupy themselves to the detriment of the morality, the order, and the well-being of society, and those who live at cost to society without rendering commensurate services unto it. Whether and to what extent capitalists and men of private means are productive shall depend upon the way in which they have come into possession of their fortunes, and upon the use they make of their incomes and their time. If they or their testators have acquired their fortune through industry, then their very ostentation shall serve to spur on all industrial classes to achieve the same goal by the same route.

If, however, the capital from which they live had been acquired by illegal or even pernicious means, then their ostentation can only serve to demoralize the industrial classes. In free and well-organized lands, distinction or honorable prosperity are only possible through the esteem of the public; this is why those of private means here strive to distinguish themselves by rendering services to the public: by showing active interest in institutions promoting the common good, by promoting the arts and sciences, by supporting new undertakings; and those people who live only for themselves, for their own interests and passions, are quite rare, for they are looked upon with scorn. In the former position, the capitalists and those of private means appear very productive, while in the latter, they are to be numbered among those classes detrimental to production.

The division of labor, the nature and the significance of which were delineated for the first time by Adam Smith in his famous *Inquiry into the Nature and Causes of the Wealth of Nations,* is at the same time cause and effect of the growing culture. In the raw state of society, man fabricates for himself the greater part of his necessities for life; he plows the field, constructs his own dwelling, and makes his own clothing. But everything is wretched and inferior, for he lacks the necessary skills and tools, and because the limited sphere in which he lives provides him with only very few and inadequate materials. He soon notices that his work proceeds more quickly and leads to greater success the more he limits his activity to bringing forth and improving such individual objects, to which end his individual skill and his natural surroundings particularly enable him.

By concentrating solely on the production of, for example, pottery or clothing, he comes to invent new tools and techniques, and acquires skills and methods that others do not possess. He then exchanges the surplus articles, of the type that he produces, for food and other things he needs; for others find it just as profitable to concentrate solely on agriculture, insofar as they can procure for themselves the implements and the articles of clothing they need much more easily by bartering their surplus produce for them than by producing them themselves. It is through this system of exchange that the division of labor is introduced; and through money, which serves as the medium of exchange, this division of labor is carried out only to the extent allowed by the given level of culture, rate of consumption, and available capital. In large cities, one can find boot makers, shoemakers, and cobblers. The first two categories can be further divided into those who work for commoners, noblemen, and the middle classes. There are men's tailors and ladies' tailors of various classes, and bakers of black bread, white bread, pastries, and confections. In small towns, on the other hand, a single class of shoemakers, bakers, and tailors supplies the entire public. Increasing trade and the facilitation of transportation bring about a division of labor among various regions, provinces, and lands. In flat, fertile country, agriculture is found to be particularly advantageous, and the surplus grain is traded for the wines of the hilly regions and the manufactured articles of the mountainous areas, which because of the considerable fall of their rivers and streams, because of their surplus of wood and because of the low fertility of their soil are particularly dependent upon the pursuit of manufacture. The products of a particularly rich mine, the implements and tools fabricated of a special type of earth or stone, the products of a skill possessed only by the populations of certain areas, and the natural products and materials peculiar each to its own region are now distributed throughout the world, and each person can trade the surplus he produces in his chosen trade for a commensurate quantity of the products and manufactured goods from the most distant lands. While in this way the division of labor puts entire regions and lands in a position to utilize in the most advantageous way the natural products and the skills peculiar to them, it enables the individual proprietor of a business to offer, by dividing the various tasks among a number of workers in such a way that the article passes from one worker to the next, better products at a lower price than if each worker were to carry out every step of the production process. In the first place, this separation allows each worker to attain specialized skills; in the second place, he saves the time and effort of having to change workplaces, positions, and instruments; in the third place, because the worker's attention is always concentrated on but a single task, he is much more apt to invent new tools, techniques, and processes.

The division of labor is keeping pace with the increases in capital, population, production, and consumption. Just as it proceeds from these, so does it exert influence upon them as well. It is more readily applicable to expensive articles requiring precise and complicated work, of greater value and lesser weight, because the market for such goods is very extensive, than to rough articles that are heavy in proportion to their price, the market for which is limited. The least likely sphere of application for the division of labor is that of agriculture. The division of labor is least developed among the savage peoples; after them come those lands that practice agriculture, the affluence of which lands is correspondingly limited (although the so-called domestic manufacture which takes place in such lands does have its advantages). The highest stage of its development is to be found in lands in which agricultural, industrial, and commercial production are fully developed and are found in the optimal proportion to each other. There is admittedly a disadvantage to the division of labor in the fabrication of individual articles; namely, that when it is carried out to too great an extent, it undermines the independence of the worker, insofar as each one represents but a part of a whole.

Workers and Wages. Just as labor is one of the main sources of wealth, the workers' wages, along with capital profits and ground rent, are one of the main elements of the cost-price and of the original value of the articles. Wages are defined as that quantity of useful things that someone receives in compensation for the physical activity he has performed. This compensation is known as an honorarium or a salary when the services rendered are more of an intellectual than of a physical nature. The physical activity can take the form of menial labor, whereby it is chiefly bodily exertion that is called for, and not any particular preparation; or it can take the form of skilled labor, for which more or less practice, skill, and ability are required.

For menial labor exist the greatest supply and demand; training therein requires the least outlay, thus making its price the lowest as well. Menial labor always regulates itself, just as does the price of every other service and every other thing, according to the relationship of the supply to the demand. When the demand for workers climbs, wages climb. When the demand for work climbs, wages fall. But the demand for workers climbs when the demands for production and for manufactured goods increase, and when the capital increases—i.e., when agriculture, trade, and commerce experience a greater upswing—and this demand falls when the reverse is true. The lowest price for labor is reached when it barely suffices to support the worker and his family and to provide him with security for the future; for as soon as this lowest limit is transgressed, the number of workers is reduced, since the worker who is struggling with poverty will either himself starve, or else will be unable to nourish and rear the children who would then replace him. This reduction in the number of workers leads in turn to a renewed rise in the demand for workers, and insofar as the price of the wages is thereby raised, the number of workers again increases. The highest price of a menial labor wage is that, as is the case in North America, which enables the worker not only to secure for himself and his family all the necessities of life, but to put aside savings as well, which allow him to attain in the course of time his independence and to insure himself against possible future illness and against the infirmities of age. This high wage level and the favorable position of the worker in North America can be explained in part by the quantity of yet-uncultivated, fertile, and inexpensive land to be found there, which makes it easy for the worker to become a landowner and thus his own worker; and in part by the rapid upswing in agriculture, trade, commerce, and capital growth, a result of the cultivation of these wild and fertile lands and of the massed productive forces in this nation, which is causing the demand for labor to steadily increase; and in part by the circumstance that the taxes, which are quite low, incidentally, paid to the state, are for the most part levied on capital profits, ground rents, and the consumption of luxury articles; the consumption tax that exists in other countries, which is levied on the consumption of the most essential necessities of life and which is deducted from the wages, does not exist there. In countries that do not enjoy similar favorable conditions, the conditions always depress the menial labor wage to the lowest point, even if in occasional periods it is driven higher by the concurrence of fortunate circumstances. A significant difference in this normal wage level from one European country to another does however exist, insofar as we can observe that in states whose agriculture, trade, and commerce are particularly flourishing, and that enjoy a high degree of liberty, the normal wage level is far greater than in countries poor in trade and commerce; this is due not only to the fact that in the former countries the monetary value is lower (as for example is the case in England over and against Poland), but also to the fact that the workers in those countries expect more from life, and reckon more and better things to the necessities of common life. Furthermore, there exists between the workers of the various classes the principle that holds that the more they occupy themselves with the production of things for the common life, the lower their wages, but the more secure their jobs, while those who occupy themselves with the production of luxury articles or with large-scale manufacturing in general find themselves at the mercy of the frequent market fluctuations, the effect of which upon them is often adverse to the highest degree. The highest degree of security in this respect is enjoyed by the class of workers occupied with agriculture, who of all classes of workers are the most assured of receiving a regular wage and least likely to starve, but who on the other hand receive the lowest wages. It must be mentioned here, just as with the majority of phenomena that affect the productive forces, that a high wage is at the same time cause and effect of a high level of prosperity in a nation, for just as this prosperity raises the worker's wage, so does a high worker's wage make possible for the majority of the population a high level of consumption of primary products and of those manufactured goods that constitute the most basic necessities of life, through which process agriculture and the most important branches of manufacture are in turn promoted.

Wages climb in proportion to the extent to which outlay, effort, special skills, and talents are required to learn and carry out the task at hand, to the arduousness, unpleasantness, danger, and unhealthiness of the work, and to the extent to which the work is subject to change, accident, and interruption.

Intelligent legislation must keep above all the welfare of the working classes in mind, not only because these classes constitute a clear majority of the nation, but because their condition exerts the greatest influence upon the order, the power, and the welfare of the nation.

Labor Saving Machines. The energy necessary for the production of primary products and manufactured goods and for the operations of commerce is produced by men, by machines, and by nature. The ship is a machine guided by men and driven by the power of wind or steam. The plow is a machine set in motion by animal energy (i.e., natural energy) and guided by men. The more man learns, through the perfection of the sciences, by means of invention or improvement of machines, to utilize the forces of nature to achieve his ends, the more he will produce, the less bodily exertion will be required of him, and the more bodily exertion will become intellectual exertion, insofar as it will in the end be only a matter of directing the forces of nature. With a wooden spade, man can already accomplish more than with a wooden stick, such as is utilized by a number of savage peoples to scratch open the ground and to make it thus receptive to seeds. A spade of iron enables him to do more work than with the one of wood; a plow set in motion with human energy accomplishes more work than an iron spade set in motion with human energy; a horse or a steer set before a plow guided by a man accomplishes ten times the work accomplished by a plow pulled by men, and the work is far less strenuous for the men involved. The more the plow corresponds to the laws of mechanics, the greater its efficacy, the easier the work. The plow recently invented by a French farm laborer by the name of Grangé requires no man to guide it whatsoever and yet it accomplishes more work than any plows previously known. Insofar as natural energy consumes far less and produces far more than pure human energy, it affords a far greater net yield and provides for a far greater number of people the necessities and the amenities of life. This is the main reason why in our times the same area is inhabited by a far greater number of people and why the majority of these people are far better nourished and clothed than in the days of antiquity. Those who inveigh against new machines do not realize that the plow, the grist mill, the wheel, the saw, the hatchet, yes, even the spade, were at one time themselves newly invented machines, and that if the invention of new machines had always been considered a misfortune, we would still be tilling the soil with wooden sticks, grinding the grain by hand with two stones, and bringing the flour to town on the backs of packhorses. The only difference between those old machines and our new ones is that the former have by now become inextricably intertwined with our social and industrial structure, whereas the introduction of the latter, initially and for the time it takes for the process to run its course, robs a number of people of their accustomed occupation and compels them to switch over to other lines of business or to exchange their previous technique for a new one yet to be learned, or to change their place of residence and seek work elsewhere. The grievances of these people, which are undeniably justified inasmuch as their livelihood is thereby temporarily endangered or at least encroached upon, induce shortsighted persons to view all machines as an evil, as though the birth of a child were an evil because it entails pain for the mother. Such people do not realize that the pains are transient, but the benefit remains, and grows from generation to generation. Far from limiting the working classes' opportunities for work, they expand these opportunities in an extraordinary way. For by helping to lower the cost-price of manufactured goods and products, machines lower the market prices of these things as well, thereby increasing the consumption and thereby the demand, and thereby the production in such a manner as to provide work for far more people than before in the branch of industry in question, in some cases for ten times as many workers, regardless of the fact that every single one of these workers is now producing ten times more than before.

A striking example of this is the so-called cotton gin and the machinery for spinning and weaving cotton. When in the 1780s the first samples of cotton were brought from Charlestown in North America to Liverpool, the customs officials refused to believe that they were American product, since that country had never been known to produce cotton; and for a long time afterwards the cotton production of the United States was quite insignificant, for the seeds of the cotton grown there are very difficult to separate from the lint. The cleaning of such cotton, as long as it had to be done by hand, required too much work, making the product far too expensive. At the beginning of this century, however, the cleaning machine known as the cotton gin was invented, which represented a savings in labor approximately analogous to that of the grist mill as compared to the hand mill. The cost-price of raw cotton was thereby lowered so drastically that as a result of the increased production the price of raw cotton fell by 200 to 300 percent. This low price, combined with the effects of the cotton-spinning and weaving machinery invented in England, machinery that depressed to an even greater extent the cost-price of cotton textiles and consequently their market price, resulted in an enormous consumption of cotton textiles, causing since that time the demand for such textiles and as a result of *that,* the manufacture and the production of cotton to increase a hundredfold, and the number of workers previously employed in the cotton industry to increase tenfold. The North American cotton harvest for the year 1834 has been estimated at no less than 1,150,000 bales, or over 400 million pounds, of which the greater part has been exported to England. The factories of England have been thereby enabled to process approximately 300 million pounds of cotton and thus to employ, directly and indirectly, approximately 1.5 million people.

In the year 1781, in contrast, England's entire cotton imports amounted to no more than between 4 and 5 million pounds, whereby barely one-tenth of the number of people employed now had been employed. In the 1780s, the price of cotton goods was so high that they could be purchased only by the rich, while in our day, the poorest class knows no cheaper dress material. Similarly, the invention of the printing press increased by a thousandfold the number of those previously occupied at copying manuscripts and the number of instructional materials. In the course of time, we shall experience to a greater or lesser extent the same results from all machines whose purpose is to facilitate and lessen work or to improve the quality of manufactured goods.

There is no image that would be better suited to illustrate the boundless advantages of machines than that of a steamboat being operated by two people and flying past another ship being rowed upstream by a hundred workers. How strenuous for the workers, how wretched and miserable in their performance does the work here appear; and how wondrously powerful, how victorious, how great the performance, how dignified and effortless the position of the men on the steamboat! But what should those ninety-eight men do, whose work is made superfluous when two of them with the help of a new steamboat are able to accomplish ten times more than the original hundred could with nothing but the weight of their bodies? The answer is easy: for the time being, they shall help build the new steamboat; after that, they shall use their strength to help produce that surplus of products and manufactured goods that has been made necessary by the improvement in water transportation brought about by steam power; thereupon shall they work in those coal mines made accessible for the first time by the steam engine; finally, they shall find employment in the transportation of this surplus production of coal and in all of the thousand new industries that this surplus production has launched.

For those dwelling inland, there is in our day certainly no machine better suited to save work and increase production than the railroads. The following are also to be regarded as labor-saving machines: roads, bridges, canals, steam tractors, and some institutions as well, such as banks, insofar as they spare the merchant the effort of collecting and disbursing money, of paying it out, storing it, carrying it back and forth and having it transported.

Translated by Daniel Theisen

Ernst Abbe

Profit Sharing in Large Industry

The supporters of profit sharing, if I understand them correctly, approach their case essentially from three different perspectives. Three different courses are followed that are not mutually exclusive and in fact often go hand in hand. They must, however, be logically differentiated.

The first group, which is represented by Jean Leclaire, the man who first introduced the arrangement, aspires to very lofty social ideals. According to this approach, the arrangement should aim at nothing less than a gradual transformation of the fundamental bases of economic activity. In other words, profit sharing should be the preparatory and preliminary step toward a cooperative economy and the gradual acquisition of all working capital by the workers and employees. Profit shares are utilized in such a way that this eventuality seems not to be merely disclosed as a possibility, but rather as the expressed goal of the arrangement. This is a concept of considerable significance. It involves the revival of the old cooperatives that provided the form of collaboration for free individuals in the earliest beginnings of shipping, mining, and even agriculture in part.

There is absolutely no question that endeavors of this sort, even if they were in large part successful, would necessarily have revolutionary implications. For they aim at gradually eliminating the separation of worker from implement, the division of labor from capital, and the historically connected conflict between employers and employees. While we must acknowledge the importance of these efforts themselves, our final approbation depends entirely on the answer to the following question: to what extent is cooperative action possible in industry today—cooperative action, that is, on which both employers and employees agree completely? It is my own personal opinion that this possibility is extraordinarily limited and in fact only exists where cooperation is more possible without a sophisticated organization, an extensive structuring of the operations, and an integration of very heterogeneous elements. This position is shared, I believe, not only by academic economists, but also by the theoreticians of social democracy. For they also are currently discussing the conditions and prerequisites on which the possibility of successful cooperative formation in industry depends.

As I have already mentioned, the initiator of profit sharing introduced and implemented it with this approach. Originally, these innovations seemed to have been accomplished with lasting success. But apart from another moment that influenced this achievement, which I will address shortly, this success was contingent, I believe, upon the fact that these cooperative organizations were restricted to a small number of selected persons, the majority of whom were employees before and who essentially remained in the same position of dependency after. I do not know much of the successes of other efforts, namely in England and America, which aim ultimately at the gradual transfer of complete enterprises into the possession of the employees. The only known effort of this type in Germany, which was implemented in 1868 in the Borchert Brass factory in Berlin, failed completely.

Recently the question has again been explored in the context of this general approach. And yet again, the discussion proceeds without any consideration of the conditions and prerequisites upon which the feasibility of the notion depends, under the naive assumption that what was possible a thousand years ago must also be possible today. To the originators of these latest suggestions we can only say that while their intentions are most honorable, their thinking is most simplistic.

In contrast to the lofty ideals appealed to by this first group of supporters of profit sharing, a second group has adopted a more rational and commonsensical position. This approach essentially conceives of profit sharing as a bonus system, which is in turn understood as a means for encouraging the employees to work more sparingly and prudently, and to use their time more efficiently. Each year, a share of a company's net profits would be allocated to the employees based on how much more profit was earned due to their prudence, frugality, and industriousness. The value of the oil, for example, which is saved by drivers and mechanics is expanded to a general bonus for the prudence and industriousness of all the employees.

It is undeniable that profit sharing of this nature, as far as the effectiveness of the bonus system is concerned, will have a certain economic impact. But this advantage is of a more mercantile nature. It has nothing to do with the economic relationship between employer and employee and thus loses its social meaning. However, this purely economic effect has often played a significant role in the successful profit-sharing ventures. Even Leclaire doubtlessly ascribes a large part of his success to the effect generated by profit shares distributed as bonuses. The employees in that case were painters, workers who by the very nature of their occupation are not very accustomed to careful stewardship and efficiency. It is thus entirely understandable that, for these workers, profit sharing in the form of a general bonus for time not squandered and for paint not spilled would have the desired effect. But such conditions are more the exception than the rule. In the majority of cases the effective consequences of a bonus system that rewards a prudent frugality and the more efficient use of time on the job would be far more limited. In fact, as far as efficiency is concerned, the effects of a bonus system would in no way exceed the effects of a rational piece-rate system. For in a bonus system the worker, even in the best possible case, receives only a portion of that saved by their industriousness and carefulness. Further, they receive this portion only when their coworkers perform similarly. With a piece-rate system, however, the savings go directly into the worker's pocket.

Profit sharing as a bonus system, however, can in no way claim to effect any changes of broad social significance.

Finally, a third approach to profit sharing recommends the arrangement without the call for a profound change in economic activity intended by the supporters of cooperatives, but also, on the other hand, without a particular emphasis on the purely economic advantages maintained by the second approach. This approach recommends profit sharing as a reform that is socially valuable and useful. Profit sharing should, according to this approach, be "one of the most effective means both for the improvement of the economic standing of workers and for the reconciliation of differences between workers and employers." These are more or less the words used recently by the most famous supporter of profit sharing in Germany (Freese). The arrangement referred to with this characterization consists of the distribution of a certain quota of an enterprise's annual net profits among its employees. This quota is normally around 10 percent of the profits and is distributed either equally or variously according to some particular sort of hierarchy. I must examine this approach more closely. For as is typically the case, this innovation involves an unjust claim to the integration of a social element into economic life.

How should we address this? Let us first examine the assumption that this form of profit sharing would provide a means for improving the economic standing of workers. This would, of course, only be possible when either due to the profits shared the workers' final salaries were larger than they would have been prior to the innovation or if the workers were ensured salaries that were more certain than they would otherwise be. The latter is impossible because the profit quota is less certain than the customary salary. The positive effect can thus only be explained as an increase in the workers' final salaries. This seems at first to be entirely clear: a salary and a share of the profits is more than a salary alone. This is correct, but only as long as the salary itself is not reduced in order to compensate for the profit shares. If indeed the intended effect of the arrangement is a cumulative increase in salary, there must be a guarantee that those profits shared by the employer with the employees at the end of the year must not have been previously retained from the salaries themselves. Current profit-sharing arrangements of this nature, however, provide no such guarantees. According to current commercial legislation, employers are free at any time to reduce salaries. This can be done either directly or by dismissing the employee and hiring another, whether on the following day or fourteen days later, who is eager to work for a diminished salary. Other than goodwill then, the only objective regulator of salary adjustment is the supply and demand relationship in the labor market. Salaries are not adjusted in and of themselves. Rather, the cumulative income of the employees, which in the case of a profit-sharing arrangement is the sum of the salary and profit share, is the variable. Whether conscious or not, the probable amount of profits to be shared will become a factor in the determination of salaries.

The fact that in the vast majority of enterprises the payroll constitutes by far the largest expense and thus influences the net profits more than any other expense must also be considered. The smallest savings in this area therefore means a rather considerable increase in net profits. In most enterprises then, a savings of only three percent gleaned from the payroll results directly in an increase of at least ten percent in net profits. This savings can in turn be distributed. In the absence of a measure that would free earnings from the merely arbitrary regulations of supply and demand and bring constancy to the determination of salaries, there exists nothing to prevent the introduction of profit-sharing arrangements that save every last cent to be distributed as profit shares from reductions in salaries.

When we consider that in almost every case a small savings in salary payments produces a considerable savings in profit quotas, it is undeniable that profit sharing can have a tendency in certain cases to lead to an overall decrease in workers' earnings. As a reform profit sharing maintains the appearance of magnanimity and progressiveness. But it is precisely in this appearance that a danger lies that should not be underestimated. Much can be concealed behind this facade that would be easily recognizable without its protection.

These observations can only lead to the conclusion that a profit-sharing system that in no way includes regulations aimed at stabilizing salaries absolutely cannot result in an ultimate increase in the incomes of economically dependent workers. In fact, such an innovation would more likely be an obstacle to this objective. This does not mean that we must maliciously oppose, puritanically reject, and refuse any good that may come of this type of profit-sharing arrangement. Indeed, it may be better if barriers in the economic sector reveal themselves coldly and without adornment. For then the structure and materials of these barriers themselves become clear. When these barriers are whitewashed and decorated in finery, we do not see them for what they are.

This third approach to profit sharing is also praised for its improvement of the personal relationships between employees and employers. It is said to moderate class conflict.

Certainly, this profit-sharing arrangement, when implemented free from pressure and thus due purely to the voluntary initiative of the employers, will be accepted in good faith by employees to the extent that they perceive the intention of the actions to be benevolent and congenial. The conciliatory effect depends then not on the arrangement itself, but on the perception of its fundamental underlying motive. The positive effect, in short, is limited to the level of effects generated by liberal gratification and other acts of personal charitableness. Hopefully there are no longer many today who expect a reconciliation or moderation of social class conflict to occur in this way.

A more profound effect of this form of profit sharing, although it could only be described as indirect, would be the dialogue necessarily instigated between workers and employers. Interestingly, it is this effect that so horrifies the primary opponents of profit sharing mentioned at the outset. For as soon as such an arrangement is implemented, the employees certainly achieve a moral, even if not a formal right to demand explanations and justifications for the profits or losses on which their share depends. This then introduces an element of critique and commentary that the representatives of the employer's perspective do not desire. In my opinion, however, this exchange is a very positive effect that is very well suited to moderate class conflict. For discussions of the most various situations, even if they do not always take the most agreeable form, imperatively encourage each side to discern the other's perspective and to understand their ideas. This in turn leads the representatives of oppositional interests in peaceful directions.

Once profit sharing has been introduced into our local enterprises, I expect completely that we also will experience this consequence. When I do experience it, I will not fear it. I cannot, however, also say I will be gratified. For this effect will only occur when bad years come, which no one desires. As long as all goes well and a share of the profits can be counted, all involved will quietly claim them and say nothing. But the first time this profit share fails to appear, or is less than expected, they will come and ask, how can this have happened, and who is to blame? Even then, though, it will be good to have to provide information and explanations.

This then would be the only advantage that could be ascribed to profit sharing as a reform of real social interest.

The supporters of profit sharing, however, can refer to a practical fact that appears to be directly opposed to my critical assessment of the arrangement up to this point. For statistics show that almost everywhere the system has been implemented it has been accompanied by good results. Profit sharing has shown itself to be connected everywhere both to relatively high salaries and to a particularly good relationship between employers and employees. It is thus argued that this connection cannot be coincidental and that it in fact proves the effectiveness of the new salary system. This seems indeed to be very illuminating. Nevertheless, I can perceive in this manner of argumentation a confusion of *cum hoc* with *propter hoc*.

I also am of the opinion that this connection is not coincidental. But there is a completely different explanation for this. Apart from a few dubious cases, the profit-sharing arrangement has until now been introduced only by very decent employers who have been expressly committed to advancing the general interest of their personnel, creating and maintaining fair salary structures for their employees, and sustaining amiable and peaceful relationships between themselves and their employees. In fact, the implementation of a profit-sharing arrangement itself seems to be a symptomatic expression of this type of intention. How then, in the situations where profit sharing has been implemented, could conditions other than these most favorable ones have resulted? And, rather than being the successful effect of the profit-sharing arrangement, could these conditions not be the effect of a more fundamental and general relationship? Indeed, if the profit-sharing arrangement had been forced on recalcitrant employers who would not and will not have implemented it for good reasons, the experience might seem entirely different. The statistics in such a case might have provided material for the notion that profit sharing merely provides a veneer for the malicious repression of real wages.

If, however, one is still capable of doubting the validity of the above explanation, this doubt would increase as one scrutinizes the statistics more closely. For these statistics show that even in cases where the profit shares are exceedingly small, and even homoeopathic, the positive effects claimed by the supporters of profit sharing are validly achieved. In some cases, for example, the profit shares over several years average little more than one or perhaps two percent of the workers' regular salary in a particular year. But if one claims this effect to be a success of the system, it can only be of a most obscure nature. While there are still people in the medical profession who believe in the effectiveness of minimal doses, homoeopathy has no place in the social sciences.

In view of the obvious weaknesses of the position criticized here, the question arises as to how so many maintain it while ardently recommending profit sharing as a reform that is of general social interest and will serve as a means of improving the situation of workers. The explanation, I believe, lies in the continuous introduction of philanthropic and humanitarian ideas into the assessment of economic as well as social innovations. The expansion of participation in the assessment and resolution of social matters among educated people, while in itself positive, is unfortunately confined in large part to the ideals of Christian altruism. Whether they advocate them collectively or alone, those whose interest in economic innovations arises from motives of this sort instinctively propose them, if not from mercifulness and Christian love, then from goodwill and humaneness.

The measures that have real social meaning, however, correspond little to this sentiment. They in no way express goodwill and humaneness. On the contrary, if one considers their direct results for many individuals, such measures almost without exception bear the stamp of coldheartedness, inconsideration, and severity. I recall, for example, the obvious severity that for many accompanied the prohibition of child labor and the restrictions on working women. Does it not seem dreadful to prevent poor people from allowing their children to work to ease their suffering from hunger? But it is similar with almost everything that aims at social progress. We simply do not recognize it so easily. Even such measures, for example, as the shortening and strict regulation of the working day and the fixation of minimum wages are full of trials and tribulations for many of those, particularly the weak and less productive, who are affected. Indeed, this is the nature of the situation. For social action concerns itself not with the relationship of individual to individual, but rather exclusively with the relationship of class to class—the class of salaried workers to the class of owners, for example, or to the class of managers. In the assessment of the effects of social reforms, therefore, the higher justice and ethics of the welfare of the whole must assume priority over the welfare of individuals where their interests are at odds. The harsh necessity of social reforms must be recognized, for social progress is achieved only at the expense of the lives of those too weak and unable to come along.

All this, however, is for the most part very disagreeable to those whose personal participation in these economic matters is rooted in Christian, ethical, and humanitarian impulses. For this reason they become interested exclusively in those matters that evidence humaneness in their motivation and clear satisfaction in their effects. With the salary system considered here, both of these are evident as in almost no other economic reform. For freely giving a portion of one's wealth that could just as deservedly be kept to those less fortunate is equally as beneficent as it is pleasant for the recipients to receive something that could not have been demanded. But in assessing such a seemingly attractive situation, the critique can be too hastily ended.

In fact, the disagreement on the question of profit sharing illustrates the variance of entirely different perspectives on economic reforms in general. The philanthropic approach favors charity for all, that all might be happy and satisfied. The Christian approach favors crutches for the weak, so they can stumble along rather than collapse. The social approach offers protection for the strong, so that workers can assert their position and maintain resilience and vitality. It is only in the case of the latter perspective that the significance and effect of reform is evaluated in terms of its economic impact on the whole of society. Both of the other approaches propose laws and assess reforms in terms of how they affect individuals and their interactions with each other. The objective is thereby subordinated to moral norms.

My examination of profit sharing to this point expresses a fundamental rejection of this approach. It is not that I wish to deny this approach of any advantage or usefulness, but rather that I dispute its claims to any significant general impact in terms of the economic interests of workers. However, so that the following argument does not seem to be contradictory, let me refer expressly to the fact that my critical judgment is conditional and in no way sweeping. I reject this approach only because it is inadequate. For the salary system itself to which the profit share will be added contains no guarantee of constancy. There is thus nothing to prevent the subtraction of these profit quotas from the regular salaries. According to the logic of my assessment then, the reform could be judged differently if the premises for my negative judgment were themselves modified.

Without any particular reason for taking this eventuality into consideration, I had not considered the arrangement any further until recently. Occasionally I am asked why, in the optical workshop where so many reforms exist that benefit the personnel, profit sharing also has not yet been implemented? I have always answered that while this also may come with time, there are in the meantime more important things to do.

About two years ago, however, I was provided with the opportunity to form a new approach to the matter when I joined the preparatory work for the "Statutes of the Carl Zeiss Foundation," which had been established in the previous year. I was charged with the task of defining principles for the regulation of salaries, which had evolved in the optical workshop over time, in order to ensure their lasting recognition in the future. To my surprise, it became clear to me in the process that I, although not conscious of it myself, had become a supporter of profit sharing. It turned out that the standards for the establishment of the personnel's economic interest, which had until then merely been pursued practically and without legal obligation in the local enterprise, could only be transformed into legally binding regulations that guaranteed that in the future the workers' income would to some defined extent be dependent on the enterprise's net profits. The workers, in short, would receive a share of the profits.

The essential features of the salary structure that I am referring to here are characterized, in Title V of the "Statutes of the Carl Zeiss Foundation," sections 67 and 77, by the following regulations:

Every employee must be guaranteed a fixed salary, whether it be weekly or monthly, which serves as a minimum wage and is unaffected by whatever piece-rate arrangement exists.

This salary, once it has been received for a year or longer, can not be reduced again by the company, even if business is bad and work limited.

While the employer does retain the right in such a case to terminate the workers' contract, this is permissible only for those who have only been employed by the enterprise for a short time. All those employed for three years or longer can only be terminated, if they themselves are not to blame, due to particular consideration of the company's best interests (like, for example, a general reduction of operations). Further, those whose positions are terminated are entitled to a certain compensation. This must be at least a half-year's salary, but increases according to the duration of the worker's employment and, in the case of older workers, is even more than a full year's salary.

In the area of salary arrangements, these regulations contain a considerable restriction of the commercial contractual freedoms that apply in other cases. The obvious intention of this restriction, however, is both to provide a moment of stability for the salary system and to ensure the workforce of a certain minimum earnings on which they can depend for the most part, even in unprofitable years. For the alternative, which is either to continue paying the complete fixed salary or to terminate positions and pay the resulting compensation, places the employer under the heavy pressure of two extremes, so that in bad times at least the majority of the workforce can be maintained at a certain income level.

I had then to clearly ascertain the consequences which could result from such a reform if, once the legal regulations had been implemented, it in no way served as a corrective.

The framework of these regulations for the salary structure of an enterprise would have to be adapted in keeping with the average business trends for the industry concerned, so that over time a lasting and reasonable balance between the economic interests of both the personnel and the employers would result. If such an average period were followed by a period of depression, as long as the reform conforms to the intentions previously described the irrevocability of the previously established base salary would ensure that the personnel's final income would not sink below the levels determined for average business trends. This should be expected of employers. And employers will be in a position to afford this if the previously determined balance leaves them surplus enough to provide sufficient reserves that can then be added, if necessary, in the case of bad years.

Let us assume, however, that this first period of average profitability were followed by one of considerably increased activity for the entire industry concerned. What then? If this activity is not entirely transitory, the personnel's income at all levels must be increased until, if the favorable trend continues, it gradually reaches an appropriately high point. It is absolutely impossible for any enterprise to evade this consequence. To wish to withhold from the personnel a share of the obvious advantages produced by a profitable business trend would not only be a glaring injustice and be perceived as such, but would also be the type of action that, considering the increased demand in such times for efficient workers, places the employer in direct danger of losing his most important assets just when they are most pressingly needed.

If the growth of income necessarily assumes the form of salary increases in such times, the previously described regulations would operate like a wheel with a mechanism built in to allow forward, but no backward motion. And if the period of economic upswing is followed by a period of lasting depression, the enterprise would necessarily remain burdened with a payroll that corresponds not to an average, but rather to an extraordinarily favorable economic situation. And in this way even a well-consolidated company could easily become bankrupt.

There is then only one way of implementing the regulations for salary adjustment and avoiding these aforementioned consequences. The workers' actual income must be separated into two components. The first of these is the salary. It should be immutable and must not be subordinated to considerations of economic boom or profitability. Rather, this salary must be determined according to the enterprise's normal, or average economic conditions. With this salary serving as the cornerstone, the other component must conform to the company's upswings and provide the personnel with a share in the advantages resulting from increased profitability.

This reasoning leads us then to a profit-sharing arrangement where the regular salary is supplemented by a quota that is based on net profits. For a company's net profit is the single objective measure of their favorable or less favorable financial situation. As described in Section 98 of the aforementioned statutes, the nature of this profit share is clearly stipulated. A supplemental percentage is allocated accordingly at the conclusion of each business year and added throughout the year to the wages and salaries of all employees. Each employee's share is determined according to the actual wage or salary for the previous year. Only the members of the company's board of directors, the very people in whose hands the profit quota is actually determined, are excluded from the profit shares, in order to maintain the appearance of impartiality.

In circumstances like those described here and implemented last year in local optical shops, profit sharing assumes an entirely different connection to workers' economic interests than those ascribed by the other approaches to profit sharing that I have criticized. In good years the profit share should in no way provide the workers with more than they would otherwise receive. The salary plus the profit share should result in the same amount that would, without any innovations, have been provided by the salary alone. The reform, however, is an important, although indirect improvement of the economic situation of the workers. For it makes allowance for bad years, when there is no talk of profit quotas. As already explained, it produces a fixed salary structure that insures the workers against seeing their earnings drop below a certain level when times are bad. According to this approach, profit sharing is understood as an indispensable, but supplementary part of a determinate salary system, which provides a regular, minimum salary even in unprofitable times. This then will preclude the possibility that the great number of existences who rise on the wave of upswings in economic activity will ebb sporadically back into the proletariat.

In the economic structure of the optical workshops there are two columns that support the important interests of the workforce. The one is a securely fixed salary structure, which obligates the employer to pay a certain minimum salary, even in economically unprofitable periods. The other is the financial vitality of the enterprise, on which the implementation of the salary structure depends. As long as both of these columns hold up, the workforce should, it is hoped, have a firm footing even in bad times and the municipality in Jena will be permanently spared the burdens that have in other cases grown out of the development of large industry. So that these two columns hold together, they must be firmly connected with a particular bolt. This is the profit quota, which in good times makes a portion of the workers' income dependent on the company's financial fluctuations. Visible only from outside, this bolt is adorned with a rose, signifying the happiness the profit quotas evoke from all involved. What is most important, however, is not this rose, but the bolt itself.

Translated by Daniel Slager

Joseph von Fraunhofer

Of the Refractive and the Dispersive Power of Glass

It would be most advantageous if one could measure for every kind of glass the dispersion for every color; but the different colors in the spectrum have no definite limits, and so this cannot be determined immediately from the color-image. The uncertainty is so great that the experiments are useless. It could be done more exactly if colored pieces of glass or colored liquids could be found which would transmit light of only one color—e.g., one which transmitted only blue, another only red, etc.; but I have not been so fortunate as to discover any such substances. With all I tried, the white light which was transmitted was broken up into all colors, the only difference being that the particular color which the glass or the liquid had was the strongest in the spectrum. Colored flames, also, which are obtained by the combustion of alcohol, sulphur, etc., do not give in their spectra homogeneous light which corresponds to their color; yet with these, as well as with oil and tallow light, and in general with light of all flames, I found in the spectra a bright, sharply defined streak in the region between the red and the green, which is in exactly the same position in all the spectra, and which will be most useful in what follows. This bright band appears to be formed by rays which are not dispersed further by the prism, and are therefore homogeneous. There is a similar streak in the green, which is, however, not so well defined and is much more feeble, so that in some cases it is recognized with difficulty; on this account it cannot be of much service.

In order to determine more accurately the refraction of the different colored beams, partly also to see if the action of the refracting medium was the same on sunlight as on artificial light, I devised an apparatus which could be used with sunlight, just as the one before described was with lamplight. This was soon seen to be superfluous.

In the window-shutter of a darkened room I made a narrow opening—about 15 seconds broad and 36 minutes high—and through this I allowed sunlight to fall on a prism of flint-glass which stood upon the theodolite described before. The theodolite was 24 feet from the window, and the angle of the prism was about 60 degrees. The prism was so placed in front of the objective of the theodolite-telescope that the angle of incidence of the light was equal to the angle at which the beam emerged. I wished to see if in the color-image from sunlight there was a bright band similar to that observed in the color-image of lamplight. But instead of this I saw with the telescope an almost countless number of strong and weak vertical lines, which are, however, darker than the rest of the color-image; some appeared to be almost perfectly black. If the prism was turned so as to increase the angle of incidence, these lines vanished; they disappear also if the angle of incidence is made smaller. For increased angle of incidence, however, these lines become visible again if the telescope is made shorter; while, for a smaller angle of incidence, the eye-piece must be drawn out considerably in order to make the lines reappear. If the eye-piece was so placed that the lines in the red portion of the color-image could be plainly seen, then, in order to see the lines in the violet portion, it must be pushed in slightly. If the opening through which the light entered was made broader, the fine lines ceased to be clearly seen, and vanished entirely if the opening was made 40 seconds wide. If the opening was made 1 minute wide, even the broad lines could not be seen plainly. The distances apart of the lines, and all their relations to each other, remained unchanged, both when the width of the opening in the window-shutter was altered and when the distance of the theodolite from the opening was changed. The prism could be of any kind of refractive material, and its angle might be large or small; yet the lines remained always visible, and only in proportion to the size of the color-image did they become stronger or weaker, and therefore were observed more easily or with more difficulty.

The relations of these lines and streaks among themselves appeared to be the same with every refracting substance; so that, for instance, one particular band is found in every case only in the blue; another is found only in the red; and one can, therefore, at once recognize which line he is observing. These lines can be recognized also in the spectra formed by both the ordinary and the extraordinary rays of Iceland spar. The strongest lines do not in any way mark the limits of the various colors; there is almost always the same color on both sides of a line, and the passage from one color into another cannot be noted.

With reference to these lines, the color-image is as shown on page 269 (Fig. 5). It is, however, impossible to show on this scale all the lines and their intensities. (The red end of the color-image is in the neighborhood of A; the violet end is near I.) It is, however, impossible to set a definite limit at either end, although it is easier at the red than at the violet. Direct sunlight, or sunlight reflected by a mirror, seems to have its limits, on the one hand, somewhere between G and H; on the other, at B; yet with sunlight of great intensity the color-image becomes half again as long. In order, however to see this great spreading-out of the spectrum, the light from the space between C and G must be prevented from entering the eye, because the impression which the light from the extremities of the color-image makes upon the eye is very weak, and is destroyed by the rest of the light. At A there is easily recognized a sharply defined line; yet this is not the limit of the red color, for it proceeds much beyond. At *a* there are heaped together many lines which form a band; B is sharply defined and is of noticeable thickness. In the space between B and C there can be counted 9 very fine, sharply defined lines. The line C is of considerable strength, and, like B, is very black. In the space between C and D there can be counted 30 very fine lines; but these (with two exceptions), like those between B and C, can be plainly seen only with strong magnification or with prisms which have great dispersion; they are, moreover, very sharply defined. D consists of two strong lines which are separated by a bright line. Between D and E there can be counted some 84 lines of varying intensities. E itself consists of several lines, of which the one in the middle is somewhat stronger than the rest. Between E and *b* are about 24 lines. At *b* there are 3 very strong lines, two of which are separated by only a narrow bright line; they are among the strongest lines in the spectrum. In the space between *b* and F there can be counted about 52 lines; F is fairly strong. Between F and G there are about 185 lines of different strengths. At G there are massed together many lines, among which several are distinguished by their intensity. In the space between G and H there are about 190 lines, whose intensities differ greatly. The two bands at H are most remarkable; they are almost exactly equal, and each consists of many lines; in the middle of each there is a strong line which is very black. From H to I the lines are equally numerous. In the space between B and H there can be counted, therefore, about 574 lines, of which only the strong ones appear on the drawing. The distances apart of the strongest lines were measured by the theodolite and transferred according to scale directly to the drawing; the weak lines, however, were drawn in, without exact measurement, simply as they were seen in the color-image.

I have convinced myself by many experiments and by varying the methods that these lines and bands are due to the nature of sunlight, and do not arise from diffraction, illusion, etc. If light from a lamp is allowed to pass through the same narrow opening in the window-shutter, none of these lines are observed, only the bright line R [*referred to before*], which, however, comes exactly in the same place as the line D (Fig. 5), so that the indices of refraction of the rays D and R are the same. The reason why the lines fade away, or even entirely vanish, when the opening at the window is made too wide is not difficult to give. The stronger lines have a width of from five to ten seconds; so, if the opening of the window is not so narrow that the light which passes through can be regarded as belonging to one ray, or if the angular width of the opening is much more than that of the line, the image of one and the same line is repeated several times side by side, and consequently becomes indistinct, or vanishes entirely if the opening is made too wide. The reason why the lines and bands are not seen when the prism is turned, unless the telescope is made shorter or longer, will be seen from the following considerations:

It is only when rays fall upon a prism in such a way that the angle of incidence equals that of emergence that they proceed, so far as divergence is concerned, just as they fall upon the prism; if the angle of incidence is greater, the rays, after refraction through the prism, diverge from a more remote point; if the angle is smaller, the rays diverge from a nearer point.

The reason is that the rays which pass through near the edge of the prism have a shorter path through the prism to traverse than those which pass through farther from the edge. This does not change, it is true, the angle of the refracted rays; but the sides of the triangle for the emerging rays become greater in the one case, less in the other. This difference should vanish when the rays fall upon the prism parallel to each other which is in accord with experiment. Since the violet rays through the objective of the theodolite telescope have a shorter focal length than the red rays, it is evident why the eye-piece must be displaced in order to see plainly the lines in the different colors.

Since the lines and bands in the color-image have only a very small width, it is evident that the apparatus must be most perfect in order to avoid all aberrations which could make the lines indistinct or entirely scatter them. The faces of the prism must therefore be perfectly plane. The glass to be used in such prisms should be entirely free from waves and streaks; with English flint-glass, which is never free from streaks, only the stronger lines are seen. Common glass and English crown-glass contain many streaks, even if they are not visible to the naked eye. If one does not possess a prism of perfect flint-glass, it is better to choose a fluid which has a great dispersive power—e.g., aniseed oil—in order to see the lines; yet in this case the prismatic vessel must have faces which are perfectly plane parallel. With all prisms the faces should make an angle of 90 degrees, or nearly so, with the base; this must be placed horizontal, in front of the telescope, if the axis of the latter is horizontal. The narrow opening through which the light enters must be exactly vertical, etc. It is easy to understand why the lines become indistinct if one or the other of these precautions is neglected.

Since the lines and bands are seen in the color-image of every refracting medium of uniform density, I have used them in order to measure the refraction of a medium for each colored ray; and this could be done with great accuracy, because the majority of the lines are sharply defined. Since with refracting media which have feeble dispersion or with prisms of small angles it is only with difficulty that the fine lines can be recognized even with strong magnification, I selected in these experiments, for all refracting media, the stronger lines, viz., B, C, D E, F, G, and H. The lines at *b* I did not take, because it is too near F; and I tried to come more in the middle between D and F. Since the eye-piece must be displaced in order to see distinctly the lines in the different colors, no large arcs such as BH could be measured, *only the small ones* such as BC, CD, etc.

On seeing the number of lines and bands in the spectrum of sunlight, one can perhaps with difficulty avoid the conjecture that diffraction at the narrow opening in the window-shutter has something to do with these lines, although the experiments which have been described do not in the least indicate this, but, on the contrary, refute it. Partly in order to be perfectly sure on this point, partly also in order to make further observations, I changed the experiment in the following manner:

If sunlight coming from a small *round* opening, 15 seconds in diameter, in the window-shutter is allowed to fall upon a prism placed in front of the theodolite telescope, it is clear that the color-image which is seen through the telescope can have only an inappreciable width, and therefore will form only a line; in a colored line, however, no fine cross-lines can be seen. In order to see the many lines in this color-image, all that is necessary is to make the spectrum broader without altering its length in the least. I accomplished this by placing against the objective a piece of glass which was plane on one side and curved on the other, so as to be a portion of a cylinder of large diameter. The axis of the cylinder was placed parallel to the base of the prism; consequently, the length of the spectrum could not be changed, and only its breadth was increased. With this arrangement I recognized again in the spectrum all the lines exactly as they are seen when the light comes through a long, narrow opening.

I applied this form of apparatus at night-time to observe Venus directly, *without making the light pass through a small opening;* and I discovered in the spectrum of this light the same lines as those which appear in sunlight. Since, however, the light from Venus is feeble in comparison with sunlight reflected from a mirror, the intensity of the violet and the extreme red rays are very weak; and on this account even the stronger lines in both these colors are recognized only with difficulty, but in the other colors they are very easily distinguished. I have seen the lines D, E, *b*, F perfectly defined (Fig. 5), and have even recognized that *b* consists of two lines, one weak and one strong; but the fact that the stronger one itself consists of two I could not verify owing to lack of light. For the same reason the other finer lines could not be distinguished satisfactorily.

I have convinced myself by an approximate measurement of the arc DE and EF that the light from Venus is in this respect of the same nature as sunlight.

With this same apparatus I made observations also on the light of some fixed stars of the first magnitude. Since, however, the light of these stars is much weaker than that of Venus, it is natural that the brightness of the spectrum should be much less. In spite of this I have seen with certainty in the spectrum of Sirius three broad bands which appear to have no connection with those of sunlight; one of these bands is in the green, two are in the blue. In the spectra of other fixed stars of the first magnitude one can recognize bands; yet these stars, with respect to these bands, seem to differ among themselves. Sine the objective of the telescope has an aperture of only 13 lines,* it is clear that these observations can be repeated with much greater accuracy. I intend to repeat them with suitable alterations, and with a larger objective, in order to induce, perhaps, some skilled investigator to continue the experiments. Such a continuation is all the more to be desired, because the experiments would serve at the same time for the accurate comparison of the refraction of the light of the fixed stars with that of sunlight.

The light of electricity is, with respect to these lines and bands, markedly different from sunlight, and also from the light of flames. Several lines are found in the spectrum of this light; some are very bright, and among these one in the green is almost dazzlingly bright in comparison with the rest of the spectrum. There is another line in the orange which is not quite so bright; it appears to have the same color as the bright line in the spectrum of lamplight. If, however, the angle of refraction is measured, it is found that its light is refracted much more—about as much as the yellow rays of lamplight. Near the red end of the spectrum there is a line which is not very bright; its light is refracted, so far as I could be sure, exactly the same as that of the bright line of lamplight. In the rest of the spectrum four other lines can be recognized easily.

If lamplight is allowed to pass through a very narrow opening of 15 to 30 seconds' width and then to fall upon a strongly dispersive prism placed in front of a telescope, it is seen that the reddish-yellow bright line of this spectrum consists of two very fine bright lines which in intensity and distance apart are like the two dark

---

*1 centimetre equals 4.43296 lines.

lines D (Fig. 5). But, regardless of the width of the slit, if the point of the flame and the lower blue end are covered, and so only the brightest portion of the flame exposed, the reddish-yellow lines of the spectrum appear less bright, and therefore are recognized with more difficulty. These lines, consequently, seem to be formed mainly by the light from the ends of the flame, especially by that from the lower one.

In the spectrum of the light caused by the combustion of hydrogen and alcohol, the reddish-green line is very bright in comparison with the other portions. When sulphur is burned it is seen with great difficulty.

I intend to repeat these experiments which have reference to the perfecting of achromatic telescopes, using a new instrument by means of which I hope to obtain at least twice the accuracy. I shall be able also to make new experiments with this instrument for which my present one is not adapted, and which will be of interest perhaps for practical optics.

In all my experiments I could, owing to lack of time, pay attention to only those matters which appeared to have a bearing upon practical optics. I could either not touch other questions, or at most not follow them very far. Since the path thus traced in optical experiments seems to promise to lead to interesting results, it is greatly to be desired that skilled investigators should devote attention to it.

Translated by J. S. Ames

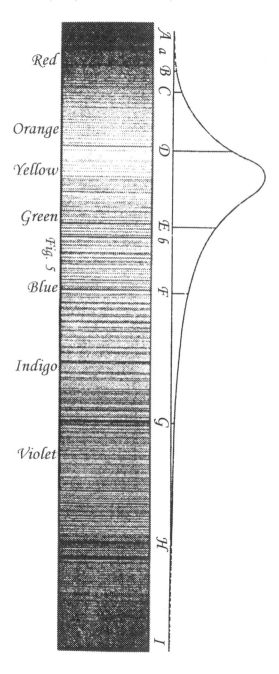

Gottfried Daimler

On the Novelty of My Patent Number 28022: A Reply

The Deutz Gas Engine Works, by contesting with their petition from February 7 of this year the novelty of my ignition process protected by Patent Number 28022, and by maintaining that this process does not constitute in any way a new invention, gives this revocatory action in its very first sentence a thoroughly incorrect and untenable foundation with the inexplicable, completely erroneous allegation that my Patent Claim 1 represents nothing but the mere description of a physical phenomenon. Deutz has completely overlooked that Claim 1 does not cover the already known compression phenomenon in and of itself, but rather the process by which the compression of the mixture charge (compression which at the time the motor is started is not sufficient to bring about ignition) occurs immediately in a hot, enclosed space which in the manner described in the patent provides the impulse for igniting the charge in the very first compression stroke.

Accordingly, Patent Claim 1 does not represent the verification of a physical fact, but contains the description of a new process for the free, untimed ignition of compressed mixture charges, detailing thereby the means necessary for bringing about this process.

Claim 2 covers the particular part, conceived as and fashioned into an ignition cap, of the hot, enclosed compression chamber referred to in Claim 1, with the important new feature that this ignition cap remains in continuous, open contact with the combustible mixture, as elaborated in the description of my novel ignition process covered by Patent Number 28022.

The entire process covered by Claims 1 and 2 constitutes the object of my patent and the essence of my invention.

As far as this matter is concerned, the Imperial Patent Office has already determined with sufficient clarity that the patent covering my ignition process, specifically the continuously open ignition cap of Claim 2, shall together with Claim 1 retain its validity unchanged.

Deutz's Claim 2 of my Patent Number 28022 does not cover an ignition cap as such, it covers the ignition cap whose interior remains in continuous, open contact with the combustion chamber (cf. description), and which is heated from the outside long enough (cf. description) for self-ignition to take place. Consequently, the continuously open ignition cap can be used—as long as no self-ignitions occur—whenever one needs it or wants to use it for ignition purposes.

In practice as well, the chief benefit of the process protected by my Patent Number 28022 has been found to lie in the use of the ignition cap that remains in open contact with the compression chamber, as per Claim 2. This previously unpracticed and previously unknown procedure of permanent ignition at glow zones without slide valves is the basis of a new type of high-speed gas and gasoline engine, which has by virtue of this ignition process been invented and brought to life; even with low-speed engines of all strengths and sizes, my ignition method maintains its superiority and its inherent advantage over the ignition forms otherwise used.

I have never maintained that Claim 2 protected the ignition cap as such. This claim does, however, protect literally and expressly the ignition cap that remains in continuous open contact with the combustible mixture in the compression chamber, and likewise protects the hot zone where start-up and continued operation take place without timed ignition.

Furthermore, the initiators of the revocatory action should have realized from the start that they could not contest the novelty of my invention as per Patent Number 28022 by simply pointing out that compression theory on the one hand and glow-tube ignition on the other were already common knowledge.

Even if my method is based on the application of commonly known physical facts, Deutz, in emphasizing this circumstance, is completely overlooking the fact that the utilization of commonly known means to fulfill a new technical purpose presents no hindrance to patentability according to patent law. Particularly in regard to this patent, the gentlemen at Deutz may well have come to the realization that the mere knowledge of available means that are capable of bringing about a certain new effect when applied in the appropriate, previously unknown manner, does not by itself suffice to actually bring about this effect or fulfill the intended purpose. This is the very task of the inventor who comes up with the new application. According to the well-known rule, it is not the discoverer of scientific premises that might serve as the foundation for new inventions, nor the dabbler who breaks ground with fruitless attempts and unpractical experiments who are entitled to the protection afforded by the patent and by the notion of intellectual property. Only the true inventor, who teaches and demonstrates new practical applications by coming up with commercially practicable designs, has a legitimate claim to such protection.

My process, protected by Patent Number 28022, meets these requirements in every respect.

Success is always the best criterion for judging the practicability and the quality of a new invention or process, particularly when such success can be demonstrated to be as unquestionable and lasting as it is in the case of my invention.

At first, even experts were highly skeptical of the efficiency and the utility of my new ignition process. Only when the eminent advantages of my new, patented ignition method had been established by my demonstration of practical applications and concrete designs did subsequent inventors come to accept the significance of my new process. They thought they could simply take possession of my invention by claiming that the principles upon which it was based were common knowledge, making repeated reference to Beau de Rochas as the theoretician of abstract compression ignition (whose simplistic theory could never be used as the basis for a commercially practicable or even workable engine), and citing other, older patent documents that described the use of glow tubes for ignition purposes. None of these predecessors' methods, however, correspond to my perfected process protected by Patent Number 28022. These predecessors were never able to come up with a commercially practicable means of manufacturing a good engine, for the simple reason that the practical application of their process was inadequate in light of this goal.

This is particularly true of Beau de Rochas, who from the very beginning has been convinced that the only way to bring about ignition is through compression, as he suggests in his treatise on thermodynamics, and who can only think of activating an engine by means of ignition through mere compression, which he wants to bring about with the help of a steam engine, no less. . . . No, only my invention, after countless attempts, of the process combining compression with an externally heated glow zone—which functions in a state of continuous, open contact with the compression chamber in such a way that the charge is ignited under rapid compression only at the end of the compression cycle, as described in my Patent Number 28022—has made possible the creation of a new type of gas and gasoline engine, known as the Daimler engine, with all of its inherent advantages.

This invention has led to the attainment of a new, technically and commercially practicable goal, a goal that until now no one has even thought to set; namely, the construction of gas and gasoline engines with free, untimed compression ignition, a feature that permits an almost unlimited engine speed while insuring an absolutely safe, uniform operation, even at the highest speeds. Success has taken the form of a new type of engine, unexcelled in performance, simplicity, and economy of manufacture. Because of its extreme compactness of form, uncommon simplicity of construction, economy of moving parts, the latter having been particularly augmented by my newly introduced cam plate timing (protected by Patent Number 28243), and correspondingly low net weight, this engine is most particularly suitable for providing even the smallest of vehicles with a convenient, economical source of power. This has led to the creation of an entire new industry: that of motor-coach vehicles, motorcycles, motorized rail inspection cars, motorized tramways, motorized fire engines, motorized pleasure and utility boats, and other such objects, even the smallest of which, most importantly, can be equipped without a significant increase in load for motorized operation.

Automotive vehicles, equipped in this way with small, powerful engines, were previously unknown: in this respect, too, my claim to priority can be upheld, since my motor-coach vehicles and motor boats were introduced to the public as early as 1885 and 1886, with the other motorized vehicles mentioned above following soon thereafter—only to be quickly copied in a slapdash fashion by my competitors, I might add.

Thus, if the patents (Clayton Number 2202, Watson Number 4608, Watson Number 1723) appealed to by Deutz in their revocatory action against me had made it possible to create without any further inventive thought—i.e., without the new process of combined compression ignition covered by my Patent Number 28022—an engine of the same quality and efficiency as mine, then it would seem rather strange that the initiators of this revocatory action have neglected until now, that is, for the past ten years, the opportunity to utilize these advantages, despite the purported fact that the latter are common knowledge. It would appear that the gentlemen at Deutz (and a host of other imitators as well), who had been unaware of the advantages of my new ignition method until they learned of my practical success, cannot come up with anything better than to usurp my invention without cost to themselves, with the help of their revocatory action based on specious arguments; to reap where they have not sown, while I, despite the years I have spent conducting experiments at great sacrifice to myself, despite the hundreds of thousands of marks I have spent on prototypes of new products, find myself about to be robbed of the sacrifices I have made thus far and even of my honor as an inventor, all because of Deutz's revocatory action, built up on the flimsiest of pretexts and initiated at such a late date.

If Deutz or anyone else for their part believes that my invention Number 28022 consists in nothing more than the simple omission of the slide valve and the direct attachment of the ignition tube, and that in this way the closed ignition can be made into a practicable open ignition, as it might appear at first glance to the uninitiated, then they are vastly mistaken.

If others had been able to do anything with the free, untimed, more or less independently operating ignition, and had been able to come up with a workable design for it, the invention would have been made long before me: Watson, Clayton, and perhaps even Deutz would already have built this motor and brought it onto the market. Before me, however, nothing has been done along these lines.

It has been a long road, requiring endless experimentation and the unrelenting, single-minded efforts of the experienced engineer to keep from losing heart in the face of the completely discouraging results to which these experiments with free ignition at first gave rise: the dangerous premature ignitions that occurred again and again, that during the expansion stroke and the compression stroke before dead center forced the flywheel backwards instead of driving it forwards, tearing the starter crank out of the experimenter's hand as though by electrical shock and making the goal of free self-ignition seem unattainable. Resolutely continuing the experiments, varying the forms and dimensions of the combustion chamber, varying the mixture charge, etc., led eventually to the production of acceptable diagrams, then finally to good, consistent ones. The practicability of my untimed ignition was thus positively established, the goal I had set for myself was reached.

Considering the extremely high speeds at which these processes took place, and since it was not possible to observe them by putting myself inside the combustion chamber, all I could do was to keep working and keep experimenting, since no theory explaining such phenomena had yet been formulated, and not even the most learned professor could be of any help.

After I have thus taken practice beyond theory, after I have finally hit the nail on the head and created with these engines the foundation for a brand new industry, I am all the more appalled at the attacks I have been receiving, first from others, and now from the Deutz Gas Engine Works—attacks whose purpose is to rob me of my work as an inventor and the protection of my patent.

I must again point out that as insignificant as my invention may appear at first glance, it has indeed assumed the greatest import: it constituted the foundation not only for the first high-speed gas engine, but for the modern high-performance gasoline engine as well, which in every resect, including the lowered manufacturing costs and simplified construction made possible by my process, are unthinkable without my invention. This invention represents a true, fundamental advance in the construction of gas engines; the new Daimler engine constitutes a new, independent member in this nascent stage of gas and gasoline engine construction. In performance, the Daimler engine compares to the "Otto engine" and the other previously known systems (the latter, however, can for the most part always be placed in a category with the Deutz engine) in the same way as the repeating rifle does to the old flintlock, in which the spark had to be introduced from the outside and the individual firings could only be brought about very slowly. Not the loading procedure, but the ignition was always the weak spot of the explosion engine; my permanent ignition brought about the perfect solution to this problem.

No foreign sponsors gave me the impetus for my invention; it came about through my single-minded efforts, for just as the development of gas and gasoline engines has been characterized by well-defined phases, whereby Lenoir's gas engine was followed by Langen's and Otto's atmospheric gas engine, and this by the so-called " O t t o engine," my new, high-speed gas and gasoline engine must now be regarded as yet another advance of universal import for the construction of gas and gasoline engines. In particular, it was my oil engine that was built according to Patent Number 28022, the first engine that solved the problem of the efficient use of liquid hydrocarbons, doing so in the simplest manner and solving thereby the problem of creating workable, first-class gasoline engines. This engine gave rise to the gasoline engine industry in its imitating, bandwagon-jumping entirety. The first unscrupulous step in this direction after filing of my patents was made by the honorable Mr. Emil Captaine, who then had the audacity to refer to himself thereafter as "The Watt of Gasoline Motors."

I cannot suppress the remark, particularly since the present attack is coming from Deutz, that this very establishment has to no small degree my assistance as technical director to thank for its rapid expansion and for the good reputation of its products. Under my direction from 1872 to 1882, the small shop that it was became a systematically equipped, well-organized model factory, an establishment of world renown. When I arrived, all they were making was a somewhat outdated version of the Langen & Otto atmospheric gas engine; under my direction, the first directly operating 1-horsepower gas engine and the world's first 100-horsepower gas compression engine were designed and built. Only thanks to my modesty was the latter named exclusively after Otto.

The gentlemen at Deutz are certainly aware that while the first atmospheric engine had previously been described and designed by Meatucci, Barsanti, and others, it did not attain recognition and begin to benefit industry until a workable model was built by Langen and Otto. Furthermore, the gentlemen at Deutz know quite well that despite the many old English patents and despite the Beau de Rochas paper from 1860 dug up by Körting, Deutz did not develop the truly workable, so-called Otto engine until 1876, and then only after endless experiments, tests, and studies carried out by Deutz at great expense. They must also be aware that this engine did not exist before the time mentioned above; since that time, it is known and used in every nation of the earth.

Neither is it likely that the purported prior inventors named in the revocatory action, Watson, Clayton, etc., etc., would have neglected to contest my patent if they themselves had not recognized the autonomy and the novelty of my invention, qualities that have in fact been confirmed by thorough testing of all of its decisive characteristics. Watson as well as Clayton must doubtlessly have been convinced that my invention neither falls within the bounds of nor does it infringe upon their claims.

Clayton, who has a particular stake in this matter, was so little concerned about a violation of or an infringement upon his own patents that in his letter from January 29, 1892, he expressed his desire to take over production and marketing of my engines in England. He would not have been able to make such an offer if he were not convinced of the autonomy of my engines and their superiority to his models.

Finally, I should like to criticize the tactics employed by the party initiating the revocatory action by mentioning that in a letter from February of this year, they demanded the right to free use of Patent No. 28022, threatening at the same time to initiate revocatory action if their demand was not met forthwith.

The Daimler Motor Company, as holder of my patents, was naturally well within their rights when they turned down this completely unmotivated request from the Deutz Gas Engine Works.

It can be readily inferred from the previous demand made by the party initiating the revocatory action, that the rights to free use of my patent be confirmed in writing, that this party recognizes the rightful existence of the patent. As I have thoroughly demonstrated, the revocatory action is based on nothing but specious pretexts. The party initiating it has only gradually, over the course of time—i.e., only when they found themselves confronted with my success—come to realize the import of my invention. This was not always the case, for it is a fact that the same gentleman whose signature appears on the revocatory action had referred to the matter at an earlier time, as I offered my patented process to the Deutz Gas Engine Works so that they could exploit and market it, as "cabbage," while now they are scrambling for it with ardent desire.

Allow me then to submit to the Imperial Patent Office with all due respect the request that I be protected in my rights as the actual inventor, and that the revocatory action be ruled upon accordingly.

Cannstat, April 1894

Translated by Daniel Theisen

Werner von Siemens

Science, Technology, and Organization

The war of 1866 had removed the obstacles that opposed the longed-for unity of Germany, and had at the same time restored internal peace in Prussia. A new support was thereby given to the idea of nationhood, and the hitherto vague, as it were tentative, efforts of German patriots now obtained a firm foundation and definite direction. It is true, the Main boundary still divided Germany into a Northern and a Southern half, but no one doubted that its removal was only a question of time, if it was not rigidly fixed by external force. That France would make that attempt appeared certain, but there was a growing confidence that Germany would successfully stand this trial also. As a consequence of this great revolution of popular sentiment there resulted the general endeavor to consolidate quickly what had been attained, to strengthen the feeling of solidarity of North and South despite the Main boundary and to prepare for the coming struggle.

This buoyant feeling was evidenced by increased activity in all departments of life, nor did it fail to react on our business affairs. Magneto-electric mine-exploders, electric range-finders, electric apparatus for steering unmanned boats, furnished with explosives, against hostile ships, as well as numerous improvements of military telegraphy, were the offspring of this stirring time.

I will here only give a detailed account of a nonmilitary invention of this time, as it has become the foundation of a new and important branch of industry, and has exerted and still continues to exert a stimulating and transforming influence in all departments of the industrial arts; I refer to the invention of the dynamo-electric machine.

As early as the autumn of 1866, when I was intent on perfecting electric exploding apparatus with the help of my cylindrical inductor, the question occupied my mind, whether it would not be possible by suitable employment of the so-called extra-current, to intensify considerably the induction-current. It became clear to me that an electromagnetic machine, whose working power is very much enfeebled by the induced currents arising in its coils, because these induced currents considerably diminish the energy of the galvanic battery, might conversely strengthen the power of the latter, if it were forcibly turned in the opposite direction by an external force. This could not fail to be the case, because the direction of the induced currents was at the same time reversed by the reversed movement. In fact, experiments confirmed this theory, and it appeared that there always remains sufficient magnetism in the fixed electro-magnets of a suitably contrived electromagnetic machine to produce the most surprising effects by gradually strengthening the current generated by the reversed rotation.

This was the discovery and first application of the dynamo-electric principle underlying all dynamo-electric machines. The first problem, which was thereby practically solved, was the construction of an effective electric exploding apparatus without steel magnets, and such exploding apparatus is still in general use at the present day. The Berlin physicists, among them Magnus, Dove, Ries, Du Bois-Reymond, were extremely surprised when I laid before them in December 1866 such an exploding inductor, and showed that a small electromagnetic machine without battery and permanent magnets, which could be turned in one direction without effort and with any velocity, offered an almost insuperable resistance when turned in the opposite direction, and at the same time produced an electric current of such strength, that its wire-coils became quickly heated. Professor Magnus immediately offered to lay a description of my invention before the Berlin Academy of Sciences, but, on account of the Christmas holidays, this could only be done in the following year, on January 17, 1867.

The priority of my application of the dynamo-electric principle was afterwards impugned in various quarters, when its enormous importance came to be seen during its further development. At first, Professor Wheatstone was almost universally recognized in

England as simultaneous inventor, because at a sitting of the Royal Society on the February 15, 1867, at which my brother William produced my apparatus, he immediately exhibited a similar apparatus, which was only distinguishable from mine by the wire-coils of the fixed electromagnet being differently disposed in their relation to those of the rotating cylindrical magnet. Next, Mr. Varley came forward with the assertion, that already in the early part of the autumn of 1866 he had given orders to a mechanician for just such an apparatus, and also subsequently handed in a "provisional specification" of the same. My first complete theoretical establishment of the principle in the printed Transactions of the Berlin Academy, and its previous practical elucidation, have however finally been taken to be decisive in my favor. The name given by me to the apparatus, "dynamo-electric machine," has also become general, although frequently corrupted in practice into "the dynamo."

Already in my communication to the Berlin Academy, I had pointed out that the industrial arts were now in possession of appliances capable of producing electric current of any desired tension and strength by the expenditure of energy, and that this would prove of great importance for many of its branches. In fact large machines of the kind were immediately constructed by my firm, one of which was exhibited at the Paris Universal Exhibition of 1867, whilst a second was employed in the summer of the same year by the military authorities for electric lighting experiments in Berlin. These experiments indeed proved quite satisfactory, with the drawback, however, that the wire-coils of the armatures rapidly became so hot, that the electric light produced could only be allowed without interruption for a short time. The machine exhibited in Paris was never actually put to the test, as there were no appliances for the transmission of power in the space allotted to my firm, and the jury, to which I myself belonged, did not subject the exhibits of their members, which were "*hors concours,*" to any trial. All the greater was the sensation caused by an imitation of my machine exhibited by an English mechanician, which produced from time to time a small electric light. It was considered sufficient recognition that the order of the Legion of Honor was awarded to me at the close of the exhibition.

When at a later time the dynamo machine, after considerable improvement, especially by the introduction of Pacinotti's ring and Hefner's coiling system, had received the most extensive application in practice, and both mathematicians and engineers had developed its theory, it seemed almost self-evident and hardly to be called an invention, that one should arrive at the dynamo-electric machine by merely reversing the rotation of an electromagnetic machine. Against this it may be said that the most obvious inventions, of primary importance, are commonly made very late, and in the most round-about way. For the rest it would not have been easy to have arrived by accident at the discovery of the dynamo-electric principle, because electromagnetic machines only "excite," i.e., continuously and spontaneously strengthen their electromagnetism, on reversing the rotation, when their dimensions and the disposition of the coils are perfectly correct.

To this period also belongs my invention of the alcoholmeter, which very successfully solved an extremely difficult problem, and accordingly excited much attention at the time. The problem consisted in constructing an apparatus to register continuously and automatically the quantity of absolute alcohol contained in the spirit flowing through it. My apparatus solved this problem so completely, that it indicated the quantity of alcohol, reduced to the customary normal temperature, as accurately as could be determined by the most exact scientific measurements. The Russian Government has employed this apparatus for almost a quarter of a century in levying the high tax which is imposed on the production of spirit, and many other European states have also subsequently adopted it for the same purpose. Apart from a few important practical improvements due to my cousin Louis Siemens, the apparatus is still supplied in the original form as a regular article of manufacture by a factory specially erected for the purpose in Charlottenburg. No imitation has hitherto been successful anywhere, although the apparatus is unprotected by a patent.

The dimensions which the firm of Siemens and Halske gradually attained naturally required a corresponding organization of the management and the help of able technical and administrative assistants. The friend of my youth, William Meyer, who filled the post of chief engineer and confidential clerk from the year 1855, had, by his considerable organizing talent, not only rendered valuable service to the Berlin firm, but also to its branches in London, St. Petersburg, and Vienna. Unfortunately he fell ill of a serious disorder after eleven years in the business, and died after prolonged sickness, deeply lamented by me as a personal friend and faithful partner.

Not long afterward, in the year 1868—my old friend and partner Halske retired from the firm. The favorable development of the business—this will hardly appear credible to many at first sight—was the determining reason for his taking this step. The explanation lies in Halske's singularly constituted nature. He took great pleasure in the faultless productions of his clever hand, as well as in everything that he could entirely overlook and control. Our common activity was thoroughly satisfactory for both parties. Halske always gladly adopted my constructive plans and designs, which with remarkable mechanical tact he at once most distinctly apprehended, and to which he often first gave their full value by his practical skill. At the same time Halske was a clear-headed cautious man of business, and I have him alone to thank for the good business results of the first years. Circumstances altered, however, when the business increased and could no longer be managed by the two of us alone. Halske regarded it as desecration of his cherished establishment that strangers should have rank and rule in it. Even the installation of a bookkeeper gave him pain. He could never get over the fact that the well-organized concern should exist and work without him. Finally, when the designs and undertakings of the firm became so large that he could no longer overlook them, he no longer felt satisfied, and resolved to retire, in order to devote his whole activity to the administration of the city of Berlin, which afforded him personal satisfaction. Halske remained a dear and faithful friend to me till his death, which occurred last year, and always, even to the last, retained a lively interest in the establishment of which he was joint-founder. Today his only son takes an active part in the management of the present business as confidential clerk.

As Meyer's successor we appointed the former director of the Hanoverian telegraph system, Herr Carl Frischen, who after the annexation of Hanover passed into the service of the North German Confederation, and had for several years filled the office formerly held by Meyer as chief telegraph engineer of the Government telegraphs. The business gained in Herr Fischen an eminent technical worker, who had already distinguished himself by many original inventions. Further it was now of great advantage to the firm that excellent departmental managers and constructors had been

286 · German Essays in Science in the 19th Century

found among its junior assistants, who had received their training in the firm. I shall only mention Herr von Hefner-Alteneck, whose achievements as head of our construction office have earned for him a worldwide reputation. Supported by such able coadjutors I was able more and more to confine myself to the general management of the business, and with full confidence to leave the details to our assistants. In this way I obtained greater leisure to occupy myself with scientific and such social problems as I had particularly at heart.

My domestic life underwent a complete transformation as a result of my second marriage, which took place on July 13, 1869, to Antonie Siemens. She was a distant relative, the only child of the meritorious Professor Carl Siemens of Hohenheim near Stuttgart who was well-known in agricultural technology. I have often jokingly said in after-dinner speeches and the like, that this marriage with a Suabian lady should be looked upon as a political act, as the Main line was bound to be bridged, and this could best be done by as many alliances of affection as possible being concluded between North and South, which must then of themselves soon be followed by political ones. Whether my patriotism was not considerably influenced by the amiable qualities of the fair Suabian herself, who has again brought warm sunshine into my somewhat gloomy and laborious life, I shall not here more closely enquire.

On the July 30, 1870, just as the news arrived by telegraph in Charlottenburg that the Emperor Napoleon had crossed the German frontier at Saarbrück and the fateful war between Germany and France had actually begun, my wife presented me with a little daughter, to be followed two years later by a son. I gave our daughter the name Hertha, in pursuance of a vow to give her this name, if the German warship so called, which the French fleet were pursuing in all waters, escaped capture. My four elder children were in Heligoland at the time of the declaration of war, and had to flee as speedily as possible with the whole troop of visitors, in order not to be prevented from returning by the blockade. The telegram from my eldest son, then sixteen, from Cuxhaven may pass as a sample of the deep emotion and courage that had taken possession of all Germany—"I must join too," words that happily could not be translated into action, as no one is accepted in the Prussian army before reaching seventeen years of age. The war with France, like that of 1866, was speedily carried to a victorious issue for

Germany, after a struggle of tremendous proportions. The joyful consciousness that for the first time in the course of their history Germans from all parts fought and conquered side by side under the same flag, made the heavy sacrifices, with which the glorious victories had to be purchased, appear more endurable, and lightened the profound mourning and misery which the war entailed. It was a glorious and elevating time, which has left impressions never to be effaced on all who lived through it; and coming generations will assuredly never allow the feeling of devout gratitude, which the nation owes to the great leaders who put an end to its ignominious discords, and which made it united and powerful, to die out.

Although I had entirely renounced political activity after the year 1866, I still continued to take the greatest interest in public affairs. One question, to which I had long before paid particular attention, was that of patent right. It had long become clear to me that one of the greatest obstacles to the free and independent development of German industry lay in the lack of protection for inventions. It is true that in Prussia, as also in the other large states of Germany, patents were granted for inventions, but the grant entirely depended on the good pleasure of the authorities and lasted at the most only for three years. Even for this short time they afforded only a very unsatisfactory protection against imitation, for it rarely paid to take out patents in all the states belonging to the Zollverein, since every state applied its own test of originality, and indeed strictly speaking it was impossible, as many of the smaller states did not grant patents at all. The consequence was that inventors, as a matter of course, sought in the first instance to turn their inventions to account in foreign countries, especially England, France, and the United States. Altogether therefore the youthful German industry was thrown upon the imitation of foreign productions, and by only dealing in imitations thereby indirectly strengthened still further the preference of the German public for foreign manufactures.

As to the worthlessness of the old Prussian patents there could not be two opinions. Indeed they were as a rule only applied for in order to obtain a certificate that an invention had actually been made. Furthermore, the then dominant thoroughgoing Free Trade Party regarded the patenting of inventions as a relic of the old monopoly rights, and incompatible with the principles of Free Trade. In this sense in the summer of 1863 a circular letter was sent by the Prussian Minister of Commerce to all the chambers of commerce of the state, in which the uselessness, nay even injuriousness, of the patent system was set forth and finally the question propounded, whether the time had not come to abolish it entirely. This led me to draw up a memorandum to the Berlin Chamber of Commerce, the council of Berlin merchants, which adopted the diametrically opposite point of view, to set forth the necessity and utility of a patent law for the promotion of the industry of the country, and to sketch the outlines of a rational patent law.

My detailed statement was approved by the Council, although the latter consisted of very pronounced free traders. It was unanimously adopted as the opinion of the Chamber of Commerce, and at the same time communicated to the other chambers of commerce of the state. Of the latter, those which had not yet sent in a reply assenting to the abolition of patents expressed their sympathy with the Berlin decision, and as a consequence the proposal for abolition was abandoned. This favourable result afterwards encouraged me to initiate a serious agitation for the introduction of an imperial patent-law, on the basis proposed by me. I sent a circular to a considerable number of men, who I supposed would have a special interest in the matter, and asked them to form a "Patent Protection Union," with the object of procuring a rational German patent law. The call was generally responded to, and, a short time after, the Union was called into existence under my presidency. I remember with pleasure the stimulating debates of this Union, to which eminent legal authorities such as Professor Klostermann, Mayor André, and Dr. Rosenthal belonged. The final result of the discussions was the draft of a patent law, which essentially rested on the foundation laid by me in my statement of 1863. This consisted of a preliminary inquiry in regard to the novelty of the invention and subsequent public exhibition of the specification, thereby affording an opportunity for objections to the grant; further, the grant of the patent for the term of fifteen years, with yearly increasing impost and complete publication of the patent granted; finally, establishment of a patent tribunal, which on application could always declare the nullity of the patent, if the originality of the invention was afterward successfully disputed.

These principles gradually gained approval with the public also, and even the Free Trade Party of the most rigid principles was quieted by the economic basis of the proposal, which consisted in the protection appearing as a reward for the immediate and complete publication of the invention, whereby the new ideas underlying the patented invention became themselves industrial common property, and might even bear fruit in other fields. It took a long time however before the imperial government resolved to take legislative action in the matter. I fancy that a memorandum, which as president of the Patent Protection Union I addressed to the imperial Chancellor, had a considerable influence on the decision for the promulgation of an imperial patent law. In this memorandum I laid stress on the inferior condition and the slight estimation of German industry, its productions being everywhere styled "cheap and shoddy"; and at the same time I pointed out that a new firm bond for the young German empire would be created, if thousands of manufacturers and engineers from all parts of the country could find in the institutions of the empire the long desired protection for their intellectual property.

In the year 1876 a meeting of manufacturers as well as of administrative officials and judges was called together from all Germany, which made the draft of the Patent Protection Union the definite basis of their deliberations. The bill resulting from these deliberations was adopted by the Reichstag with a few modifications, and has very materially contributed to strengthen German industry, and procure respect for its productions both at home and abroad. In almost all its branches our industry has since been well on the way to losing the stigma of "cheap and shoddy," which Professor Reuleaux rightly gave to its productions at the Philadelphia Exhibition in 1876.

I will now take up my account of the development of the businesses established by us from the point where I described the changes which our London house had to go through after the unhappy cable undertakings between Spain and Algeria in the year 1864. The firm of Siemens Brothers, from that time separated from the Berlin business, had quickly and regularly developed under brother William's direction, both as a manufacturing and as a contracting concern. As William had also at the same time great success in the engineering business carried on by him privately, and his time and energies were thereby very much taken up, it was desirable at the end of the sixties that brother Carl should undertake the special management of the London telegraph business. Carl consented as, since the expiration of the Russian maintenance contracts, he no longer found any considerable sphere of activity in Russia.

Halske's resolution to retire from the Berlin firm was taken about the same time, and we three brothers decided accordingly upon an entire reform of the business-connection of our different firms. A joint business was formed which embraced them all. Each firm retained its independence as regards administration and financial methods, but its profit and loss account was carried over to the joint business, of which we three brothers were the sole proprietors and partners. The St. Petersburg concern was placed under an able manager, whilst Carl went to England to undertake the special management of the London firm. How splendidly the London house, now named "Siemens Brothers," prospered in the period immediately following has been described at length in the above-mentioned book by Dr. Pole on my brother William. I therefore confine myself here to some remarks on my own and my brother Carl's personal cooperation.

When in the year 1869 Carl transferred his residence to London, the factory at Charlton was already in full production as a mechanical workshop for the construction of electric apparatus of every kind; a cable-sheathing shop was also combined with it, in which important cables had already been manufactured. The principle employed by me in the testings of the English Government cables, that the permanence of a cable could only be assured if it were tested at all stages of its manufacture with scientific thoroughness and accuracy, had borne good fruit, and the system of cable testings, then elaborated, has as a consequence answered admirably well.

The remarkable success of the Malta-Alexandria line, which we tested according to this system for the English Government, had considerably raised our technical reputation in England, and perhaps for this reason the only factory in England which then turned out wires coated with seamless gutta-percha according to my method, threw difficulties in the way of supplying the purified gutta-percha which we ordered from it. We accordingly resolved to establish our own gutta-percha factory, and accomplished this with complete success. In this manner we were enabled ourselves to undertake great cable-layings, and thereby to break down the monopoly of the great cable-ring which had meanwhile been formed, and whose purpose was to monopolize the whole field of submarine telegraphy. In reality my brothers succeeded in calling a Company into existence, which entrusted to us the production and the laying of an independent direct cable between Ireland and the United States. The requisite capital was subscribed on the Continent, as the English market was closed to us by the overwhelming competition. Brother William showed his great constructive ingenuity by designing a large steamship expressly destined for the laying of cables, which was christened by us "Faraday." Brother Carl undertook the command of it for laying the cable. I considered Carl specially fitted for this task, as he was cool and deliberate, besides being a good observer and resolute in action. I myself was not to be deterred from sailing in the Faraday, laden with the deep-sea cable, to the starting-point of the laying, Ballinskellig Bay, on the west coast of Ireland, and there undertaking the direction of the operations of the land-station during the laying.

It was tolerably favorable weather, and everything went well. The difficult abrupt descent of the Irish coast into deep water was successfully overcome, and according to the electrical testings the state of the cable was faultless. Then suddenly there occurred a small defect in the insulation, so small that only extremely sensitive instruments, such as we were employing, could have detected it. According to previous cable-laying practice, this defect would have been allowed to pass, as it was without any influence on the signalling. But we wished to lay down a perfectly faultless cable, and determined therefore to take the cable up again to the point of the fault, which must be immediately behind the ship. This indeed went off well in spite of the great depth of 18,000 feet, as was continuously telegraphed to us from the ship. Suddenly however the scale of our galvanometer flew out of the field of sight—the cable was broken! Broken at a depth, from which to fish up the end again appeared quite impossible.

It was a hard blow, which threatened our personal reputation as well as our business credit. The intelligence spread through all England in the same hour, and was received with very different feelings. Nobody believed in the possibility of recovering a detached piece of cable from so great a depth, and even brother William advised by telegraph to abandon the paid-out cable, and to recommence the laying. I was convinced however that Carl would not return without having made the attempt to pick up the cable, and calmly watched the continual fluctuations of the scale of the galvanometer to detect any signs pointing to the movement of the cable-end by the search-anchor. Such indications indeed frequently occurred, without having further consequences, and two anxious days passed without any news from the ship. All at once a violent mirror-vibration! The end of the copper-wire must be in metallic contact. Then for several hours feeble regular twitching of the reflected image of the scale, from which I referred a jerky lifting of the cable-end by the grapnel. However, long hours of silence caused hope to sink again. Then once more strong mirror-vibration produced by a current from the ship, which was greeted with repeated hurrahs by the workers at the station. The incredible had been realised. From a depth exceeding the height of Mont Blanc the cable had been found by a single operation, and what is more, had been brought up to the surface unbroken. Many favourable circumstances must have combined to make this possible. Good sandy sea-bottom, fine weather, suitable appliances for seeking and lifting the cable, and a good manageable ship with a skillful captain, happily concurred, and made possible the apparently impossible with the help of much luck and self-confidence. Brother Carl, however, confessed to me afterwards that during the uninterrupted lowering of the grapnel, which took seven hours to reach the sea-bottom, giving him for the first time a clear idea of the known depth, he had lost all hope of success and was himself astounded when it came.

After successful removal of the fault and re-establishment of connection with the land the laying was continued for some days without disturbance. Then the ship reported rough weather, and, soon after, a small fault again occurred in the cable, which was left however till reaching shallow water off Newfoundland, in order to seek and remove it when the weather was more favourable. The recovery proved to be very difficult however, as the sea-bottom was rocky and the weather persistently bad. Much cable was thereby lost, and the Faraday was obliged to return to England without finishing her task, to ship fresh cable and coals. Yet even the following expedition led only to the more accurate localization, but not to the removal of the fault, and a third attempt was necessary, in order to render the cable communication perfectly faultless.

This first transatlantic cable laying of ours was not only exceedingly instructive for us, but in point of fact led for the first time to the completely clear apprehension and mastery of cable-layings in deep water. We had shown that even in unfavorable weather and at a bad time of year cables can be laid and repaired, and that too in very deep seas and with a single but well-constructed and sufficiently large ship. The loss of cable which we had had in the repairings was attributed by brother Carl to the unsuitability of the construction of the cable, which was identical with that adopted for the first successful transatlantic cable. To diminish the specific gravity of the cable, steel wires had been used for the covering and protection of the conductor, surrounded with hemp or jute. On a strong pull these twisted the cable and produced kinks in the cable on the bottom of the ocean, which very much impeded or altogether prevented the recovery. In accordance with Carl's suggestion we afterward used only a closed steel-wire sheathing and thereby removed all the difficulties which so considerably hampered our first deep-sea laying.

On the further technical improvements in the method of laying cables in deep water, to which the preceding enterprise led us, I cannot here enlarge. I will only mention that my theory, propounded on laying the Cagliari-Bona cable in 1857, has held its ground very well. As already mentioned, I have further developed and mathematically treated this theory in an essay laid before the Berlin Academy of Sciences and the Society of Telegraph Engineers and Electricians in London, and believe that it may now be regarded as fairly settled. The laying of this our first transatlantic cable brought us brothers many exciting incidents, one of which occurred at a very unfavorable moment and profoundly agitated me.

In the year 1874 the Royal Academy of Sciences in Berlin had elected me one of its ordinary members, an honor which hitherto had only fallen to the lot of professed *savants*. On the day fixed for the purpose I was about to give my prescribed inaugural address at a special meeting of the Academy, when on leaving the house I received a telegraphic message from London to the effect that according to a cablegram the Faraday had been crushed by icebergs and had gone down with all hands. It required no slight self-control on my part, oppressed as I was by this terrible intelligence, still to deliver my address, which I did not admit of postponement. Only a few intimate friends had perceived my violent emotion. Certainly

I had hopes from the first moment that it was only a "love-token" of our opponents to cause this dread intelligence to be concocted in America, whence it was telegraphed. And indeed so it soon turned out to be. How the story originated could never be discovered, and after the lapse of several anxious days the Faraday was reported safe and sound from Halifax. It had been detained at sea for a considerable time by a thick fog.

At a stroke the successful completion of the American cable raised the London firm to a far higher level of English business-life than it had occupied hitherto. The testing of the electric properties of the cable by the highest authority in this department, Sir William Thomson, had proved that it was entirely faultless and possessed a very high signalling capacity. It was of great importance that the cable ring, which had been formed under Sir John Pender's auspices, was now broken. It is true the attempt was made to restore it by subsequently admitting to the ring the cable laid by us. This however was to our advantage, for there was soon formed another, and this time a French, company, which gave orders to our firm to lay an independent cable. After a short time this also was purchased by the Globe, as the cable ring was called, but this led to American capital being attracted to cable telegraphy. In the year 1881 brother William received a cablegram, in which the well-known railway king Mr. Gould ordered a double cable to America, which was to be constructed entirely like the last laid by us—the French so-called Pouyer-Quertier cable. It is a sign of the credit which our firm also enjoyed on the other side of the ocean that Mr. Gould declined to receive a representative to conclude the contract, "as he had perfect confidence in us," and confirmed this by the remittance of a large instalment. This was the more noteworthy, as Mr. Gould is well known in America as a very cautious and keen man of business, and it was a matter of some millions. At any rate, however, he had correctly speculated, for his unlimited confidence constrained my brothers to propose the most favorable conditions possible and to execute the work in the very best fashion. After some competitive contests the Gould cables were also united with the Globe, but it was America that again broke through the monopoly. In the year 1884 the well-known Americans, Mackay and Bennett, gave orders to Siemens Brothers for two cables between the English coast and New York, which were faultlessly manufactured and laid within a year, and have up till now maintained their independence of the cable ring.

These six transatlantic cables have all been laid by the Faraday, which proved a most satisfactory ship for cable-laying, and as such has served as a model for the competing firms. The double screw with axes inclined to one another, which was first employed in it, gave to the great ship of five-thousand tons a degree of mobility hitherto unattained, which made it possible to carry out cable-laying and repairing work in every season and even in unfavorable weather.

Brother Carl had already returned to St Petersburg in the year 1880, after the London firm had at his instigation been transformed into a private limited liability company. In the year 1883 brother William was, alas, torn from us and his untiring activity by a quite unexpected and sudden death. Herr Löffler, an official of many years standing, was installed as managing director of the London firm, and has been recently succeeded by a younger member of the family, Mr. Alexander Siemens.

My appointment as ordinary member of the Berlin Academy of Sciences was not only very honorable in itself for the favored individual, who did not belong to the class of professional *savants*, but it also had a profound influence on my later life. As my friend Du Bois-Reymond, who as presiding secretary of the Academy acknowledged my inaugural address, rightly pointed out, by natural endowment and inclination I belonged in a far higher degree to science than to practice. Scientific research was my first, my early love, and it has retained my affection to the advanced age, which I now—I can hardly say—enjoy. At the same time I have certainly always felt the impulse to make scientific attainments useful for practical life. I expressed that in my inaugural address, when I enlarged on the theme that science does not exist for its own sake, merely to satisfy the thirst for knowledge of the limited number of its votaries, but that its office is to increase the treasures of knowledge and power of the human race, and thereby to raise mankind to a higher level of civilization. It was noteworthy that friend Du Bois in his reply to my address at the end bade me welcome "into the circle of the Academy, which only pursues science for it own sake." In every truth scientific investigation must not be a means to an end. The German *savant* has always been justly distinguished by this, that he pursues science on its own account, for the satisfaction of his thirst for knowledge, and in this sense I have always been able to consider myself more of a *savant* than an engineer, since the prospective profit has either not at all, or only in special cases, guided me in the choice of my scientific work. The entrance into the narrow circle of distinguished men of science could not therefore but elevate me in a high degree and spur me to scientific activity. Moreover the statutes of the Academy exerted a beneficial constraint upon me. Every member must in rotation give a lecture, which is then printed in its Transactions. As it was very disagreeable to evade this obligation, it compelled me to complete and publish researches, which under other circumstances I should perhaps have postponed in favor of others seemingly more interesting, or have left altogether unfinished. While therefore before my reception into the Academy I seldom got as far as the publication of a piece of scientific work, and usually contented myself with the enlargement of my own knowledge—not without subsequent vexation, if my results were discovered and then made public by others—I was now obliged every year to finish and publish one or two contributions. To this state of things is also to be ascribed the circumstance that in my academic lectures I dealt less with matters of my special department, electrical industrial arts, than with subjects of general scientific interest. They were partly detached thoughts and reflections, jotted down in the course of my life, which were now brought together and scientifically worked up, partly novel phenomena, which aroused my particular interest and called for special investigation. I shall once more return to these purely scientific publications at the close of these reminiscences. Although since my reception into the Academy I had been far more occupied than heretofore with purely scientific problems, unrelated to my business calling, I did not omit to continue to devote the necessary time to the latter also. The superior management of the Berlin firm, and the technical work connected with it, usually claimed my whole working time during the day. The difficulty of my task was much augmented by the multifarious character and the far-reaching dimensions which the firm's operations had gradually assumed; and although able coadjutors relieved me of a considerable portion of the burden, yet there still remained for me much arduous and unceasing work.

It had become clear to me very early that a satisfactory development of the continually growing firm must depend on securing the hearty, spontaneous cooperation of all the workers for the furtherance of its interests. To attain this it seemed to me essential that all who belonged to the firm should share in the profits according to their performances. As my brothers acceded to my view this principle came to be adopted in all our establishments. Arrangements to that end were settled at the celebration of the twenty-fifth anniversary of the original Berlin firm in the autumn of 1872. We then determined that a considerable portion of the yearly profits should regularly be set aside for allowing a percentage to officials proportionate to their salaries and bonuses to workmen, and as a reserve fund for necessitous cases. Moreover we presented the collective body of workers with a capital stock of nine-thousand pounds for an old age and invalid fund, the firm agreeing to pay every year to the account of the managers of the fund, chosen directly by those interested, fifteen shillings for each workman and thirty shillings for each official who had served in the business uninterruptedly for one year.

These arrangements have worked remarkably well during the nearly twenty years of their existence. Officials and workmen regard themselves as a permanent part of the firm and identify its interests with their own. It is seldom that officials give up their position, since they see their future assured in the service of the firm. The workmen also remain permanently attached to the firm, as the amount of the pension rises with the uninterrupted period of service. After thirty years continuous service the full old age pension commences with two thirds of the wages; and that this is of practical importance is proved by the respectable number of old age pensioners who are still strong and hearty, and apart from their pension continue to receive their full wages. But almost more than the prospect of a pension it is the endowment fund for widows and orphans connected with the pension fund that binds the workmen to the firm. It has been proved to be the case that this endowment is still more urgent than the invalid pension, as the uncertainty of the future of those dependent on him commonly weighs more heavily on the workman than his own. The aging workman nearly always love his work, and does not willingly lay it down without actual and serious need of rest. Accordingly the superannuation fund of the firm, in spite of a liberal use of the pensions by the workmen themselves, has only consumed the smaller part of the income from the interest of the funded capital and the contributions of the firm towards pensions; the larger part could be applied for the support of widows and orphans as well as for increasing the capital stock of the fund, which is destined to secure the workman's claim for pensions in the event of the possible liquidation of the business.

The criticism has been made of this arrangement that it binds the workman too much to a particular workshop, since by his leaving it he loses the advantages gained. This is quite true, although the hardship is considerably mitigated by the circumstance that with dismissal for want of work every dismissed workman receives a paper, giving him a preferential claim to readmission over other workmen. Certainly the workman's freedom to strike is considerably restricted by the conditions regarding pensions, for, by the rules, on his leaving voluntarily his old age claims lapse. It is however in the interest of both parties that a permanent working staff should be formed, for only thereby is the firm enabled to maintain the workmen even in unfavorable times and to pay them wages affording adequate subsistence. Every large factory ought to form such a pension-fund, to which the workmen contribute nothing, but which they themselves manage, of course, under the control of the firm. The strike mania, which seriously injures industry and especially the workmen themselves, is best coped with in this manner.

It is certainly somewhat hard that the provisions of the Workmen's Old Age Insurance Law of Germany have no regard to the already existing or prospective private pension funds, and thus oblige the particular factories to pay double for pensioning their workmen. However, the peaceful relations between employers and employees, which are secured by the private pension fund, as well as a permanent staff of workmen, are so important that such an excess of expenditure is amply justified.

The esprit de corps produced by the arrangements described, which binds together all the fellow workers of the firm of Siemens and Halske, and gives them an interest in its welfare, explains in great part the commercial success which we achieved.

This leads me to the question whether it is altogether in the general interest that large commercial houses should be established, which permanently remain in the possession of the family of the founder. It might be said that such large firms are hindrances to the rise of many smaller undertakings and therefore act injuriously. That is certainly pertinent in many cases. Wherever it is possible to maintain an export trade by the productions of handicraftsmen, large competing factories have a prejudicial effect. Wherever, on the contrary, the development of new branches of industry or the opening of the markets of the world for those already in existence are concerned, large centralised business undertakings with abundant capital are indispensable. At the present day such capital can certainly be brought together most easily in the form of joint stock companies, but these can nearly always be only purely gain-seeking companies which, by their own regulations, are only allowed to have in view the attainment of the largest possible amount of profit. They are therefore only adapted for reaping advantage from already existing well-tried methods of working and organization. The opening of new paths is on the contrary nearly always troublesome and attended with great risk. It requires also a larger store of special knowledge and experience than is to be found in joint stock companies, which are for the most part short-lived and often change their management. Such an aggregation of capital, knowledge, and experience can only be formed and maintained in long-established commercial houses, remaining by inheritance in the same family. Just as the great commercial houses of the Middle Ages were not only money-making institutions, but considered themselves called upon and bound to serve their fellow-citizens and the state by seeking out new commodities and new highways of commerce—the obligation being transmitted as a family tradition through many generations—so at the present day in this awakened scientific age the large technical business houses are called upon to put forth their whole strength, that the national industry may take the lead in the great contest of the civilized world, or at least the place assigned to it by the nature and situation of the country itself. Our political institutions still rest almost everywhere on the feudal system, according to which the landed proprietor was almost exclusively regarded and honored as the supporter and maintainer of the power of the State. Our time can no longer recognize the validity of this privilege. The social forces maintaining the state today and henceforth will not consist of possessions, whatever they may be, but of the spirit which animates and fertilizes them. Although it is conceded that inherited possession of the soil binds the owner by tradition and education more firmly to the state, and is therefore a better preserver thereof than the possession of land easily transferable and of capital altogether movable, yet it no longer suffices to protect the state from impoverishment and decay. This protection can only be secured today by the conscious cooperation of all the spiritual forces of the nation, the maintenance and further development of which is one of the most important problems of the modern state.

Translator unknown

Biographies

ABBE, ERNST (b. Eisenach 1840, d. Jena 1905), physics professor, microscope constructor, co-owner of ZEISS (a leading manufacturer of optical instruments), and social reformer. Studied mathematics, physics, astronomy, and philosophy at the universities of Jena and Göttingen. Professor of physics in Jena, Marburg, and Berlin. From 1875, technical and scientific collaboration with Carl Zeiss in Jena. Promoted fairness and justice in business and society, and created, in 1891, the Carl Zeiss Foundation, instituting workers' co-ownership.

BACHOFEN, JOHANN JACOB (b. Basel 1815, d. Basel 1887), law professor and classicist. Studied law in Basel, Berlin, Göttingen, Paris, London, Cambridge. Professor of Roman law as well as criminal court judge in Basel. Research in Italy with emphasis on antiquity and prehistorical age. Proposed that in ancient societies the mother was the source of culture and power. Author of *The Mother Right,* (1861), *The Lycian People,* (1862), *The Saga of Tanaquil,* (1870), and *Myth, Religion, and Mother Right.*

BREHM, ALFRED EDMUND (b. Renthendorf 1829, d. Renthendorf 1884), explorer and zoologist who undertook an eighteen-member expedition to Africa that lasted five years. Studied zoology at the universities of Jena and Vienna. Director of the Hamburg Zoo and founder of the Berlin Aquarium. Further expeditions to Africa, Spain, Scandinavia, and Siberia. Eighteen-eighty-three lecture tour in the United States. After his death at fifty-five, fame as "father of animals." Author of *Brehm's Animal Life* (1864–69).

BURCKHARDT, JACOB (b. Basel 1818, d. Basel 1897), philosopher of culture and professor of art history. Studied art history and history (with Leopold von Ranke) at Berlin University 1838–43. Professor of art history in Basel 1844–97. Author of *The Age of Constantine the Great* (1853), *The Civilization of the Renaissance* (1860), *History of the Renaissance in Italy* (1867), *History of the Greek Culture* (1898–1902), *Force and Freedom: Reflections on History* (1905).

CHAMISSO, ADELBERT VON (b. Boncourt, Champagne, 1781, d. Berlin 1838), Romantic poet, natural historian, and botanist. Born as Louis-Charles Adelaide in France, he was reared in Berlin, entered the military, serving until 1807. A poet and Madame de Stael's friend, discovered his love of botany and at thirty-two enrolled in the natural sciences at Berlin University. A voyage of discovery to the Pacific shores (1815–18), many years before Darwin; brought back rich botanical collections. Curator of the Royal Botanical Gardens and Herbarium in Berlin and editor of *Deutscher Musenalmanach* (1832). Author of *The Strange Story of Peter Schlemihl* (1814; *The German Library, volume 35, German Romantic Stories*), and *Voyage around the World with Romanzov Discovery Expedition* (1821).

CLAUSEWITZ, CARL VON (b. Burg 1780, d. Jena 1831), Prussian general and military strategist. Author of *On War* (1832). Entered the Prussian army in 1792 and in 1801 the War College in Berlin. Studied philosophy and literature at Berlin University and after 1808 became one of the leaders of the resistance against Napoleon. Director, 1818–30, Berlin War College. "War is nothing but a continuation of political intercourse with the admixture of different means," is a concept central to his doctrine of *total war*, which targets not only the enemy's armed forces but also its economic resources and will to fight.

DAIMLER, GOTTLIEB (b. Schorndorf 1834, d. Cannstatt 1900), mechanical engineer and automobile inventor. Studied engineering at Stuttgart Polytechnic, patented high-speed internal-combustion engines in 1883, and founded Daimler-Motoren-Gesellschaft in 1890, building the first Mercedes in 1899.

EHRLICH, PAUL (b. Strehlen 1854, d. Bad Homburg 1915), medical scientist and bacteriology professor known for his pioneering work in hematology, immunology, chemotherapy. Studied medicine at the universities in Breslau, Straßburg, Freiburg, and Leipzig. Worked at Robert Koch's Pathology Institute in Berlin from 1882. A professor at Berlin University from 1891, he was appointed in 1896 director of a new Center for Serum Research in Steglitz, which was transferred to Frankfurt am Main and renamed the Royal Institute for Experimental Therapy. Nobel Prize in Physiology or Medicine in 1908. In 1910 discovered the first effective treatment for syphilis and became a full professor at Frankfurt University in 1911.

EULER, LEONHARD (b. Basel 1707, d. St. Petersburg 1783), mathematician and astronomer. Studied mathematics and physics (with Johann Bernoulli). In 1727, professor at the Academy of St. Petersburg, director of the Academy of Sciences in Berlin in 1741, returned to St. Petersburg in 1766. Author of *Introduction to Mathematical Science* (1768) and *Letters to a German Princess* (1768–72).

FRAUNHOFER, JOSEPH VON (b. Straubing 1787, d. Munich 1826), optician and physicist. Trained in optics at the Utzschneider Optical Institute at Benedictbeuern, of which he became director in 1818. A pioneer in spectroscopy, he developed achromatic lenses and studied the dark lines of the sun's spectrum, now known as Fraunhofer lines. Appointed corresponding member of the Royal Bavarian Academy of Sciences in 1817 and professor in 1823. Author of *Prismatic and Diffraction Spectra* (1898).

GAUSS, KARL FRIEDRICH (b. Brunswick 1777, d. Göttingen 1855), mathematician. Studied mathematics and classical philology at the University of Göttingen. Appointed professor of astronomy at the University of Göttingen and director of the Göttingen observatory in 1807. Applied mathematics to astronomy, geodesy, and physics, as demonstrated in the twelve volumes of his *Collected Works* (1863–1933).

HELMHOLTZ, HERMANN VON (b. Potsdam 1821, d. Berlin 1894), physiologist, physicist, and philosopher who helped develop thermodynamics with his law of conservation of energy. Studied chemistry, clinical medicine, and physiology at the University of Berlin. Appointed professor of physiology at the universities in Königsberg, Bonn, Heidelberg and, in 1871, director of the Physics Institute at the University of Berlin. Fundamental contributions to physiology, optics, electrodynamics, meteorology, and philosophy of nature. Author of *The Conservation of Force* (1847), *Treatises on Physiological Optics* (1856–1867), and *Treatises on Physiological Acoustics* (1863).

HUFELAND, CHRISTOPH VON (b. Langensalza 1762, d. Berlin 1836), physician who counted Wieland, Herder, Goethe, and Schiller among his patients. Studied medicine at the universities of Jena and Göttingen. Appointed professor of medicine at the University of Jena in 1793 and founded the *Journal der praktischen Arzneikunde und Wundarzneikunst* in 1795. From 1800, Royal Physician and director of the Charité hospital in Berlin. Hufeland helped establish the faculty of medicine at the University of Berlin. Pioneer of natural medicine and author of "Macrobiotics" (1796).

HUMBOLDT, ALEXANDER VON (b. Berlin 1769, d. Berlin 1859), natural scientist and explorer who is one of the founders of earth science and biogeography. Younger brother of Wilhelm v.H., studied engineering, botany, mineralogy, and geology at the universities of Berlin and Göttingen. In 1790, he entered the School of Mines in Freiberg and in 1792 joined the Mining Department of the Prussian government. Expedition to the Spanish colonies in Central and South America (1797–1804) resulted in the "scientific discovery of America." At the end of his journey, Humboldt informed President Jefferson and members of his cabinet in Washington. He lived in Paris from 1804 to 1827 and published his data in twenty-three volumes. Trip to Siberia, 1829. Back in Berlin and Paris, he wrote *Cosmos* (1845–62), a popular account of his discoveries, in five volumes. Author of *Aspects of Nature in Different Lands and Different Climates* (1808) and *Personal Narrative of Travels to the Equinoctial Regions of the New Continent during the Years 1799–1804* (1814–29).

IHERING, RUDOLF VON (b. Aurich 1818, d. Göttingen 1892), legal scholar who founded the branch of sociological jurisprudence emphasizing the needs of society. Appointed professor of Roman law in Basel in 1845, he later taught at the universities of Rostock,

Kiel, Gießen, Vienna, and Göttingen. Author of *The Spirit of Roman Law* (1852–65), *The Struggle for Justice* (1872), and *Law as a Means to an End* (1877–83).

LICHTENBERG, GEORG CHRISTOPH (b. Ober-Ramstadt 1742, d. Göttingen 1799), physicist, astronomer, and writer. Studied literature, history, and natural science at the University of Göttingen, where he was appointed professor of philosophy in 1769. In 1780, he was the first to erect a correct version of Benjamin Franklin's lightning rod. Lichtenberg published Mayer's detailed map of the moon and wrote a biography of Copernicus. From 1775, as professor of experimental physics, Lichtenberg discovered the basic process of photocopying as well as the first electrostatic recording process by which he produced the so-called Lichtenberg figures. In 1793, elected member of the Royal Society in London and in 1795 of the Academy of Sciences in St. Petersburg. His witty literary work, composed of aphorisms as well as commentaries on the engravings of Hogarth, was devoted to enlightenment. Author of *Letters from England* (1776–78), *On the Pronunciation of the Muttonheads of Old Greece* (1782), *Full Explanation of Hogarthian Copper Engravings* (1794–99), *Aphorisms* (1902–8).

LIEBIG, JUSTUS VON (b. Darmstadt 1803, d. Munich 1873), chemist who was the founder of organic chemistry and inventor of artificial fertilizer. Studied chemistry at the universities of Bonn and Erlangen and did postdoctoral work with Joseph-Louis Gay-Lussac in Paris. At the recommendation of Alexander von Humboldt, appointed professor of chemistry at the University of Gießen in 1824. Established a university laboratory with emphasis on agricultural chemistry and biochemistry. From 1852, professor at the University of Munich. Author of *Instructions for Chemical Analysis of Organic Bodies* (1839), *Organic Chemistry in Its Application to Agriculture and Physiology* (1840), *Animal Chemistry* (1842), *Letters on Chemistry* (1844).

LIST, FRIEDRICH (b. Reutlingen 1789, d. Kufstein 1846), economist who favored tariff protection and a railroad system. Without formal education and with special permission, studied economics at the University of Tübingen. Secretary of the German Association of Industrialists in 1819 and elected delegate to the Württemberg Council in 1820. Accused of treason, he served a prison sentence of five months at Asperg and was exiled in 1825. Emigrated to the United States where he became a newspaper editor and owner of a coal mine. President Andrew Jackson appointed List United States Consul at Leipzig in 1834. Advocated a German railroad system and was involved in building the line between Leipzig and Dresden. Travels to Belgium, Hungary, Austria, and England to promote his tariff protection concept. Author of *Outlines of American Political Economy* (1827), *On the Railroad System in Saxony* (1833), *The National System of Political Economy* (1841).

MÜLLER, ADAM (b. Berlin 1779, d. Vienna 1829), law professor and economist. Studied law at the University of Göttingen and natural sciences at the University of Berlin. Friendship with Friedrich Gentz and the Schlegel brothers. In 1805, public lectures on "German Literature and Science" and Romanticism in Dresden. In 1808 editor of "Phöbus" (together with Heinrich von Kleist). Conservative critic of Adam Smith's economic theory. Austrian Consul in Leipzig, 1815–25; from 1827 adviser to the Austrian government in Vienna. Author of *Elements of Statesmanship* (1809), *Treatise on a New Theory of Money* (1816), *Twelve Lectures on Rhetoric* (1967).

OKEN, LORENZ (b. Bohlsbach 1779, d. Zurich 1851), natural scientist and philosopher of nature who established the genetic principle in natural history. Influenced by Immanuel Kant and Friedrich Wilhelm Schelling, a leading philosopher of German Romanticism and professor of medicine at the University of Jena 1807–19. From 1816 editor of *Isis,* an encyclopedic journal, and in 1822 founder of the Society for German Naturalists and Physicians. In 1832 appointed professor of medicine at the newly founded University of Zurich where he served as its first rector in 1833. Author of "Handbook of Natural Philosophy" (1812–26) and *General Natural History* (1833–45).

PESTALOZZI, HEINRICH (b. Zurich 1746, d. Brugg 1827), educational reformer and writer who advocated a natural method of learning in elementary education and favored formal teacher training. Studied theology for a short period but under the influence of Jean-Jacques Rousseau's philosophy decided to go "back to nature." In 1769, he became farmer in Birrfeld; 1771 in Neufeld where he started a pedagogical project with poor children, self-

Biographies · 307

supported by spinning and weaving. In 1798, director of an orphanage in Stans; in 1799, teacher at the Elementary School in Burgdorf where he was appointed director of the Helvetian Seminar on Teaching in 1800. Founder and head of the Yverdon Institute 1805–25 where Friedrich Fröbel, J. G. Herbarth, and Carl Ritter became visiting educators. Author of *The Evening Hour of a Hermit* (1780), *Leonhard and Gertrude* (1781–83), *My Inquiries into the Course of Nature in the Development of Mankind* (1797), *How Gertrude Teaches Her Children* (1801), *Letter from Stans* (1807), *Swan Song* (1826).

RANKE, LEOPOLD VON (b. Wiche 1795, d. Berlin 1886), historian who established modern historiography by emphasizing historical continuity and a search for objectivity. Studied theology and classical philology at the University of Leipzig. Schoolteacher in Frankfurt/Oder, 1818–25. Appointed professor of history at the University of Berlin in 1825 where he became a close adviser of the Prussian kings. Research sojourns in Vienna, Florence, Rome 1827–29. Influenced by the philosophers J. G. von Herder, F. W. Schelling, and G. W. F. Hegel, Ranke developed a scholarly method combining historical facts and philosophical ideals. His goal was a universal world history that "demonstrates how it really happened." Author of *History of the Latin and Teutonic Nations from 1494 to 1514* (1824), *The Roman Popes in the Last Four Centuries* (1834–36), *History of Reformation in Germany* (1845–47), *Memoirs of the House of Brandenburg and History of Prussia* (1849), *Civil Wars and Monarchy in France in the Sixteenth and Seventeenth Centuries* (1852), *A History of England in the Seventeenth Century* (1875), *World History* (1881–88), *The Secret of World History* (1881).

RITTER, CARL (b. Quedlinburg 1779, d. Berlin 1859), geographer who founded geography as an empirical science. Studied mathematics, physics, chemistry, history, and philology at the University of Frankfurt. Influenced by Heinrich Pestalozzi as well as J. G. von Herder and greatly inspired by Alexander von Humboldt, he was appointed professor of geography at the University of Berlin in 1820 and became a member of the Academy of Sciences in 1822. Author of *Earth Science in Relation to Nature and the History of Man* (1817–59) in nineteen volumes.

SAVIGNY, FRIEDRICH CARL (b. Frankfurt am Main 1779, d. Berlin 1861), jurist who founded modern German civil law and advocated the historic school of law. Studied at the universities of Göttingen and Marburg. Appointed professor of law at the universities of Heidelberg, Landshut, and Berlin. Prussian Minister of Justice 1847–48. Influenced by German Romanticism, he stressed that the law must be in accord with the spirit of the people. Author of *Treatise on Possession* (1803), *History of Roman Law in the Middle Ages* (1815–31), *On The Vocation of Our Age for Legislation and Jurisprudence* (1831), *System of Modern Roman Law* (1840–49), *The Law of Contracts* (1851–53).

SIEMENS, WERNER VON (b. Lenthe 1816, d. Berlin 1892), industrialist and electrical engineer who discovered the dynamo-electrical principle. Trained in engineering at the Prussian Artillery and Engineering School in Berlin. In 1841, appointed to the artillery workshop in Berlin where he became a specialist on the electric telegraph. With Johann Georg Halske started a telegraph factory in Berlin and invented the self-excited generator in 1866. Established factories in London, St. Petersburg, Vienna, and Paris. In 1866 member of the Prussian Chamber of Deputies. Author of *Personal Recollections* (1892).

VIRCHOW, RUDOLF (b. Schievelbein 1821, d. Berlin 1902), pathologist who founded cellular pathology and liberal politician who advocated public health. Studied medicine at the University of Berlin 1839–43. As an intern at the Charité hospital he published a paper describing one of the earliest cases of leukemia. In 1847, established a journal *Archives for Pathological Anatomy and Physiology, and for Clinical Medicine,* after 1852 renamed "Virchow's Archives." In 1848, appointed by the Prussian government to investigate an outbreak of typhus fever in Upper Silesia, he blamed the social conditions and joined the barricades in the March revolution of 1848. In 1849, appointed professor of pathological anatomy at the University of Würzburg and in 1856 at the University of Berlin. Virchow stressed as one of the first that every cell is derived from a preexisting cell. In 1859, elected to the Berlin City Council and in 1861 to the Prussian Chamber of Deputies. In 1869, he founded the Berlin Society for Anthropology. An outspoken politician of the Liberal Party, he was a member of the German Parliament from 1880 to 1893 and an archenemy of Chancellor Otto von Bismarck. Author of *Handbook of Special Pathology and Therapeutics* (1850), *Cellular Pathology as Based upon Physiological and Pathological Histology* (1858).

Translated by Virginia Cutrufelli

Bibliography

Ackerknecht, E. H. *Rudolf Virchow: Doctor, Statesman, Anthropologist*. Madison: University of Wisconsin Press, 1953

Aron, Raymond. *Clausewitz: Philosopher of War*. London: Routledge & Kegan Paul, 1993

Cahan, David, ed. *Hermann von Helmholtz and the Foundations of Nineteenth-Century Science*. Berkeley: University of California Press, 1993

Gay, Peter. *Style in History*. New York: Norton, 1988

Hall, Tord. *Carl Friedrich Gauss*. Cambridge, Mass.: MIT Press, 1970

Henderson, William O. *Friedrich List: Economist and Visionary*. London: Frank Cass, 1983

Iggers, Georg G. and James M. Powell. *Leopold von Ranke and the Shaping of the Historical Discipline*. Syracuse; Syracuse University Press, 1990

Johnson, Jeffrey A. *The Kaiser's Chemists: Science and Modernization in Imperial Germany*. Chapel Hill: University of North Carolina Press, 1972

Jungnickel, Christa and Russell McCormack. *Intellectual Masters of Nature: Theoretical Physics from Ohm to Einstein*. vol. 1. Chicago: University of Chicago Press, 1986

Knight, David. *The Age of Science: The Scientific World View in the Nineteenth Century*. London: Basil Blackwell, 1986

Rossiter, Margaret W. *The Emergence of Agricultural Science: Justus Liebig and the Americans*. New Haven: Yale University Press, 1975

Schweizer, Nikolaus Rudolf. *A Poet among Explorers: Chamisso in the South Seas*. Bern: Lang, 1973

Stern, Joseph Peter. *Lichtenberg: A Doctrine of Scattered Occasions*. Bloomington: Indiana University Press, 1959

Terra, Helmut R. *The Life and Times of Alexander von Humboldt*. New York: Knopf, 1955

Acknowledgments

Every reasonable effort has been made to locate the owners of rights to previously published translations printed here. We gratefully acknowledge permission to reprint the following material:

"Foundations of Mathematics" by Carl Friedrich Gauss appeared in *Inaugural Lecture on Astronomy and Papers on the Foundation of Mathematics*. Translated and edited by G. Waldo Dunnington. Baton Rouge: Louisiana State University Press, 1937.

"On the Art of Listening" by Adam Müller from *Lectures on Rhetoric. A Translation with a Critical Essay* by Dennis R. Bormann and Elisabeth Leinfellner. Reprinted by permission of Dennis R. Bormann and Elisabeth Leinfellner.

"The Art of Human Education" by Johann Heinrich Pestalozzi is reprinted by permission of Walter de Gruyter & Co.

Bachofen, Johann Jakob; "My Life in Retrospect" from MYTH, RELIGION, AND MOTHER RIGHT, translated by Ralph Manheim (Bollingen Series LXXXIV). Copyright © 1967 (renewed) by Princeton University Press. Reprinted by permission of Princeton University Press.

Clausewitz, Carl von; "On Military Genius" from ON WAR, edited and translated by Michael Howard and Peter Paret. Copyright © 1976 by Princeton University Press. Reprinted by permission of Princeton University Press.

"On the Novelty of my Patent No. 28022. A Reply" is reprinted by permission of the Mercedes-Benz Archiv in Stuttgart, Germany.

THE GERMAN LIBRARY

in 100 Volumes

Wolfram von Eschenbach
Parzival
Edited by André Lefevere

Gottfried von Strassburg
Tristan and Isolde
Edited and Revised by
 Francis G. Gentry
Foreword by C. Stephen Jaeger

German Medieval Tales
Edited by Francis G. Gentry
Foreword by Thomas Berger

German Mystical Writings
Edited by Karen J. Campbell
Foreword by Carol Zaleski

German Humanism and Reformation
Edited by Reinhard P. Becker
Foreword by Roland Bainton

*German Poetry from the Beginnings
 to 1750*
Edited by Ingrid Walsøe-Engel
Foreword by George C. Schoolfield

Seventeenth Century German Prose
Edited by Lynne Tatlock
Foreword by Günter Grass

German Theater before 1750
Edited by Gerald Gillespie
Foreword by Martin Esslin

Eighteenth Century German Prose
Edited by Ellis Shookman
Foreword by Dennis F. Mahoney

Eighteenth Century German Criticism
Edited by Timothy J. Chamberlain

Sturm und Drang
Edited by Alan C. Leidner

Immanuel Kant
Philosophical Writings
Edited by Ernst Behler
Foreword by René Wellek

Friedrich Schiller
*Plays: Intrigue and Love
    and Don Carlos*
Edited by Walter Hinderer
Foreword by Gordon Craig

Friedrich Schiller
Wallenstein and Mary Stuart
Edited by Walter Hinderer

Friedrich Schiller
Essays
Edited by Walter Hinderer
    and Daniel O. Dahlstrom

Johann Wolfgang von Goethe
The Sufferings of Young Werther
and Elective Affinities
Edited by Victor Lange
Forewords by Thomas Mann

Johann Wolfgang von Goethe
Plays: Egmont, Iphigenia in Tauris,
Torquato Tasso
Edited by Frank G. Ryder

German Romantic Criticism
Edited by A. Leslie Willson
Foreword by Ernst Behler

Friedrich Hölderlin
Hyperion and Selected Poems
Edited by Eric L. Santner

Philosophy of German Idealism
Edited by Ernst Behler

G. W. F. Hegel
Encyclopedia of the Philosophical Sciences in Outline and
   Critical Writings
Edited by Ernst Behler

Heinrich von Kleist
Plays
Edited by Walter Hinderer
Foreword by E. L. Doctorow

E. T. A. Hoffmann
Tales
Edited by Victor Lange

Georg Büchner
Complete Works and Letters
Edited by Walter Hinderer and Henry J. Schmidt

German Fairy Tales
Edited by Helmut Brackert and Volkmar Sander
Foreword by Bruno Bettelheim

German Literary Fairy Tales
Edited by Frank G. Ryder and Robert M. Browning
Introduction by Gordon Birrell
Foreword by John Gardner

F. Grillparzer, J. H. Nestroy,
   F. Hebbel
Nineteenth Century German Plays
Edited by Egon Schwarz in collaboration with
   Hannelore M. Spence

Heinrich Heine
Poetry and Prose
Edited by Jost Hermand and Robert C. Holub
Foreword by Alfred Kazin

Heinrich Heine
The Romantic School and other Essays
Edited by Jost Hermand and
   Robert C. Holub

Heinrich von Kleist and Jean Paul
German Romantic Novellas
Edited by Frank G. Ryder and Robert M. Browning
Foreword by John Simon

German Romantic Stories
Edited by Frank G. Ryder
Introduction by Gordon Birrell

German Poetry from 1750 to 1900
Edited by Robert M. Browning
Foreword by Michael Hamburger

Karl Marx, Friedrich Engels, August Bebel, and Others
German Essays on Socialism in the Nineteenth Century
Edited by Frank Mecklenburg and Manfred Stassen

German Lieder
Edited by Philip Lieson Miller
Foreword by Hermann Hesse

Gottfried Keller
Stories
Edited by Frank G. Ryder
Foreword by Max Frisch

Wilhelm Raabe
Novels
Edited by Volkmar Sander
Foreword by Joel Agee

Theodor Fontane
Short Novels and Other Writings
Edited by Peter Demetz
Foreword by Peter Gay

Theodor Fontane
Delusions, Confusions and The Poggenpuhl Family
Edited by Peter Demetz
Foreword by J. P. Stern
Introduction by William L. Zwiebel

Wilhelm Busch and Others
German Satirical Writings
Edited by Dieter P. Lotze and Volkmar Sander
Foreword by John Simon

Writings of German Composers
Edited by Jost Hermand and
    James Steakley

Arthur Schnitzler
Plays and Stories
Edited by Egon Schwarz
Foreword by Stanley Elkin

Rainer Maria Rilke
Prose and Poetry
Edited by Egon Schwarz
Foreword by Howard Nemerov

Robert Musil
Selected Writings
Edited by Burton Pike
Foreword by Joel Agee

Essays on German Theater
Edited by Margaret Herzfeld-Sander
Foreword by Martin Esslin

German Essays on Art History
Edited by Gert Schiff

German Novellas of Realism I
Edited by Jeffrey L. Sammons

German Novellas of Realism II
Edited by Jeffrey L. Sammons

Hermann Hesse
Siddhartha, Demian,
  and other Writings
Edited by Egon Schwarz
  in collaboration with Ingrid Fry

Friedrich Dürrenmatt
Plays and Essays
Edited by Volkmar Sander
Foreword by Martin Esslin

German Radio Plays
Edited by Everett Frost and Margaret Herzfeld-Sander

Max Frisch
Novels, Plays, Essays
Edited by Rolf Kieser
Foreword by Peter Demetz

Gottfried Benn
Prose, Essays, Poems
Edited by Volkmar Sander
Foreword by E. B. Ashton
Introduction by Reinhard
   Paul Becker

Hans Magnus Enzensberger
Critical Essays
Edited by Reinhold Grimm and Bruce Armstrong
Foreword by John Simon

All volumes available in hardcover and paperback editions at your bookstore or from the publisher. For more information on The German Library write to: The Continuum Publishing Company, 370 Lexington Avenue, New York, NY 10017.